Confucian Thought in Korea

Confucian Thought in Korea

A Study Based on the Cardinal Principles of Confucianism

Youn Sa-soon

Translated by Sohn Yoo-taek & Yoon Hee-ki

KOREA
UNIVERSITY
PRESS

Korea University Press
82-2-3290-4230 (Tel.) 82-2-923-6311 (Fax)
http://www.kupress.com kupress@korea.ac.kr
145, Anam-Ro, Seongbuk-Gu, Seoul, 02841 Korea

Published July 2017

ISBN 978-89-7641-938-5 93150

PRINTED IN REPUBLIC OF KOREA

Preface

When I published *A History of Korean Confucianism* (Vol. I, II) in 2012, I undertook to write a book which would illuminate the philosophical attributes of Korean Confucianism. This text, *Confucian Thought in Korea*, is the result of that commitment.

While planning this book, the first aspect requiring consideration was the methodology that would be most appropriate to the investigation. Ultimately, I decided on an analysis structured around the cardinal principles of Confucianism.

In any country that adopts Confucianism, the doctrine's cardinal principles are the fundamental factors that constitute its strand of Confucian thought. Therefore, the Confucian thought of Korea is the product of the application of its principles to the distinctive cultural climate of Korea on the part of Korean Confucian scholars. This is the reason I decided on the above-mentioned methodology.

The cardinal principles of Confucianism are generally considered to be benevolence (仁), righteousness (義), propriety (禮), wisdom (智) and fidelity (信), the concepts which have been most frequently debated since Confucius' own time. I believe that these are the ideological principles that have constituted the core of Confucianism.

It seems that this is the first time a methodology structured around these principles has been adopted in the entire Confucian region of East Asia. However, at the risk of possible error, which is usually committed in any first attempt, I believe that the fundamental Confucian concepts can best be understood through this methodology.

I discuss the application of the cardinal principles so that they may reveal the characteristics and idiosyncrasies of Korean Confucianism, and in this way persuasively explicate the contours of Korean Confucian thought. However, I have omitted the principle of fidelity from my discussion because, as a subsidiary idea, it has never been conceptualized as an independent quality, but only in tandem with the other principles. On the other hand, I discuss the principle of sil (實, substance or practicality), which was an indispensable concept in the development of Silhak (實學, Practical Learning), in grasping the characteristics of 'Neo-Confucian Silhak' and 'De-Neo-Confucian Silhak'.

Whether or not this book faithfully reflects my original intention depends on the reader's judgment, and I myself recognize the need for critical reflection on this work.

I will now briefly introduce some of the most significant results of my analysis.

Korean Confucian scholars faithfully observe the principle of benevolence, which they believed allowed them to be the primary force upholding the nation. On the basis of benevolence, with the spirit of devotion to the people, they sacrificed their lives in the purges of Confucian scholars in order to achieve rule by the people and for the people. Their sacrifice is strong evidence of the unique application of the principle of benevolence to the governance of the people.

Korean Confucian scholars were also preeminent in applying the principle of righteousness to the contemporary situation of Korea in various periods. Their belief that they were the primary intellectual and spiritual bulwark of the nation presupposed their adherence to righteous conduct. The outstanding evidence of Confucian scholars' practice of righteousness was the fact that beginning in 1592 they fought against the Japanese invaders for many years as soldiers of the righteous army. This was a distinctive phenomenon that could not be found in other Confucian countries in East Asia.

Another distinctive feature was the focus on propriety. Since the Goryeo Dynasty Korea has had the reputation of being 'the country of courteous people in the East'. During the Joseon Dynasty in the 17th century Confucian scholars intensively studied and practiced propriety, and this eventually gave rise to a partisan struggle called 'Yesong' (禮訟, disputes on the observance of propriety), which demonstrated the political ramifications of the excessive focus on decorum. This was also a characteristic that could not be found in other Confucian countries.

The main effect of the adherence to the principle of 'knowledge or wisdom (智)' in Korean Confucian thought was to give impetus to the study of Neo-Confucianism and the development of De-Neo-Confucian Silhak in the late Joseon Dynasty. Neo-Confucianism originated in the study of Cheonmyeong (天命, The Mandate of Heaven) in the 16th century. The core idea of this doctrine was that the human being is the supreme creature, and is one which can autonomously engage in moral action. It is not an exaggeration to say that all Neo-Confucian theories until the 19th century derived from continuous engagement with this core idea. In addition, 'the theory of human nobility (人尊思想)' became established as a significant locus of Confucian thought as a result of this focus.

In contrast to the abstraction of Neo-Confucianism, De-Neo-Confucian Silhak scholars in the late period of Joseon pursued thoroughgoing reforms aimed at the improvement of the welfare of the people and the enhancement of national wealth and power. They focused on the transformation of the land taxation, educational and slave systems, based on the proposition that all human beings were created by Heaven. Just as was the case with Neo-Confucianism, this doctrine also developed into 'the theory of human nobility', which in turn constributed to the formation of more modern theories such as 'human rights endowed by Heaven' and 'the equality of human beings'.

As we have seen, there is a case to be made that the diverse strands of Korean Confucian thought converge in 'the theory of human nobility'. This theory is clearly related to the 'humanitarian spirit' elaborated by Confucius and 'devotion to the welfare of mankind' advanced by the Dangun (the forefather of the Korean people) Myth. Ultimately, I believe that Korean Confucianism has bright prospects, as it is fundamentally based on 'the theory of human nobility'.

At the outset, I was conscious of the risk that my investigation, based on each of the several cardinal Confucian principles, could result in divergent kinds of understanding and could conversely also be more monotonous than a general survey which was not structured around the cardinal principles. Bearing this in mind, I begin this work with a survey of the history of Korean Confucianism. In addition, the investigation of each cardinal principle and its application have been carried out in the light of the contemporary historical situation in which it emerged. As a result, those who read this book in a linear fashion from start to finish may gain a general understanding of the subject.

Korean Confucian thought, based on the idea of human nobility, is not an obsolete intellectual remnant but a source of wisdom applicable to the task of living. An age-old philosophy is like a gemstone that reveals its true mettle after repeated polishing. In dealing with the venerable currents of Korean Confucianism, I have honed in on their unique characteristics because I have sought to excavate some pristine or jewel-like ideas worth polishing repeatedly, and I have underlined them whenever they merit special attention.

In particular, in the conclusion of this book, I anticipate that the theory of four beginnings and seven feelings, the status of human nature and the thing's nature relative to each other, and Neo-Confucian *simjeukri* (心卽理, Mind is *ri*) might contribute greatly to the development of 'the philosophy of mind'. I hope my expectation may be borne out, and that this book may play a part in strengthening Korean Confucian thought.

Anticipating unreserved criticisms from fellow scholars, I undertake to produce a more comprehensive work on Korean philosophy in the future. Finally, I am grateful to Kim Ji-eun, a student in the doctoral program in Korean Philosophy at Korea University, for her scrupulous proofreading and to the staff of the publishing company who spared no effort in readying this book for publication.

Youn Sa-soon,

at Silsangjae
June, 2017

CONTENTS

Chapter V.

A Revaluation of Neo-Confucian Theories

Chapter VII.

The Characteristics of De-Neo-Confucian Silhak

Chapter VIII.

Reflection on Korean Neo-Confucianism

Chapter I.

The Subject and Methods of Inquiry

1. Definition of Korean Confucianism

Korea has a long history of more than 4,300 years, and has preserved and developed its own variegated and priceless cultural heritage. Given its geopolitical position, of course, it cannot be denied that Korean culture has shared some common qualities with those of other East Asian countries. Nevertheless, Korean culture has its unique values and characteristics, which is evident in the fact that approximately 10 of its cultural artifacts and sites, including the Korean alphabet (Hangul), have been registered on UNESCO's World Cultural Heritage List.

At first glance, much of Korean culture has been based on its 'intellectual culture,' including its language and alphabet, religion, philosophy, education, politics, and so on, although 'folk culture,' consisting of native customs, folk plays and recreations, has also been very significant. Korea's intellectual culture has evolved around shamanism, Confucianism, Buddhism and Taoism. Korean shamanism, a type widely propagated in the Siberian region, is one of the oldest forms of religion in Korea and, as such, has played a role as one of Korea's native ideas and a primary foundation of national religion as well; moreover, Confucianism, Buddhism and Taoism, which were mainstreamed around two thousand years ago, have developed on the basis of shamanism and have been central to Korean history.

Among these traditional matrices of Korean thought, this book deals only with Confucianism. More specifically, I focus my inquiry on Korean Confucianism, especially Korean Confucian thought, that is, Confucianism as a field of learning, differentiated from Confucianism as a religion.

The term 'Confucianism' generally refers to Confucianism as a type of learning, 'Yuhak' (儒學), not as a religion, 'Yugyo' (儒教). However, Confucianism as a religion does not differ greatly in its content from Confucianism as a field of learning. In fact, considering that a religion *per se* entails a belief in an absolute being such as a god, we cannot say that Confucianism is a religion proper. As Confucius himself had an antipathy to the notion of divinities or spirits, Confucianism had little conventional religious inflection from the beginning. Moreover, 'gyo' (教) in 'Yugyo' refers originally to 'teaching' or 'education' rather than to 'religion.' In this sense, as I said above, the generic term Confucianism may be properly understood as a field of learning, and hereafter, it is referred to as such.

Confucianism comprises the elements Confucius compiled from the important cultural strains that had been shared by the school of the scholars called 'Yuka' (儒家) in the Spring and Autumn Period (春秋時代) of ancient China, which he consolidated into a system of learning. Many scholars called 'Yuja' (儒者) at that time studied and immersed themselves in their culture, including the arts and literature, rituals and music, astrology and calculation of planetary movements, numerology, and so on. It was very natural that these elements of the culture were assimilated into Confucius' system of learning. In short, Confucianism embraces various aspects of the Spring and Autumn Period's culture and integrates them into a complex system of learning. In this sense, Confucianism, constructed primarily on the basis of diverse areas of the culture such as literature, history, philosophy and science, is a complex, multi-faceted amalgam.

The main basis of the scholars' intellectual milieu in the Spring and Autumn Period was the Yellow River culture, and it was developed and expanded through its interaction with its neighboring cultures, such as that of the Dongyi (東夷族, Eastern Barbarians). It is beyond dispute that this cultural interchange contributed greatly to the formation of Confucianism. In this book, however, I will not deal with the origin or formation of Confucianism in ancient China, since, as I said above, my primary concern is Korean Confucianism.

In its generic sense, Confucianism is a Chinese system of thought. Therefore, the question is how to define Korean Confucianism. I define it as a strain of Confucian thought which has developed and flourished in a specific area of the Korean Peninsula, and whose scholars are Koreans. It should also be noted that the Korean people had not only received Confucianism from China and maintained it, but also modified and supplemented it according to their shifting circumstances and needs. Through this process, the Korean people adopted Chinese Confucianism on a widespread basis, and accordingly, Korean Confucianism has its own unique characteristics. This is not to say that it has no elements in common with Confucianism(s) in China and other countries. If it hadn't, we would have to delete the term 'Confucianism' from Korean Confucianism. In this regard, I will inquire into Korean Confucianism from the two perspectives of its unique aspects and those it shares with other Confucianism(s).

2. Methods of Inquiry

Any studies in Korean Confucianism must necessarily consider both some common aspects that it shares with Confucianism in other countries and its own distinctive aspects. Of these two, of course, the latter aspects should be underscored, because they are the special features that differentiate Korean Confucianism from other Confucianism(s).

As previously mentioned, it should also be noted that Confucianism is a complex edifice of learning, comprising politics, economics, sociology, literature, history, philosophy, and even science. Korean Confucianism is not an exception. However, when we analyze it, it is very important that both its phenomenal aspects (its application to or influence on actual realities) and its deeper aspects (its informing doctrines) should be considered. However, traditional or conventional approaches toward Confucianism have focused mainly on politics and ethics among its phenomenal aspects. Of course, such aspects are important, and the fact is that Korean Confucianism has helped form and develop Korean politics and public morality during some periods, which I will deal with in this book. However, my primary concern and the main focus of this research lies in the philosophical underpinnings of such phenomenal aspects. This is the reason I have entitled this book 'Confucian Thought in Korea.'

My research will be presented in the following order. First, I will point out some characteristics which the history of Korean Confucianism has displayed since the introduction of Confucianism, which constitutes chapter II. For this chapter, it will be sufficient to briefly survey the uniqueness of Korean Confucianism, revealed in the specific phases of its historical development.

Second, I will analyze the cardinal virtues of Confucianism. Many Korean scholars isolated its five cardinal virtues as ideological, guiding principles and applied them to the politics and morality of their time. As is well known, the five cardinal virtues which had been cherished as the bedrock of Confucianism since Confucius and Mencius are *in* (仁, benevolence or charity), *ui* (義, righteousness or justice), *ye* (禮, courtesy or propriety), *ji* (智, wisdom or knowledge) and *shin* (信, fidelity or sincerity). In chapter III, I will deal with how the three virtues, 'benevolence,' 'righteousness' and 'propriety' among these five virtues were realized in real world politics and moral education. Then I will describe the appearance of the new concept *sil* (實, substance or practicality) which came to the fore as an equivalent principle to the cardinal virtues. The realization of 'wisdom' will be considered in the subsequent chapter, while the virtue 'fidelity' will not be separately dealt with because it is a virtue which applies to the full realization of 'benevolence,' 'righteousness' and 'propriety.'

Third, chapter IV discusses a unique theory which Korean Confucian scholars elaborated regarding the virtue of 'wisdom.' The theory was based on Simhak (心學, the study of the mind), developed by Wang Shou-ren (王守仁, also known as Wang Yang-ming). Although the fact that Wang Shou-ren's philosophy was neglected or rejected by major Korean Confucian scholars may be a weakness in the history of Korean Confucianism, I think it is very important that at least one Korean scholar engaged himself in Wang's philosophy and established his own theory based on it. After this chapter, I will deal with Korean scholars' debates on complicated ideas such as *ri* (理, principle), *gi* (氣, material force), *sim* (心, mind or heart), *seong* (性, human nature) and *jeong* (情, feeling), along with the ideas of *in*, *ui* and *ye*.[1]

Fourth, another topic related to the virtue of 'wisdom' is Neo-Confucianism, the result of Korean Neo-Confucian scholars' theoretical research, which will be discussed in Chapter V. As a matter of fact, Neo-Confucianism, which had been established by Zhu Xi (朱熹, 1130-1200) and other representative Chinese Neo-Confucian scholars, was adopted as the reigning ideology of the Joseon Dynasty and, as such, it served as the representative strain of Korean Confucianism during the long period from the late fourteenth until the early twentieth centuries. In any case, Korean Neo-Confucianism enjoyed a long heyday, and accordingly brought forth the most colorful and abundant research of all Korean Confucian thought. In a sense, it may be said that Korean Neo-Confucianism was the intellectual field where the virtue of 'wisdom' was most fully realized.

Fifth, Chapters VI and VII deal with the other topics related to the virtue of 'wisdom', post Neo-Confucian Silhak (實學, Practical Learning),

1 Neo-Confucianism and Practical Learning in the Joseon Dynasty also prioritized the virtue of 'wisdom.'

which was conceived by some scholars of the late Joseon Dynasty who criticized the Neo-Confucian social order and governance in that period. Here, it is notable that, while the study of mind pursued by the Lu-Wang School (陸王學派), as opposed to the orthodox Neo-Confucianism of Zhu Xi, was in effect disregarded, post Neo-Confucian Practical Learning, a theory native to Korea, developed steadily in this era and came into full bloom. It can be asserted, however, that in cases where the concept of 'the practical' was applied as a principle, both Neo-Confucianism and post Neo-Confucianism may be regarded as 'Practical Learning'. On the other hand, there is a school of thought that these two departures can be distinguished in their content and character from each other even if they were both schools of 'Practical Learning.' I will also discuss these two conflicting ideas.

Previously I have published several books and articles dealing with Korean Confucianism. Among them are the two-volume *A History of Korean Confucianism* (Jisik Sanup Publications, 2012) and "A Study on the Specialties of Korean Confucianism" included in Volume 1 of *An Outline History of Korean Confucian Thought* (Advanced Center for Korean Studies, 2014). I should note that in this book I have recalibrated and rearranged the ideas contained in these previous studies and added new materials, in order to develop a new descriptive structure focusing on the cardinal principles of Confucianism.

Chapter II.

The History of Korean Confucianism : A General Outline

1. The Interregnum between the Introduction of Confucianism and Its Widespread Adoption

(1) The Introduction of Confucianism into Korea

When was Confucianism first introduced into Korea? This question has not been clearly answered, for there are no historical documents concerning the issue. Unlike Buddhism and Taoism, which were officially introduced into Korea through a series of political and (or) diplomatic decisions that were recorded in official documents, it is possible or even likely that Confucianism was introduced on an *ad hoc* basis by some Korean scholars who interacted with their counterparts in China, a process that did not produce any official documentation. As a result, the traces of the early introduction of Confucianism into Korea are difficult to discern. For this reason, the estimate of the period of Confucianism's introduction into Korea is unavoidably based on my own analysis.

Given that Confucianism found its way to Korea through personal contacts between Korean and Chinese scholars, we may assume that several preconditions had to be fulfilled. First, it was necessary for

Korean scholars to have competence in reading Chinese characters. Second, the canonical Confucianism texts such as *The Analects of Confucius* (論語) and *The Book of Mencius* (孟子) must have already been completed and achieved recognition. Lastly, there must have been ongoing interchange between Chinese Confucian scholars and Korean scholars, even if only on a personal basis. Given these preconditions, I suggest that Confucianism was first introduced into Korea at around the same time as they had been fulfilled.

Chinese characters along with epigraphic letters were known in Korea around the fifth century BC. About one century later, Chinese characters began to be used to designate proper nouns such as a person's name in the Three Kingdoms of Goguryeo, Baekje and Silla. On the other hand, the main texts, including *The Analects of Confucius* and *The Book of Mencius*, which constitute the traditional Confucian canon, are known to have been completed before the end of the Warring States period (戰國時代) (247 BC), and many Chinese scholars and intellectuals began to move from China to Korea around 246-240 BC during the early Qin (秦) Dynasty. Given these considerations, it can be said that Confucianism became known in Korea in approximately 240 BC, between the end of the Qin dynasty and the early days of the Han (漢) Dynasty. Therefore, I believe that Korean Confucianism was established in this period.

(2) The Belated Adoption of Confucianism

In general, it sometimes happens that no sooner has a doctrine or an ideology been introduced than it is accepted and widely diffused. This, however, was not the case with the beginnings of Confucianism in Korea. Full-fledged acceptance and propagation of Confucianism in Korea took place many centuries after it was introduced.

In fact, a noticeable example of Confucianism being genuinely accepted was the establishment of both private and public educational institutes. Despite the slowness of its diffusion, some private educational institutes used Confucian classics as the main textbooks or included Confucianism in their curriculum. In the Three Kingdoms, there were private schools which Korean scholars established on their own account (it is not known exactly when they were founded), for instance, Gyungdang (扃堂) in Goguryeo, and other similar private institutes in Baekje and Silla.

However, the official acceptance of Confucianism was closely related to the establishment of a central national/public educational institute in which Confucian teachings were propagated. The first national school was Taehak (太學), also called Kukhak (國學, the highest national educational institute). In Goguryeo, it was established in the 2nd year of King Sosurim's reign (372 AD); in Baekje, it is believed that a national school like a Taehak was built in the 26th year of King Geunchogo's reign (371 AD)[1]; and in Silla, much later in the 14th year of King Bubheung's reign (527 AD).

Given this historical record, there is a consensus that the first Taehak was established in 372 AD. It is noteworthy, then, that this was approximately 610 years after the introduction of Confucianism into Korea. That is, it took about six centuries to officially accept Confucianism after its introduction. This long period was, as it were, an empty interregnum in the history of Korean Confucianism. The fact that there was a centuries-long long pause in the initial phase of Korean Confucianism is a salient feature in its history, compared with that of Chinese Confucianism.

In China, the era corresponding to this period in Korea extended from the Han dynasty (206-264 AD) to the Northern and Southern Dynasties in which the Northern Wei (北魏) and Jin (晉) Dynasties wielded power. During the Han Dynasty, Confucianism had been adopted as a governing ideology. Subsequently, it underwent a period of hungo (訓詁), that is, heated debates on Confucian exegesis and began to be influenced by the thought of Laozi (老子) and Zhuang

1 Cf. Go Myung-sa, "The Development of School Education in Baekje," *The Journal of Paekche Research Institute*, Vol. 11 (Paekche Research Institute, Chungnam National University, 1982).

Zhou (莊子) during the era of the Northern and Southern Dynasties. As mentioned above, however, Confucianism in Korea was quiescent for roughly the same length of time since its introduction. The important point is, therefore, the need to explain this central phenomenon of the early development of Korean Confucianism. In the following section I will discuss this issue.

(3) Native Korean Ideas and Confucianism

I believe that the above-mentioned interregnum in Korean Confucianism's history was related to the way it was introduced into Korea. In other words, the belated official adoption of Confucianism was due to the fact that it was first introduced through personal contacts between Chinese and Korean scholars, not as a result of national policy. As a matter of fact, the introduction of an idea by isolated individuals generally has little power to further its active adoption.

Another fact may also be relevant. Confucianism was first introduced earlier than Buddhism and Taoism, and there were no negative reactions toward it in Korean society. On the other hand, Buddhism and Taoism were confronted with antipathy and resistance. In Silla, when Buddhism was introduced, there were signs of discontent from some sections of society, and in Goguryeo, Buddhist circles displayed their dissatisfaction with the introduction of Taoism. In the Three Kingdoms of Korea, however, there was no repulsion shown toward Confucianism. The reason may be that the core ideas of Confucianism didn't conflict with those of shamanism, which was deeply rooted in Korean society at that time. If Confucianism had clashed with shamanism, distaste for it may have been apparent, as occurred in the cases of Buddhism and Taoism.

In fact, the virtue of *chunghyo* (忠孝, loyalty and filial piety), one of the representative virtues of Confucianism, can be found in the ancient shamanistic society of Korea. For example, in Goguryeo, Dongmaeng (東盟), a celestial divine worship ritual based on shamanism, was performed. However, it was also a ceremonial ritual enacted in memory of King Dongmyeong, the founding father of Goguryeo. In this sense, *Dongmaeng* was an exemplary ritual of ancient ancestor worship which had a source in common with *hyo* (孝, filial piety), a virtue of Confucianism. It is, therefore, natural that *hyo* of Confucianism was never seen as an aberrant virtue in a society where ancient ancestor worship was familiar.

Likewise, *chung* (忠, loyalty), another virtue of Confucianism, was a familiar concept in ancient Korea. Before the era of the Three Kingdoms, Yemaek (濊貊), an ancient tribe who lived in the northern part of Korea and had ancestral ties to some Korean kingdoms, had struggled against China for a long period. Yemaek's fierce antagonism toward China had been succeeded by that of Goguryeo, which waged large-scale wars against China by mobilizing more than ten thousand troops in each war. Judging from these historical facts, it can be said that the Goguryeo kings were not tribal leaders but powerful heads of state kings in a centralized government, and under them, there were loyal subjects, generals and officials who rendered devoted service to their king. In that political structure, it is not likely that *chung* (loyalty) of Confucianism was regarded as a foreign, strange virtue, but was instead naturally assimilated into the native idea of loyalty of the Korean people.

In this regard, it is probable that Confucianism seeped into Korea without any obstacles, and as a result, there was no need to actively or consciously adopt it. That is, the long interregnum between the introduction of Confucianism and its official adoption paradoxically derived from the cultural or spiritual climate of the Korean peninsula, which had a close affinity with Confucianism.[2]

The last consideration that should be taken into account is the difference in the cultural situations of China and Korea at that time. In China, during the Han Dynasty, there was an effort to reconstruct

2 I discussed these facts in detail in Vol. 1 of *A History of Korean Confucianism* (Jisik Sanup Publications, 2012).

Confucian texts which had been destroyed as a result of the policy of Emperor Qin Shi Huan, the first emperor of the Qin Dynasty, which called for 'the burning of books and burying of scholars' (焚書坑儒) in order to suppress intellectual discourses. Many Chinese Confucian scholars made every effort to restructure Confucian texts through the difficult process of hungo (exegeses and historical investigation). On the other hand, it was not necessary for Korean scholars to be concerned with this task, and they were not in a position to engage in it. It may be safely said that this cultural situation in Korea was another reason Confucianism was not officially adopted for several centuries after its introduction.

2. The Characteristics of Korean Confucianism Formed in Its Early Years

(1) Education at Royal Academies Based on Their Textbooks

The Confucian classics used for educational purposes in the royal academy called Taehak in the Three Kingdoms of Korea included *The Book of Odes* (詩經), *The Book of History* (書經), *The Book of Changes* (周易), *The Book of Rites* (禮記), *The Spring and Autumn Annals* (春秋) which are the five Confucian classics (五經); *The Grand Scribe's Records* (史記), *The Book of Han* (漢書), *The Book of the Later Han* (後漢書), *Samgukji* (三國志, The Records of the Three Kingdoms), and *The Spring and Autumn Annals of the Jin Dynasty* (晉春秋), which are history books; *Munseon* (文選), a collection of poetry; *Okpyeon* (玉篇), *Jatong* (字通), and *Jarim* (字林), which are lexicons; *The Analects of Confucius*, and *The Book of Filial Piety* (孝經).[3] These were the texts commonly taught at Taehak during the Three Kingdoms era. Therefore, it can also be said that the education at Taehak did not exceed the scope of

3 "Iyeokjeon" (異域傳), *The Book of Zhou* (周書).
"Goryeo (Goguryeo)jeon" (高麗傳) and "Dongijeon" (東夷傳), *The Old Book of Tang* (舊唐書).

these books.

There are some materials from the Silla Dynasty that reveal the content of the education at its Taehak. Silla's Taehak offered the following three levels of classes (三科授業), each of which had its own texts as follows: advanced level—*The Book of Rites, The Book of Changes, The Analects of Confucius*, and *The Book of Filial Piety*; intermediate level—*Jwajeon, Mosi, The Analects of Confucius*, and *The Book of Filial Piety*; and elementary level —*Sangseo* (*The Book of History*), *Munseon*, *The Analects of Confucius*, and *The Book of Filial Piety.* In these three-levels of classes, along with *The Analects of Confucius, The Book of Filial Piety* was also regarded as important enough to be mandatory reading. At the end of the 8th century (788 AD), *Dokseosampumgwa* (讀書三品科), a three-level course of instruction, was created in Taehak. According to this system, *The Analects of Confucius* was the basis of a mandatory course both at advanced and intermediate levels, which shows the importance of this text at that time. It is clear that these mandatory courses at the Taehak reveal what were considered the core components of intellectual education at that time. This state of affiars will be discussed in detail below.

(2) Mandatory Courses: *The Analects of Confucius* and *The Book of Filial Piety*

Mandatory courses at Taehak, which was akin to today's national university, were established in order to disseminate their central ideas among the public. It seems clear that, in the early years after the official adoption of Korean Confucianism, national policies focused on inculcating the ideas contained in *The Analects of Confucius* and *The Book of Filial Piety*. Therefore, it is necessary to explore the ideas that comprise these two books.

It is well known that *The Analects of Confucius* is a book that elaborates on the philosophy of Confucius. Most scholars agree that the core idea of Confucius is *in* (benevolence). In *The Analects of Confucius, in* is explained in various ways by Confucius, but "loving people" (

愛人) is its most fundamental definition.[4] According to Confucius, *in* is realized in the attitude of *seo* (恕)—the injunction to allow others to do that which the self wants to do, and not to coerce others to that which the self does not want to do.[5] This attitude corresponds to the golden rule of Confucian ethical thought—the injunction to divine others' feelings based on what one feels (推己及人).

With respect to the realization of *in*, Yuja (有子), a disciple of Confucius, offered a more specific account: "*In* is realized as *hyoje* (孝悌: filial piety and brotherly love)[6]." This is why *hyo* (filial piety) was employed as a principle of patriarchal order in Confucianism, and the text that specified the path to its realization was *The Book of Filial Piety*. Based on these considerations, it can be said that the reason for making these courses mandatory was that the government strove to put them into practice by focusing on filial piety (*hyo*). In order to emphasize *hyoje* among many virtues, the Taehak royal academy required the teaching of *The Book of Filial Piety* as well as *The Analects of Confucius*.

Besides, *The Analects of Confucius* also includes the idea of *chung* (loyalty), which is applicable to politics and moral behavior. Confucius mentioned the principles that should be applied to the relationship between the king and his vassals. He said, "Vassals should serve the king with *chung*, and the king should rule his vassals with propriety (禮)."[7] The fact that vassals had to practice *chungseong* (忠誠: loyalty) reveals the reason for the mandatory teaching of *The Analects of Confucius*. In order to consolidate the centralization of power, the government wanted the people to learn and practice the virtue of loyalty. This logic was applied not only to the public but also to powerful parties such as tribal chiefs who might attempt to become king. The goal was that knowledge of the loyalty-mediated relationship between the king and his subjects would also transform the consciousness of an individual who wished to become king based on his ability to rule not just a

4 "Book 12" (顔淵), *The Analects of Confucius*.
5 "Book 6" (雍也) and "Book 15" (衛靈公), ibid.
6 "Book 1" (學而), ibid.
7 "Book 3" (八佾), ibid.

single tribe (clan) but all tribes. Thus, it seems that promoting changes in the consciousness of the king and the country was another reason for the focus on *The Analects of Confucius* at Taehak.

(3) Autonomy Demonstrated through the Distinctive Acceptance of Confucianism

It should also be noted that contemporary society had the characteristics of a kinship community, unlike today. Patriarchal family ethics centered on the Confucian *hyo* could effectively be applied to society thanks to the latter's nature. To ensure the authoritative rule of a king who sought to possess real power, loyalty to the king had to predominate over loyalty to tribal or clan leaders. The setting of *The Book of Filial Piety* and *The Analects of Confucius* as compulsory texts at the Taehak royal academy was the measure implemented to satisfy this imperative. This was how the foreign philosophy of Confucianism was propagated in Korean society, which demonstrates the autonomous reception of Confucianism on the part of the Korean people.

This autonomous reception can also be confirmed by the type and variety of history books published in the Three Kingdoms of Korea. The history books of the Three Kingdoms published during this period are as follows. In the initial years of the Goguryeo Dynasty (founded in 37 BC), a series of history books composed of 100 volumes, *Yugi* (留記), was created by an unknown author. They were later reorganized and republished as a five-volume work entitled *Sinjip* (新集) in the 11th year of King Yeongyang's reign (600 AD) by Yi Mun-jin (李文眞), a scholar of the royal academy Taehak. During the Baekje Dynasty, Go Heung (高興) wrote *Seogi* (書記) in the 30th year of King Geunchogo's reign (375 AD), followed by several other history books created by unknown authors, such as *Baekjegi* (百濟記), *Baekjebongi* (百濟本紀), and *Baekjesinchan* (百濟新撰). Finally, during the Silla Dynasty, Geo Chil-bu (居柒夫) and others wrote *Guksa* (國史) in the 6th year of King

Jinheung's reign (556 AD).

The history books of a country reveal the people's conception of its origin and evolution. It can be said that the history books in the Three Kingdoms of Korea were influenced by three canonical Chinese history texts (*The Grand Scribe's Records, The Book of Han and The Book of the Later Han*) and by *The Spring and Autumn Annals of China*, but their publication also revealed that the origin of the Three Kingdoms of Korea was different from that of China. Thus, these history books were the manifestation of the autonomous development of the Korean people and the adoption of Confucianism in Korea occurred based on this sense of independence.

3. Original and Sajang (詞章) Confucianism after the Adoption of Confucianism (6th-11th Century)

In terms of its content, the investigation of Korean Confucianism cannot be conducted thoroughly without understanding historical trends, which entails exploring the historical changes in Korean Confucianism. In addition, while the trajectory of Korean Confucianism did not mirror the developments in Korean dynastic history, the two were nevertheless very closely related to each other. This is the reason why it is necessary for explanations of dynastic history to accompany the examination of the historical changes in Confucianism.

To this point, this book has covered the history of the 4th to the 6th centuries, from the introduction of Confucianism into a society where ancient shamanism had prevailed since approximately 2300 BC, to the adoption of Confucianism in the Three Kingdoms of Korea (Goguryeo, Baekje, and Silla). This period was followed by the North-South States Period (669-918) when Balhae (渤海) and Silla coexisted, and then the Goryeo Dynasty (918-1392), which preceded the Joseon Dynasty (1392-1910). Korea was then temporarily occupied by force by Japan (for 36 years), and was liberated in 1945 with the end of the

Pacific War. Soon after the liberation, the Korean War occurred, and currently the Korean Peninsula is divided into South and North Korea.

According to Choe Chi-won (崔致遠, 857-?) from Silla, the trend of philosophy in the North South States Period subsequent to the Three Kingdoms Period was called *pungryu* (風流, 玄妙之道) which appropriated shamanistic elements and embraced Confucianism, Buddhism, and Taoism on the basis of the shamanistic idea of *seon* (仙, the immortal beings). The core ideas of these three religions were all adhered to to the extent that circumstances required, on the basis of Korea's shamanistic tradition. Specifically, as a result of the assimilation of the tenets of shamanism that they shared, the loyalty and filial piety of Confucianism, the perspective on virtue and vice of Buddhism, and the idea of non-action and nature of Taoism (Lao-Zhuang) were all incorporated in a delicate balance with one another.[8] This hybrid dissemination of all three religions without any priority given to one in particular was the primary trend of philosophy from the Three Kingdoms Period to the North South States Period. As a result, during this period, Confucianism was not valued above the other religions.

However, Buddhism was in fact the state religion in the Goryeo Dynasty. This dynasty also valued Taoist feng shui (風水) thought, but Buddhism was most valued as the state religion. Confucianism was disseminated as a subordinate teaching within the ambit of Buddhism. However, even in this period, a representative Confucian scholar, Choi Seung-ro (崔承老, 927-989), emerged in the early years of the Goryeo Dynasty. He pointed out the worldly limitations of Buddhism and strove to elevate Confucianism. According to him, since Buddhism only focuses on purifying oneself in order to enjoy prosperity in the afterlife, politics in this life must rely on Confucianism. He tried to limit the influence of Buddhism and to actively promote Confucianism. Partly as a result of his efforts, Confucian ideas came to predominate in the field of politics at that time, and this trend continued into the 11th century.

---

8 Choe Chi-won (崔致遠), "Introduction to Nanrangbi" (鸞郎碑,序).

Until the end of the 11th century, Korean Confucianism was a combination of the Original Confucianism (本源儒學) of Confucius and Mencius and the Sajanghak (詞章學, study of poetry and writing) of the Han and Tang Dynasties. As previously mentioned, Original Confucianism was not succeeded by Hungo Confucianism in Korea. Thus, Original Confucianism and Sajang Confucianism coexisted in Goryeo, and it is clear that this situation differed from the prevailing conditions in China.

Between the late 11th century and the first half of the 13th century, early Neo-Confucianism (also known as Northern Song Neo-Confucianism), which preceded Zhu Xi Neo-Confucianism in China, was introduced into Korea. Although this period marked only the beginning of its intellectual trajectory, Neo-Confucianism was already approached quite philosophically. Thus, it will be described separately below in more detail.[9]

4. The Rise of Early Neo-Confucianism

(1) The Background of the Rise of Early Neo-Confucianism

The emergence of early Neo-Confucianism in Goryeo from the late 11th to the early 13th century seems to have been greatly influenced by the exchanges between scholar envoys from Goryeo and Confucian scholars in the Northern Song. At that time, Kim Ryan-gam (金良監, ?) was the leader of a group of scholar envoys from Goryeo. While visiting Song, he met Su Shi (蘇軾), and learned about the academic work of the Cheng brothers, Cheng Ho and Cheng Yi (程顥 and 程頤). In addition, Yun Gwan (尹瓘, ?-1111), one of the great scholars of *The Book of Changes*, had the chance to acquire *Zizhi Tongjian* (資治通鑑) and also discussed *yeok* (易) and wrote poetry with Cheng Yi while

9 Descriptions in this chapter are based on *A History of Korean Confucianism* (Jisik Sanup Publications, 2012).

visiting Song in 1098. Yun Eon-yi (尹彦頤, ?- 1149), a son of Yun Gwan and author of *Yeokhae* (易解), gave a lecture on *The Book of Changes* to writers who studied under Cheng Yi while visiting Song. Kim Bu-sik (金富軾), author of *Samguksagi*, and Kim In-jon (金仁存), the author of *Noneoshinui* (論語新義), also visited Song around that time. These contacs contributed to the emergence of Neo-Confucianism in Goryeo during that era (12th -13th century).

The rise of Neo-Confucianism occurred at the end of the Tang Dynasty when Buddhism was the leading strand of public philosophical thought, and constituted an attempt to revive Confucianism by displacing Buddhism and the thought of Laozi and Zhuang Zhou (Taoism). For this reason, in the development of early Neo-Confucianism in late Tang, Buddhism and the thought of Laozi and Zhuang Zhou were rejected as heresy. Precisely the same phenomenon occurred in Goryeo during the 11th century.

Buddhism had been the state religion ever since the foundation of Goryeo, and Taoist learning and practices had also been permitted to the public. By the end of the 10th century, Buddhism and Taoism were thriving greatly in the lives of people throughout Goryeo, from the royal family to the general public. Even *feng shui*, a strand of thought from Taoism, was also approved by the government. In 1106, a group of scholars, including Kim Injon, Choi Seon (崔璿), and Yi Jae (李載), wrote *Haedongbirok* (海東秘錄) at the king's command. This was a comprehensive investigation into Korean geography based on *feng shui* (i.e. nature). This book was later used as a resource for the construction of roads and government offices, and was a basis of *feng-shui* theory in Korea.

However, at almost the same time (around the end of the 11th century), some Confucian scholars began to speak negatively about *feng shui*. Yi Ui (李顗, ?), a government official during that period (from King Munjong's reign to Seonjong's), stressed that not only *Bibo* (裨補), a book that artificially assimilated the concept of fortune into that of nature, but also *Pungsudocham* (風水圖讖), a text that predicted fortune based on natural conditions, were not credible.[10] He explicitly rejected *Pung-sudocham*, pointing out its absurdity in front of the King. In addition, in 1131, Yun Eon-yi even rejected the thought of Laozi and Zhuang Zhou, and proposed to prohibit its study at Taehak. As these examples show, Confucian scholars attempted to strengthen Confucianism by rejecting the thought of Laozi and Zhuang Zhou.

Ihm Chun (林椿, ?), in particular, spearheaded the rejection of Buddhism in the 12th century. In order to accomplish this, he first reminded people of Han Yu (韓愈). Han Yu was a scholar who led the effort to reject Buddhism in favor of the revival of Confucianism in the late Tang Dynasty, where Confucianism had declined due to the rise of Buddhism. Im Chun also bitterly criticized the behavior of the monks of that time. According to him, the acts of some Confucian scholars seemed somewhat undesirable, but those of the monks were odious enough to cause adverse consequences. He pointed out that not only their ignorance of family life composed of husband-wife and parent-child relationships, but also their debauchery, bad faith, and selfishness were significant problems. The primary reason why he rejected Buddhism was because he believed that it lacked the concepts of benevolence (仁), righteousness (義), and morality (道) and basically turned people into barbarians. This argument revealed the passionate desire of Ihm Chun to revive Confucianism through the rejection of Buddhism.

Yi Gyu-bo (李奎報, 1168-1241), a well-known younger writer at that time, was also a leading scholar of the Confucian canon. He insisted that people should try to resolve their daily problems through the study of scriptures, that is, 'Confucian Classics.' This was what Yi Go (李翺), a pioneer of Neo-Confucianism along with Han Yu in the late Tang Dynasty, also advocated. What Yi Gyu-bo argued for was the need to seek from the Six Classics of Confucianism (六經) a way to resolve problems related to overlordship, religion and

10 *Goryeomyeonghyeonjip* (高麗名賢集), Vol. 2, p.108, and Choi Ja, *Bohanjip* (補閑集), Vol. 1.

politics, morals, and customs. Because he considered the study of the Confucian Classics important, Yi asserted, "Writing is merely a trivial skill," despite his reputation as a great writer.[11] Yi showed his determination to evolve in terms of academic traditions from the *Sajang* tendency, which focused on sentences and literal work, to Neo-Confucianism, the so-called study of fidelity, which put more emphasis on thought. It was this will to migrate from one academic tradition to another that initiated Neo-Confucianism in Goryeo. The concrete reality of this early Neo-Confucianism is explicated below.

(2) The Theoretical Understanding of Nature and Humans

A group of scholars, including Ihm Chun, proposed a new theory, which had never been elaborated before. They had already amassed an understanding of all phenomena involving change based on first principles instead of divine power. Their intellectual project was founded on an ontological interpretation of change that applied the concept of *ri-gi* (理氣) to nature and humans, and the resulting study was Neo-Confucianism in all respects. Yi Gyu-bo expressed his philosophy as follows:

> "The creation of humans and nature, which you have asked about, is wholly determined in deep darkness and occurs naturally. Neither God nor the Creator has insight into it. Originally, the creation of humans did] not occur upon the command of God but naturally. First, the primordial *gi* (元氣) is divided into two: the upper part became the sky, and the lower part became the earth. Since humans are in the middle realm between the two, the entire system is called *samjae* (三才), which is a constant principle."[12]

11 Yi Gyu-bo, "Sangminsangsisikseo" (上閔上侍湜書), *Dongukisangukjip* (東國李相國集), Vol. 26.
12 Yi Gyu-bo, "Munjomul" (問造物), *Dongukisangukjip*, Vol. 1, 2nd Collection. (This article was first unearthed by Jeong Seong-cheol and Choi Bong-ik.)

"With the clean and strong *gi*, which was sturdily forged by the creation hammer, I was born with a soul after the five elements constituted a body based on *yin* (陰) and *yang* (陽), and twenty-eight lunar mansions were aligned in the bosom."[13]

According to this conception, the universe was not formed by God or the Creator, and neither is even aware of it. These passages emphasize the fact that the universe was naturally created. They maintain that the primodial *gi* had already existed, and, for unfathomable reasons, it was divided into heaven, humans, and the earth, forming the *samjae* (三才). This is Yi Gyu-bo's cosmogony, his creation theory.

He also stated that a human being is made up of *gi*. The only difference between humans and objects is that humans are born with a very clean and strong *gi*. This is reminiscent of what Zhou Dunyi (周敦頤) in the Song Dynasty said in his *Taegeukdoseol* (太極圖說), that "Humans are endowed with the most superior *gi* of all that consist of the five elements." These scholars believed that man, who has the most superior *gi*, is the lord of all creation.

The fact that the primordial *gi*, which can be called a kind of protyle with energy, and clean and strong *gi* were mentioned here shows that the concept of *gi* was used earlier than that of *ri* in the early Neo-Confucianism in Goryeo. Subsequently, *do* (道) or *cheondo* (天道) began to be referenced by this philosophy based on the concept of *gi*.

"If all intervening objects are removed in order to see things in depth based on *do*, fortune and misfortune are no longer noticed. However, based on *cheondo*, although sun and moon, stars, mountains and streams, and clouds are the largest of all things, they cannot avoid wax and wane, new changes, good and bad luck, and fortune and misfortune, either. This is because it is impossible to escape the law of *yin* and *yang*."[14]

---

13 Ihm Chun, "Sangyhaksajimyungseo" (上李學士知命書), *Seohajip* (西河集), Vol. 4.

14 Yi Gyu-bo, "Tongjaegi" (通齊記), *Dongukisangukjip*, Vol. 23, 2nd

The fact that all things with form must endure wax and wane, new changes, and fortune and misfortune is a result of *cheondo*, the law of nature. Since the cause of those changes is the *gi* of *yin-yang*, the law of nature *cheondo* can be seen as the law of *yin* and *yang*. In this regard, it is all but certain that the philosophy of *gi* in early Neo-Confucianism was singularly intensified in Goryeo.

(3) The Awareness of ***Ri*** (理, principle) and ***Seong*** (性, human nature) and the Establishment of the Moral Value of Scholars

During this period, Yi Gyu-bo was able to employ the concepts of not only *gi*, but also *ri* and *seong*. However, he used the concept of *ri* less frequently compared to that of *gi*. The following passages are the explanations of this emphasis:

> "While *yin* and *yang* keep changing, *ri* is often too subtle to be noticed."[15] "The sun and moon wax and wane in the sky. The fullness and emptiness of all creation is really *sangri* (常理, immutable principle). This is not an imbalance but the law of nature."[16]

He also used *ri* as a contrasting concept for the *gi* of *yin-yang*. However, as can be ascertained from the fact that even *sangri* was understood based on changes in nature, the concept of *ri* was interpreted as the law of nature. This reveals that his *ri* primarily referred to a natural and universal law. In this regard, it should be noted that this *ri* was different from the *ri* in Zhu Xi's *soiyeon* (所以然, natural principle) and *sodangyeon* (所當然, normative principle). Yi's *ri* was not only different from Zhu Xi's, but also distinct from even Cheng Yi's *ri* in *riilbunsu* (理一分殊, one principle and its instantiation in many manifestations),

---

Collection.
15 Yi Gyu-bo, "Sibiweolsakilsik" (十二月朔日蝕), *Dongukisangukjip*, Vol. 2, 2nd Collection.
16 Yi Gyu-bo, 'Woorusangwanjojeungdongyogimgun" (又樓上觀潮贈同寮金君), *Dongukisangukjip*, Vol. 16, 2nd Collection.

which was ultimately the form of *ri* that Yi believed was actualized in order to be applied to *Taegeuk* (太極, the great ultimate).

It should also be noted that Yi Gyu-bo's *ri* was not only limited to the law of nature, as it also encompassed the principle of morality. This can be seen in his characterization of it, as follows:

> "I just follow *ri* based on *seong* (human nature) departing from nature. How could such a strange creator say anything about this!"[17]

Ri in this text is not the law of nature. It is a moral principle, which aligns it with the *ri* of *sodangyeon* (normative principle). Based on his statement, "I follow *ri* based on *seong* departing from nature," this *seong* does not seem to be of a basic form, either. It corresponds to *seong* of the earth and the sky that Zhang Zai (張載) described as symmetrical to the *seong* of character, which becomes the *seong* of nature later. Yi Gyu-bo in fact differentiated between the *seong* of character and the *seong* of nature.[18] Clearly the *seong* of nature has a rational attribute, while the *seong* of character has a kind of emotional attribute. In this regard, the adoption of *ri* based on *seong* is a moral attitude that attempts to follow ethical norms in accordance with a rational nature. This becomes more evident in light of the fact that the *seong* of nature is not dissimilar to Confucius and Mencius's virtues of benevolence, righteousness, propriety and wisdom.

After being excluded from the orbit of those in power, Im Chun passed the idle hours pondering upon himself one of *Haejwachilin* (海左七人, Seven Sages of Goryeo). While discussing the appropriate condition and attitude of the scholar, Im Chun wrote a text in a poetic style, quoted below:

> "Make a knife whose spine is made up of virtue and morals, whose

---

17 Yi Gyu-bo, "Byeongjung" (病中), *Dongukisangukjip*, Vol. 16, 2nd Collection.

18 Cf. Rho Pyeong-yu, *A Study of Yi Gyu-bo's Philosophy (*Sungkyunkwan Univ. Graduate School, 1990).

> point is made up of benevolence and righteousness, and whose edge is made up of wisdom and courage. Wrap it with righteous and reliable word and deed and decorate it with exquisite and outstanding writing. If one keeps it in a chest, it will surely protect one. If one practices this skill, one can use it to meet the demands of the times."[19]

As a desirable candidate for public office, a scholar must be equipped with righteous and reliable word and deed as well as beautiful and outstanding writing ability. However, it is more important to possess the personal attributes of virtue, good morals, benevolence, righteousness, wisdom, and courage. According to Ihm Chun, when one is equipped with these attributes, one can finally become a worthwhile person, a scholar. This demonstrates that early Neo-Confucianism incorporated this perspective in what constitutes the ethical man.

Because Neo-Confucianism had originally emerged with the goal of strengthening morals, which was a more practical focus than that of Buddhism, the focus on ethical man was not unusual at all. Actually, it seemed natural, and was consistent with the fact that propriety was prioritized with the emergence of Neo-Confucianism. (This will be discussed in more detail later.[20]

As described above, early Neo-Confucianism emerged in its own unique way in Goryeo. However, it is difficult to avoid the conclusion that the intellectual breadth and depth of the early Neo-Confucianism of Goryeo was constricted compared to that of China. First of all, there were only two Neo-Confucian scholars in Goryeo. If there had been additional scholars, Korean Neo-Confucianism would have been richer during that period. It is also unfortunate that important texts were lost, including *Yeokhae* written by Yun Eon-yi and *Noneoshinui* (論語新義) written by Kim In-jon.

---

19 Ihm Chun, "Sangyhaksajimyungseo" (上李學士知命書), *Seohajip* (西河集), Vol. 4.

20 The practical application of propriety will be discussed in Chapter 3, "The Practical Implementation of the Cardinal Principles of Confucianism."

Secondly, there was no recognition of the following crucial concepts related to Neo-Confucianism in Goryeo: *saengui* (生意), the definition of benevolence proposed by the Cheng brothers who regarded *ri* as real even though its concept emerged only in theory; and *cheonjeukri* (天卽理, heaven is *ri*), *seongjeukri* (性卽理, human nature is *ri*), and *riilbunsu* (理一分殊). However, regardless of these deficiencies, after Zhu Xi's Neo-Confucianism was later introduced, Neo-Confucianism in Joseon developed to such an extent as to surpass the sophistication of Chinese Neo-Confucianism. Thus, our regret at those deficiencies will be tempered in a later chapter that examines this flowering.

5. Major Aspects of the Zhu Xi Neo-Confucian Era

(1) The Introduction of Zhu Xi Neo-Confucianism

The Neo-Confucianism of Zhu Xi in the Southern Song Dynasty, a compilation of the entire Neo-Confucian corpus since the era of the Northern Song Dynasty, could not be directly introduced into Korea. Unlike the Neo-Confucianism of the early Northern Song, Zhu Xi Neo-Confucianism entered Korea belatedly. It was first introduced by Ahn Hyang (安珦, or 安裕, 1243-1306) in 1289 (the 15th year of King Chungryeol's reign). While visiting Yanjing, the capital of Yuan, Ahn had an opportunity to read *The Complete Works of Master Zhu* (朱子書). After doing so, he transcribed it (including the portraits of Confucius and Zhu Xi) in order to disseminate it in Korea.[21]

The reason for the late introduction of Zhu Xi Neo-Confucianism to Korea was because of national and international political instability. Nationally, the military rule (under the military wing of the Choi family) that had persisted for almost 100 years since the military rebellion

21 "Sega" (世家), *The History of Goryeo* (高麗史), Vol. 30, (the 15th year of King Chungryeol's reign).

(1170) led by Jeong Jung-bu (鄭仲夫, 1106-1179) brought about academic decline. Internationally, there were the intermittent intrusions of Jin (金國) and Khitan (契丹) from the North, the repeated large-scale invasions of Yuan from 1231 to 1274, and the severance of academic exchanges with the Southern Song Dynasty, which was in decline.

However, after its introduction, it did not take long for Zhu Xi Neo-Confucianism to gain a foothold in Korea due to scholars' enthusiastic research into it. Within approximately one century, by the late Goryeo Dynasty (1392), Zhu Xi Neo-Confucianism planted its roots deep into the the world of Korean Confucianism. Through the work of representative scholars during this period, including Baek I-jeong (白頤正, 1247-1323), Gwon Bo (權溥, 1262-1346), Yi Je-hyeon (李齊賢, 1287-1367), Yi Saek (李穡, 1328-1396), and Jeong Mong-ju (鄭夢周, 1337-1392: a professor at Seonggyungwan), the theories underlying Zhu Xi Neo-Confucianism began to be studied and its customary proprieties (e.g. the three-year mourning period) began to be observed. As a result, Confucianism during the Joseon Dynasty, which had been represented by the thought of Gwon Geun (權近, 1352-1409) and Jeong Do-jeon (鄭道傳, 1342-1398) was replaced by Zhu Xi Neo-Confucianism.

(2) The Beginning of the Zhu Xi Neo-Confucian Era

The Joseon Dynasty (1392-1910) period is the era when Zhu Xi Neo-Confucianism flowered, to the extent that it can be called the Neo-Confucian era. Therefore, the unique philosophical trajectory of Korean Neo-Confucianism can be best seen in the Neo-Confucian theory in the Joseon Dynasty. Because Neo-Confucian theory consisted of profound philosophical insights, the exploration of its content does not align with the goal of this section, which is to provide an overview of a historical tendency. The content of the theory will be covered separately in Chapter IV.

Zhu Xi Neo-Confucianism (or Cheng-Zhu Neo-Confucianism: sometimes this name will be used) flourished during the Joseon Dynasty because it was selected as the governing principle of Joseon, just as Buddhism was adopted as the national religion in the Goryeo Dynasty. I will now discuss the broad principles of Zhu Xi Neo-Confucianism, which developed during this period.

During the early Joseon Dynasty in the late 14th century, the ruling classes adopted *gukgarye* (國朝五禮儀, customary proprieties of a country), *sagarye* (私家禮, customary proprieties of a family), and *samgangoryun* (三綱五倫: three fundamental principles and five moral disciplines in human relations) policies. In addition, some scholars attempted to establish a moral order by building upon the ethical theory of Neo-Confucianism, which they believed could replace the punitive theory of justice of Buddhism (the Buddhist law of cause and effect). The individual who elaborated the Neo-Confucian theory of justice was Jeong Do-jeon, who led the dynastic revolution.[22] In terms of purely scholarly work, an important contribution was *Iphakdoseol* (入學圖說), an introduction to Zhu Xi Neo-Confucianism, published by Gwon Geun. Gwon also opened up new fields of study in relation to the Confucian canon. He emphasized that all five Confucian classics (五經: *The Book of Changes*, *The Book of Odes*, *The Book of History*, *The Book of Rites*, and *The Spring and Autumn Annals*) were in an organic relationship with each other. In addition, through *Ogyeongcheongyeonrok* (五經淺見錄), an annotated edition of all five Confucian classics, he criticized all of them, referring to the opinions of Chen Hao (陳皓) and Wu Cheong (吳澄) who hailed from the Yuan Dynasty of China. He even criticized Zhu Xi's annotation of the Confucian classics, opening up an avenue for the study of Confucian classics for the first time in Korea.

(3) The Pursuit of Confucian Theory and Ritual Study

During the late 15th century while the foundation of the Joseon dynasty was being consolidated, the practice of loyalty (忠節) toward the king and the dynasty, so-called *Spring and Autumn Daeui* (春秋

22 This will be discussed in Chapter V in detail.

大義), enhanced the spirit of fidelity. The case of the six martyred ministers (死六臣), who lost their lives while resisting the usurper Grand Prince Suyang (King Sejo), increased the priority accorded to the practice of fidelity. During the middle of the Joseon Dynasty in the 16th century, scholars tended to interpret traditional ethics theories, such as *sadanchiljeongseol* (四端七情說, theories of four beginnings and the seven feelings) derived from the study of the Mandate of Heaven (天命), based upon the theory of *ri-gi* in their research.[23]

Around this time, in the late 15th century, Lu Jiu-yuan (陸九淵) and Wang Shou-ren's Simhak (the study of the mind) was also introduced into Korea. However, it failed to gain popularity due to strong opposition from eminent scholars such as Yi Hwang (李滉, 1501-1570), a representative scholar of Zhu Xi Neo-Confucianism in Joseon. Another reason for its lack of popularity was the fact that the brevity of the ruling periods of scholars who were moderately favorable toward Lu-Wang's work (少論系, the Faction of Young Doctrine called 'Soron'). Due to these factors, Lu-Wang's study of the mind could not overcome the power of Zhu Xi Neo-Confucianism and never became influential in Joseon. It was not just a matter of influence, as even those scholars who expressed an affinity for Lu-Wang's work appeared to be acolytes of Cheng-Zhu Neo-Confucianism. As a result, Lu-Wang's study of the mind was not integrated into Korean Confucianism.

In this milieu, it is not an exaggeration to say that Jeong Je-du (鄭齊斗, 1649-1738) was the only Korean scholar who gave due weight to the implications of Wang Shou-ren's study of the mind. This field finally received a little attention after the clear decline of Cheng-Zhu Neo-Confucianism caused by the collapse of Joseon in the 20th century (which will be described in more detail later). This was another significant difference in the histories of Confucianism in Korea and China.

The Neo-Confucian circles that had dominated academia and displayed great progress in theoretical research in the 16th century faced drastic changes in the 17th century. There were abundant studies

23 This will also be discussed in Chapter V in detail.

of propriety and even political disputes over related issues. It was the period in which the study of propriety (禮學) was preponderant. Such emphasis on the study of propriety and the role of propriety in political rule could not be found in any other East Asian country that adhered to Confucianism. More specifically, there was partisan strife among scholars and ministers in Joseon over the appropriate duration of the mourning period of the queen dowager in the circumstance of the king's death. During this time, the debate over what constituted reasonable grounds for determining the appropriate mourning period played an ideological role in the possible seizure of political power. This was a special case in which the sophisticated sense of moral duty (derived from Neo-Confucianism) of Neo-Confucian scholars in Joseon was projected onto the political reality. It was also a distinctive feature of Korean Neo-Confucianism.

(4) The Further Exploration of Human Nature and the Emerging Conflicts over the Theory of *Ri-gi*

During the late Joseon Dynasty in the 18th century, research into the good in human nature was conducted from a new perspective. That is, the focus turned to whether human beings and objects come into existence with equal value. It is well known that there had been heated arguments about the difference in nature between humans and objects for a long period.[24]

While this debate persisted in Neo-Confucian circles, new research tendencies emerged which focused on only one of the two key concepts of Neo-Confucianism, *ri* and *gi*. Ultimately, this caused sharp conflicts between scholars over the Neo-Confucian theory of *ri-gi*. For example, some scholars' view of the world was based solely on *gi* (唯氣說), while that of other scholars was founded exclusively upon *ri* (唯理說).[25]

---

24 These arguments will also be introduced in detail in Chapter V.
25 This will also be introduced in detail in Chapter V.

In late Joseon during the 19th century, the doctrine of *wijeongcheoksa* (衛正斥邪論, the movement to "defend orthodoxy and reject heterodoxy") emerged, which was a kind of theory of fidelity (義理論) whose implications were in opposition to the imperialist invasions of Japan and Western countries. In addition, Yang-ming's (Wang Shou-ren's) study of mind (Simhak) in Zhu Xi Neo-Confucianism was replaced by Simseol (心說, the theory of the mind).[26] All of these departures will be reviewed in detail in a later section dealing with Neo-Confucian theories.

(5) The Formation of Silhak (實學) with the Characteristics of De-Neo-Confucianism in Late Joseon

The Korean concept of Silhak, which is similar to that of the Qing Dynasty, arose in the late Joseon Dynasty. It was developed between the 17th and 19th centuries and had the characteristics of De-Neo-Confucian thought. Although Lu-Wang's study of the mind, which was in tension with Zhu Xi Neo-Confucianism, failed to gain popularity, Silhak (which can be viewed as a strand of Zhu Xi Confucianism in a narrow sense and of De-Neo-Confucianism in a broad sense) wielded considerable influence in the late Joseon Dynasty. As Chinese Silhak scholars had done, Korean Silhak scholars also emphasized *gyeongsechiyong* (經世致用: the utilization of theoretical studies in governing the country) and *iyonghusaeng* (利用厚生: the promotion of public welfare), but *silsagusi* (實事求是: seeking truth grounded on concrete evidences) was not attended to to a great extent in this period. In the Joseon Dynasty, the principle of *silsagusi* was promoted only by Kim Jeong-hee (金正喜,1786-1856) to stress the importance of proof for historical research, in a similar way to Ruan Yuan (阮元) in China. Yang Deuk-jung (梁得中, 1685-1742), a Neo-Confucian scholar, also analyzed *silsagusi*, but with a somewhat different interpretation—that of truth or sincerity without falsity. As such, it was also a unique feature of Korean Confucianism that there were only a few scholars immersed in in the field of the empirical scholarship called

26 This will also be introduced in detail in Chapter V.

Kaozheung Studies (考證學, evidence-based research) of the Qing Dynasty.

Silhak in the late Joseon Dynasty was bolstered by some reformist scholars who advocated *gyeongsechiyong,* in tandem with De-Neo-Confucian thought and Bukhakpa (北學派) scholars who supported *iyonghusaeng.* These *Silhak* scholars in late Joseon also modified and attempted to delegitimize the theories of Cheng-Zhu Neo-Confucianism through gyeonghak (經學: the study of Confucian Classics). In addition, between the 18th and 19th centuries, De-Neo-Confucian Silhak scholars succeeded in developing an independent philosophy completely distinct from Zhu Xi Neo-Confucianism through applying *gyeonghak* in the field of basic philosophy.[27] This is another characteristic of Silhak in Korean Confucianism, and it will be discussed in more detail in a later section.

27 This will also be introduced in detail in Chapter V.

Chapter III.

The Practical Implementation of the Cardinal Principles of Confucianism

1. Perspectives on the Emphasis on the Cardinal Principles

The basic principles of Confucianism, including *in* (benevolence) and *ui* (righteousness), are not objective principles of neutral value, such as the law of nature. They are the wisdom that guides people, and elements of a kind of doctrine that entails a concept of value.

Confucius stated, "My thoughts (道) are unified in one principle."[1] Most scholars have agreed that this one principle is *in*. According to Confucius, *in* refers to the act of loving people (愛人)[2], which can be accomplished through showing consideration (恕) for others over oneself.[3] Therefore, for Confucius, *in* connotes love and consideration, and has the characteristic of a mandatory (ethical) injunction. Mencius said, "*In* enables humans to be humans (仁人也)[4]," attributing value to *in*.

After their validation as crucial principles by both Confucius and Mencius, *in* and *ui* (仁義) began to be recognized as the core principles of Confucianism. In addition, Mencius also informed people that

---

1 "Book 4" (里仁), *The Analects of Confucius.*
2 "Book 12" (顔淵), Ibid.
3 "Book 15" (衛靈公), Ibid.
4 "Jinsim" (盡心), *Mencius,* Vol. 3, and Chap. 20, *The Doctrine of the Mean* (中庸).

chin (親), *ui* (義), *byeol* (別), *seo* (序), and *shin* (信), which are similar to 'sadeok' (四德, four virtues: 仁義禮智 *in/ui/ye/ji*), had already been employed since ancient times to create ethical hierarchy in various interpersonal relationships, namely father-son (父子), lord-vassal (君臣), husband-wife (夫婦), old-young (長幼), and friend-friend (朋友) relations. Later, *chin/ui/byeol/seo/shin* began to be regarded as the same principles as those of 'osang' (五常, the five constant virtues of *in/ui/ye/ji/shin*), and the ethical order established on the basis of these principles was actively implemented under the rubric of 'oryun' (五倫, the five moral disciplines in human relations). Were *sadeok* and *osang* regarded as the principles of morality simply because they allowed the moral strictures of Confucianism to be formulated as ethical principles? A half-formed consensus to this effect emerged. However, the historical trajectory of Confucianism shows that they were not just used as principles within such narrow conceptual boundaries. *In* was applied as the principle of *hyo* (filial piety) in terms of morality, but in terms of politics, it was used as basis of the principle of *injeong* (仁政: generous rule), which comprised the politics of *aemin* (愛民, loving the people) and of *wimin* (爲民, showing solicitude for the people).

With the passage of time, these principles, namely *in/ui/ye/ji*, began to evidence their practicality in Korean history. Therefore, analysis of the implementation of these principles can help us grasp the practical usefulness of Confucianism, which is why that is the focus of this study. The examination of the application of these basic principles in Korean Confucianism is a way to identify another unique aspect of Korean Confucianism.[5]

In the application of fundamental Confucian principles, there was no significant difference between Korea and China. In both countries, monarchy and patriarchy were predominant, and Confucian scholars sought to achieve the human character of the 'gunja' (君子, virtuous man)

5 The question may arise as to why *chung* (loyalty) in relation to monarchy or *hyo* (filial piety) with respect to patriarchy are not included in these principles. However, if *chung* and *hyo* are seen as analogous to *ui* and *in*, respectively, based on their characteristics, that question is resolved.

in reality. In addition, both Korea and China adopted *oryun* as the standard of morality, thereby placing emphasis on the fundamental principles of Confucianism. They also attempted to practice the principles of *The Family Rites* (家禮) and *Sohak* (小學, Elementary Learning) after the introduction of Neo-Confucianism. This commonality came about in all likelihood because significantly different phenomena rarely emerged through the application of identical principles. Some phenomena in Korea that were a little different from those of China seem to have been caused by the special circumstances of Korea in the process of the practical application of these principles, just as the performance of proprieties is influenced by prevailing conventions.

It cannot be said that the real-world application of principles is unimportant. The implementation of Confucian principles through the practical application of its philosophy played an important role in differentiating Korean from Chinese Confucianism. In the realization of ideological principles, different environments result in different application patterns and outcomes. This is the case here, as unique modalities in the application of Confucian principles caused by the distinctive Korean environment had significance in distinguishing Korean from Chinese Confucianism.

It should also be noted that not only different environments but also the varied intellectual proclivities and skills of human beings brought about differences in the Confucianism of each country. In this case, although identical doctrinal principles were put into practice, the results and implications were different. Confucianism has varied features in its structure and content according to the country and era in which it exists. This is why a preamble on the characteristics of Korean Confucianism is offered in the section where the application of fundamental Confucian principles is examined.

2. The Consequences of the Application of *In* (Benevolence)

(1) *Injeong* (仁政, generous rule) Practiced in the Original Confucian Culture

Although the concept of *in* was described above, further explanation is required. *In* refers to loving people, and it is concretely realized through *seo*, the showing of consideration for others over oneself. This intended to be shown to intimate parties, such as parents. The practice of *in* in the pursuit of *hyoje* (filial piety and brotherly love) is strong evidence of this. As ancestor worship had been practiced since the heyday of ancient traditional Korean culture, the concept of *hyo* (filial piety) derived from Confucianism gained widespread acceptance in Korea. As mentioned earlier, the concept of *chung* (loyalty) was also actively adopted. It has been confirmed that the patriarchal social system rapidly developed in Korea after the collapse of the matriarchal system. This patriarchal system was based on the increasing primacy of kinship and agriculture, which was a similar development to that of China.

It is important to remember that the *in* principle was applied to politics even after Confucius' time. In terms of politics, *in* is realized as *wimin* and *imin* (利民, benefitting the people), which can be synthesized as *aemin* (loving the people). The idealist politics of Confucius, *deokchi* (德治, ruling by virtue) and *yechi* (禮治, governing with courtesy), and the idealist politics of Mencius, *wangdojeongchi* (王道政治, ruling through benevolence and mercy) all correspond to *injeong* (generous rule) whose key principle is *in*. *Hyeolgujido* (絜矩之道, deliberation based on objective standard), which was emphasized in *The Great Learning* (大學), is the method by which *in* was applied in politics. It displays concern for others by putting them before oneself.

As the defining characteristic of *injeong* is love for people (subjects), *aemin*, it should comprise the qualities of *wimin* and *minbon* (民本: people-centered). This characteristic had been recognized by the king and the ruling class since the Three Kingdoms Period in ancient Korea.

In order to practice *aemin*, the kings of the Three Kingdoms regarded themselves as fathers, upon whom it was incumbent to love and take care of their people.

For example, while touring the country, King Yurinisageum (儒理尼師今, reign: 24-27 AD) in the Silla Dynasty encountered an old woman dying of hunger and cold. He covered her with his clothes and fed her, saying, "This is my sin because I, as the king, did not take care of my people and thereby inflicted this harsh situation on an old lady." Later, the king ordered that the poor who had no support, such as widowers (鰥), widows (寡), people without sons (獨), orphans (孤), and the sick (病者), be taken care of.[6] This is an example of the practice of *injeong*, which was depicted as the utopian politics of the egalitarian society in *The Book of Rites*. The king typically saw that he was responsible for the poverty and misery of his people, and this insight arose from the awakening of *injeong*. From this time on, the practice of *injeong* began to be regarded as the king's inherent duty. During the same period, astronomical research, originally conceived of as means of predicting of disasters and auspicious events, was also conducted to support the implementation of *injeong* by the king. This was because the onus on the king to care for his people was regarded as the result of a divine command. In Confucianism, as shown in *The Book of History*, kingship itself was believed to depend on the command of God that *injeong*, also known as *seonjeong* (善政: good governance) be practiced. Thus, political practices that deviated from *injeong* were not accepted in Confucianism.

If the king practiced *paedojeongchi* (覇道政治: ruling through force and suppression), which is the opposite of *injeong*, it was necessary for him to be ousted or put to death. This eventuality had actually come about in several instances since ancient times in Korea. The assassination of King Mobon (慕本王) and King Chadae (次大王) in 165 AD and the expulsion of King Bongsang (烽上王) in 300 AD occurred in the

6 "Sillabongi" (新羅本紀), *Samguksagi*, the 5th year of King Yurinisageum's reign

Goguryeo Dynasty.[7] These events reveal the profound value placed on *injeong* among ordinary people in the Three Kingdoms Period and their determination to actualize it.

During the Three Kingdoms Period, *injeong* was also realized through the *jindae* (賑貸) system, which was one of the *injeong* practices developed to help people through *yulmin* (恤民: relieving the suffering of the people). *Jindae* was the system through which the government lent grain during spring and summer to farmers in extremity, who were experiencing food shortages due to natural disasters, and through which the grain was repaid after the fall harvest. This began to be implemented in 194 AD by King Gogukcheon (故國川王) in Goguryeo (the 16th year of his reign). One day, on the way to his hunting ground, King Gogukcheon met a person who was dying of hunger. The king helped him, saying that he was responsible for that person's hardship (as King Yurinisageum had done). Later, King Gogukcheon implemented *jindaebeop* (賑貸法) to aid the poor throughout the nation by lending government grain to them, with their agreement to return the equivalent amount at the winter solstice.[8]

(2) *Injeong* in the *Hungo* and *Sajang* Confucian Period

Wang Geon (王建: reign 918-943), the founder of Goryeo, wrote that public sentiment regarding the king was determined by winning over the public through *injeong* in his *Hunyosipjo* (訓要十條, *The Ten Articles of Instruction*). Later, King Seongjong (成宗: reign 982-997) also pursued *injeong*, stipulating the idea of *minbon*—the basis of the nation is its people—in his agenda on farming. This agenda was devised for the purpose of improving the lives of people whose primary source of income was farming.

In this way, the precepts of *wimin* (showing solicitude for the people) based on *injeong* gradually took root over time. Consequently, the welfare

7 "Goguryeobonki" (高句麗本紀), ibid., Vol. 7, the 6th year of King Mobon's reign, and the 9th year of King Bongsang's reign.
8 Ibid., Vol. 26, the 16th year of King Gogukcheon's reign.

policy of taking care of disadvantaged elderly people, patients, and orphans was also strengthened. The kings often invited disadvantaged people to the palace and held entertaining events for them. This practice was somewhat related to the fact that Buddhism was the national religion at that time, as it could be seen as in part deriving from the emphasis placed on merciful good deeds in Buddhism.

The promulgation of welfare, based on the implementation of *injeong* with a sense of mercy, was more actively specified and striven to be sought in the Goryeo Dynasty. One example of this was the foundation of a national hospital, Dongseodaebiwon (東西大悲院). This institution was established mainly to take care of the sick, but it also administered relief to the poor who were dying of hunger. Later, this institution was called Dongseohwalinseo (東西活人署) in the Joseon Dynasty.

Needless to say, the *jindae* (賑貸) system devised in the Three Kingdoms Period persisted in the Goryeo Dynasty, and was in fact maintained until the Joseon Dynasty. During this last dynasty, the *jindae* system was called *hwangok* (還穀), and many types of *jindae* were created to provide relief to various kinds of vulnerable groups.[9] Now *jindae* could aid people in trouble caused not only by ordinary hardships in farming or self-sustenance, but also by droughts, floods, and severe cold snaps.

In the Goryeo Dynasty, despite the considerable development of Confucianism, *injeong* was not actively pursued. The civil service examination, which was influenced by Confucianism, was initiated as Dokseosampumgwa (讀書三品科) in the year 788 (during King Wonseong's reign) in the Silla Dynasty. It was developed into the civil service examination in the year 598 (the 9th year of King Gwangjong's reign) in the Goryeo Dynasty, and continued until the end of that dynasty (1392).

9 They include *eunmyeonjije* (恩免之制), *jaemyeonjije* (災免之制), *hwangwagodokjinjije* (鰥寡孤獨賑貸之制), and *suhanyeokryeojinjije* (水旱疫癘賑貸之制). However, it is also true that this *hwangok* system involved many problems caused by corrupt officials. This will be discussed in the section on De-Neo-Confucian Silhak.

Thus, the civil service examination had a history of more than 600 years. In terms of the governmental ruling structure or system, the yukjo (六曹: six ministries) system discussed in *The Rites of Zhou* (周禮) was adopted in the early Goryeo Dynasty in order to achieve more effective governance. Therefore, if the practice of *injeong* was actively introduced to Confucian scholars who had assimilated the high level of political knowledge available to them, the Goryeo Dynasty, which had a history of almost 500 years, was able to develop a highly refined state administrative system based on *minbon* and *wimin*.

As mentioned above, *injeong* was not actively promoted in Goryeo, and this was for several reasons. Firstly, Confucianism in Goryeo was not Neo-Confucianism but *Sajang* and *Hungo* Confucianism, forms which persisted until the final days of the dynasty. In addition, early Neo-Confucianism prior to Zhu Xi Neo-Confucianism, such as the Neo-Confucianism of Northern Song, also became popular in Goryeo, but it was not very influential compared to that of Northern Song.[10] Moreover, because Buddhism was the national religion of Goryeo, there were real constraints on the propagation of other strands of thought. There is no doubt that Confucianism was regarded as less important than Buddhism. Furthermore, for approximately 100 years after the rebellion of Jeong Jung-bu in 1170, fields of study, including Confucianism, could not escape some decline due to the military rule of Choi's family. Finally, in 1231 Mongolia (later Yuan) invaded and began to inflict political suppression on Goryeo. Due to these circumstances, Confucianism could not prosper in Goryeo, and thus, it could not contribute to the thorough implementation of *injeong*.

Confucianism was freed from these constraints in Joseon. After the Neo-Confucian scholar Jeong Do-jeon and others established the Joseon Dynasty through a dynastic revolution and adopted Neo-Confucianism, especially Zhu Xi Neo-Confucianism, as a ruling principle

10 Cf. Chap. 10, *A History of Korean Confucianism* (Jisik Sanup Publications, 2012).

of the new dynasty, Confucianism began to flourish. The adaptation of Zhu Xi Neo-Confucianism, a primary political principle of Joseon, resulted in the prospering and consistent implementation of Confucianism in that period.

(3) The Realization of *Injeong* during the Period of Neo-Confucian Predominance

During the Joseon Dynasty (1392-1910) when political rule was based on Neo-Confucianism, the practice of *injeong* was actively promoted from the beginning. It was closely associated with the spirit of *wimin* among virtuous scholars called 'seonbi' (士) during this period.

In this era, it was a unique feature that those with the responsibility of assisting the king also possessed significant political power. They were 'sadaebu' (士大夫), including government officials and seonbis. Because they were scholar-bureaucrats who studied Neo-Confucianism, they were keenly aware of the importance of *injeong*. Seonbis in this period were far more determined than the intellectual class of past eras to construct an ideal country through the realization of *injeong*. This was a great driving force in the promotion of *injeong* in this era. In addition, in early Joseon, the role of outstanding kings who took the lead or worked with seonbis in the promotion of *injeong*, such as King Sejong (世宗, reign: 1418-1450), should not be overlooked.

Seonbis promoted *injeong* through the unique administrative methods of governments from the early Joseon Dynasty on. These methods included the adoption of the chancellor-centered system; the establishment and use of the 'eonro' (言路, the channel of communication that enabled the open expression of opinions) system to communicate with the king; the activation of the daily lectures called 'gyeongyeon' (經筵), a type of 'eonro'; the practice of 'yeoksagamgye' (歷史鑑戒)—the recording of the acts of the king and his vassals for the purpose of learning lessons from them.

The chancellor-centered system required that all government tasks handled in the yukjo (six ministries) be reviewed not only by each minister but also by chancellors before a final decision regarding them could be taken. This rendered the king's final approval for a variety of tasks unnecessary, and this system could be seen as a proxy for the king in a sense. Therefore, the implementation of this system implied the strengthening of the authority of the vassals. The advantage of this system was that it prevented the deviation of the king from agreed-upon policy and the abuse of royal authority, especially the danger of authoritarianism. This effect was also closely related to the public application of 'eonro.'

'Eonro' refers to the method of loyal remonstration (諫言) with the king. Although the remonstration system was established in Silla and continued in Goryeo, it was primitive and not actively utilized. 'Eonro' began to be actively promoted in early Joseon as a system that included assurances of good faith.

The government offices in charge of 'eonro' were the Samsa (三司, three offices), namely — Saganwon (司諫院, Office of Censors), Saheonbu (司憲府, Office of the Inspector General), and Hongmungwan (弘文館, Office of Special Advisors). The main tasks of Hongmungwan were the handling of government documents and the management of the Confucian classics and historical records. However, some senior officials also worked as eongwans (言官, officials in charge of presenting their opinion to the king) by providing advice and suggestions to the king upon request and participating in 'gyeongyeon.' Saheonbu was an inspection office for the administration as a whole, which was mainly involved in uncovering the corruption and irregularities of officials. Since the fundamental sanctions imposed as a result of the irregularities of officials were generally within the reign of the king, the Saheonbu officials were also employed in Hongmungwan and performed the duties of eongwans. Saganwon was the major remonstration agency. During the Joseon Dynasty, eongwans who neglected their duty of facilitating remonstration were punished. As such, the activities of eongwans were systematically provided support and encouraged. This active use of the remonstration system prevented the deviation of the king from consensus decisions and increased the constraints on royal power.

It should be noted that 'eonro' was not open only to Samsa in the Joseon Dynasty. The 'eonro' system accessible to all government officials and even ordinary seonbis was the 'sangso' (上疏, a memorial to the throne). In addition, 'Sinmungo' (申聞鼓, a petitioner's drum) was incorporated for the benefit of the illiterate public who were not capable of writing a 'sangso' letter. Even 'gyeokjaeng' (擊錚, the act of striking a gong) was permitted to everybody at a royal procession. All of these opportunities were created and made accessible during the time of King Sejong.

It is clear that there were numerous ways for government officials and the general public to complain about the king or the government, or to propose new ideas. However, the active use of those systems varied depending on the king. In the event of their falling into disuse, seonbis attempted to correct the situation. They stressed the importance of the 'eonro' system, claiming that the rise and fall of the country depended on its use. Because the specific activities of those seonbis will be described in the next section,[11] in this section it is important to note only that the implementation of the remonstration system enhanced 'gunmingongchi' (君民共治), governance by both the king and his people, and thus, the practice of *injeong* became easier and more substantive.

'Gyeongyeon' refers to a lecture on politics *per se* and relevant philosophy and history through the study of scriptures or historical records, given to the king in the palace by the greatest scholars of the age, such as Daejehak (大提學, chief knowledge officer) or Jehak (提學, knowledge officer). The idealist political ideology of Confucianism, *injeong*

11 These were princepled accomplishments which seonbis achieved through the 'sarim' spirit (士林精神), which was embodied in the faction they formed called 'sarim' (士林). The seonbis' specific righteous activities will be described in the next section.

(*deokchi* or *wangdojeongchi*), was taught to the king through 'gyeongyeon.' Thus, this was an educational venue where the remonstration of vassals was transmitted to the king through the prism of ancient events and philosophical theories. This was why 'gyeongyeon' was an activity carried out by Samsa which were in charge of 'eonro.' King Sejong, a celebrated sage king in the Joseon Dynasty, almost always attended 'gyeongyeon.' *A Commentary on the Great Learning* (大學衍義) was the most frequently used textbook of 'gyeongyeon' from early Joseon because it contained the specific practices of *injeong.*

For eongwans, offering constructive criticism and education to the king was their duty and the expression of their loyalty to the king and the country. Although this weakened the king's authority, it was an essential element required to realize *injeong* for the benefit of the country and the people. Based on the historical consciousness of 'yeoksagamgye' (歷史鑑戒), which put emphasis on history, seonbis devoted themselves to recording the acts of the king and his vassals. *The Annals of the Joseon Dynasty* (朝鮮王朝實錄: 888 books; 1,893 fascicles), which contains the records of monarchy during the reign of 25 kings from King Taejo to King Cheoljong over 472 years of the Joseon Dynasty and the everyday acts of the kings and their vassals, *The Diaries of the Royal Secretariat* (承政院日記: 3,047 books), which includes the records spanning 270 years from King Injo (1623) to King Gojong (1894), and *The Records of the Border Defense Council* (備邊司謄錄: 273 books), which contains records from the 9th year of Gwanghaegun's reign (1617) to the 29th year of King Gojong's reign (1892), emerged from such efforts. The value of these texts can easily be gauged from the fact that *The Annals of the Joseon Dynasty* was designated a World Heritage artefact by UNESCO. The reason seonbis in Joseon put stress on historical records such as annals was that they pursued the realization of *injeong*. More developments that illustrate how much Joseon seonbis valued the historical consciousness of 'yeoksagamgye' will be introduced later in relation to the realization of righteousness, the topic of the next section.

Undercutting this idealistic orientation, evils far removed from the realization of *injeong* also befell Joseon. Approximately two centuries after the foundation of the dynasty (in the late 16th century), social disorder arose due to the limitations of and contradictions within various administrative systems. For instance, despite the goal of holding land in the public trust, land fell into private hands on a widespread basis. In addition, the corruption of officials who were in charge of military administration and the grain exchange system was prevalent. Those evils threatened the livelihoods of ordinary people. To make matters worse, the Japanese Invasion of Korea (壬辰倭亂, 1592-1598) and the Manchu Invasion of Korea (丙子胡亂, 1636-1637) brought about miserable conditions in rural communities. The people were so impoverished that seeing them was difficult to bear. The fundamental improvement and reform of various administrative systems were urgently required. The reform theories that emerged to meet the demands of the time were derived from Silhak (實學) and incorporated *injeong*, which had been proposed by late Silhak scholars for the relief of the poor.

In short, the implementation of *injeong* through the application of *in* during the Joseon Dynasty had both light and dark aspects; that is, it engendered both positive and negative consequences. Nevertheless, in order to grasp the unique characteristics of Korean Confucianism, some Korean Confucian scholars' determination and efforts to produce positive results should be highlighted to a greater degree. The implementation of *injeong* was, in itself, applicable to the realization of the two principles of *in* and *ui*, for *injeong* was inseparable from the seonbis' righteous actions (which will be discussed in the next section). At this point a historical example may illustrate the connection between the two.

In the early 16th century, there was a calamity that some Confucian seonbis called 'sarimpa' (士林派) suffered while striving to achieve just politics at the risk of their lives. This calamity is what is called Gimyosahwa (己卯士禍). In 1506 (the year of Gimyo), the tyrant Yeonsangun (燕山君, reign: 1496-1506), who had held sway by inflicting great oppression, was supplanted and expelled, and King Jungjong (中宗, reign: 1506-1544) acceded to the throne through a kind of coup d'état that is known as 'the Restoration of King Jungjong.' 'Restoration,' which is the process of 'returning something to its original state of rightness,' in fact has the same intention as the pursuit of *injeong*.

Jo Gwang-jo (趙光祖, 1482-1519) was a seonbi who was in the vanguard of the era in his embodiment of the spirit of restoration. He designated the ideal form of *injeong* as 'utmost governance' (至治) and sought to remedy the evils and abuses that prevailed in the field of politics. As a result of his vigorous reforms, the conservative force called 'hungupa' (勳舊派) faced a challenge. After readying themselves to retaliate against Jo Gwang-Jo, the adherents of 'hungupa' rose in opposition and even engaged in the Machiavellian reporting of false information that reflected badly on him to King Jungjong. The king, who had grown weary of Jo's sweeping reforms, succumbed to the wiles of 'hungupa,' and finally Jo Gwang-jo was exiled and sentenced to death. In addition, some of his followers, particularly conscientious younger seonbis, suffered the same fate, while others even committed suicide or were ousted from their positions.

Gimyosahwa was a calamity which ironically resulted from the seonbis' righteous actions aimed at restoring and then preserving just governance. Their ethically-informed actions were fundamentally motivated by the goal of realizing *injeong*, which is the reason it is appropriate to mention them in this context. In addition, it is note-worthy that, though the seonbi community had contracted and was dispirited due to the reaction to the restoration, their commitment to work for the benefit of the people and the country paradoxically became stronger and more unyielding. This commitment, that is, their righteous spirit, is 'the seonbi spirit of Korea' which originated in the 'sarim' spirit (士林情神). This seonbi spirit is also one of distinctive characteristics of Korean Confucianism.

3. The Characteristics of the Application of Righteousness (義)

(1) The Realization of Righteousness: Loyalty and Fidelity

The concept of righteousness is a synthesis of the ideas of 'obligation' and 'rightness.' Propriety (禮) also dovetails with the meaning of 'obligation', but it is differentiated from righteousness because it does not contain the implication of 'rightness.' As Mencius stated that righteousness is the right path (正路) for human beings, while propriety is a gate (門) built upon the path,[12] righteousness has the characteristic of an immutable norm, whereas propriety has that of a mutable or transient norm. In addition, righteousness was explained as the fruit (實) of propriety[13] in *The Book of Rites*. Thus, it can be said that the concept of righteousness contains the meaning of 'obligation' that enhances the meaning of propriety.

Originally, the concept of obligation encompassed by righteousness was realized as loyalty to the king. This was because monarchy was justified and practically supported by Confucianism. *Gunsinyueui* (君臣有義)—there should be righteousness in the relationship between the king and his subjects—in *oryun* (the five moral disciplines in human relations) is a good example. Righteousness began to be seen as loyalty between the king and his vassals in a hierarchical system. The statement of Confucius, "The king observes propriety with his vassals (君使臣以禮), and vassals serve their king with loyalty (臣事君以忠),"[14] has similar significance.

However, righteousness was not limited to the loyalty of vassals. Both the king and his vassals were obliged to practice their own righteousness. *Injeong*, described in the previous section, was also a type of righteousness required not only of vassals but also of the king. Justification for the punishment of tyrants stemmed from the same

12 "Manjang" (萬章) II, and "Iru" (離婁) I, *Mencius*.
13 "Yeun" (禮運), *The Book of Rites*.
14 "Book 3" (八佾), *The Analects of Confucius*.

understanding. One example was the Restoration of King Jungjong (中宗反正, 1506) upon the ousting of Yeonsangun (燕山君, reign: 1494-1506), who lived a frenzied life and did not attend adequately to political affairs.

A clearer explanation of the concept of righteousness is required here. As can be seen from its meaning, righteousness does not refer to rightness related to objective truth but to rightness related to obligation and justness. This is the reason righteousness had been realized through the loyalty of vassals (seonbis) to the king in the past. However, it should be noted again that loyalty was not only the king's due. The practice of righteousness, whose origin was the need to protect the dynasty and the royal line, extended its scope to the protection of the people and homeland, which will be elaborated upon below.

Jeong Mong-ju (鄭夢周, 1337-1392) from the late Goryeo Dynasty was the father of Korean Confucianism. He lost his life while resisting the dynastic revolution that deposed the Goryeo Dynasty and led to the Joseon Dynasty. His is an example of fidelity to the dynasty. During the Joseon Dynasty, King Sejo (世祖, reign: 1455-1468) usurped the throne from his nephew, King Danjong (端宗, reign: 1452-1455). Some ministers made an attempt to reinstate King Danjong, but in the process, six ministers lost their lives and six others were removed from their positions. The former were later called 'sayuksin' (死六臣), and the latter, 'saengyuksin' (生六臣). Their actions were an example of fidelity to the royal line, and were the realization of righteousness through righteous acts, such as the moral principle described in *The Spring and Autumn Annals* or *jeoleui* (節義, fidelity and loyalty). As more seonbis began to practice *jeoleui*, they began to be called 'jeoleuipa' (節義派). 'Jeoleuipa' emerged in the mid-15th century because seonbis regarded themselves as national administrators.

(2) The Strengthening of 'Eonro' and *Wimin*-based Politics Sensitive to Public Sentiment

While participating in the administration of the country, seonbis regarded their work as national in scope. This can be seen in their definition of seonbi—"The seonbi is the premier energy of the country." Seonbis considered themselves as rulers of the country along with the king, and thus, the remonstration system was highly important to them. The remonstration system was not simply devised to restrict the king's authority. It was based on loyalty, which was the duty of vassals to show towards the king, the country, and the people. That is, seonbis tried to realize righteousness, which was their duty, through remonstration. Due to this belief, they sometimes even risked their lives for the sake of the principle of remonstration, and the phrase 'loyal remonstration (忠諫)' was created on the basis of this phenomenon.[15]

As the importance of remonstration grew, 'eonro' such as 'sangso,' which was a main remonstration medium, also became more significant. The contemporary claim that the opening and closing of 'eonro' determined the rise and fall of a country shows the importance of 'eonro.' However, the 'sangso' was available only to noble seonbis with academic knowledge, and the illiterate civilians were not able to access it. In addition, the opportunity to use 'Sinmungo' or 'gyeokjaeng' was quite limited in Joseon society. Some conscientious seonbis considered *wimin* (showing solicitude for the people) their duty, a righteous act, and used 'sangso' as a tool to transmit the thoughts and needs of the people. These seonbis with a conscientious spirit played

15 There is a fable about royal remonstration. In Silla, Kim Hu-jik (金后稷), an official, entreated the king, who enjoyed hunting every day, to stop hunting, reminding the king of the statement in *The Book of History*—'If the king falls in hunting or falls in with women, the country falls.' However, the king did not listen to him. Upon his death, Kim Hu-jik left a will stipulating his desire for burial beside the road to the royal hunting ground, and his family honored his wish. One day, when passing by the tomb on the way to the hunting ground, the king heard the words, "Please don't go." After learning that the tomb was Kim's, the king was moved to tears by Kim's loyalty, and decided to stop hunting. 'Kimhujikjeon' (金后稷傳), *Samguksagi*, Vol. 45.

the role of the voice of the people through 'sangso.' The majority of these 'sangso' were concerned with the condition of disadvantaged people and the amelioration of their problems. Jo Gwang-jo and Yi I (李珥, 1536-1584) in the 16th century, who strongly emphasized 'eonro' by claiming that the opening and closing of 'eonro' determines the rise and fall of the country, wrote 'sangso' on behalf of the public. It should also be noted that 'sangso' was the reflection of 'gongron' (公論, public opinion) for Yi I because it represented the complaints and ideas of the people. According to Yi I, originally there was no dedicated remonstrator in ancient times. Everybody played a role as a remonstrator by discussing politics in the streets and markets during that period.[16] Yi elaborated upon a kind of freedom of speech in this way. Opinions formed in an atmosphere of freedom were his 'gongron.'

As will be seen below, Yi I maintained that 'gongron' was the "consensus of the people (人心所同然者)."[17]

> "If 'gongron' enters into the royal court, the country will be well managed, but if 'gongron' stays in the village, the country will be in chaos. If 'gongron' does not exist in both the upper and lower classes, the country will perish… (Therefore) 'Gongron' is the premier energy of the country."[18]

> "The locus of 'gongron' is national policy. A specific national policy refers to a priority that all the people in a country agree upon in an uncoerced way."[19]

Yi stated that a national ideology is also determined by 'gongron.' This insight was comparable to the ideology of the modern democratic republic. This was a very advanced stance at that time, but it

16 Yi I, 'Okdangroneulsawihuncha' (玉堂論乙巳僞勳箚), *Yulgokjeonseo* (栗谷全書, The Complete Works of Yulkok), Vol. 3.
17 'Okdangroneulsawihuncha' (玉堂論乙巳僞勳箚), ibid., Vol. 4.
18 'Daebaekchamchanso' (代白參贊疏), ibid., Vol. 7.
19 Cf. footnote 135.

could be anticipated as inevitable consequence of the philosophy of *injeong,* considering that Yi's thinking was derived from the philosophical underpinning of *wimin*. This way of thinking resulted from a combination of the philosophy of *injeong* and the righteous act of putting stress on 'gongron,' which were both contained in the people-oriented philosophy of Yi I.

(3) The Seonbis' Righteous Actions Strengthened through 'Sahwa' (the Calamity of the Literati)

The strong awareness of 'gamgye' (鑑戒, imbibing lessons from historical records) among Joseon seonbis was already mentioned. As seonbis realized that the utility of 'gamgye' contained in historical records was similar to that of royal remonstration, they used it as a means of realizing righteousness. A good example of this was Muosahwa (戊午士禍) occurred in 1498 (the 4th year of Yeonsangun's reign), which centered around the records described in *The Annals of the Joseon Dynasty*.

This calamity was associated with King Sejo's (Grand Prince Suyang) usurpation of the throne from his young nephew, King Danjong. This constituted an injustice because it disrupted the royal line. In the process of resisting it, 'sayuksin', and 'saengyuksin' emerged, and formed 'jeoleuipa' (節義派) in Confucian circles. Their spirit of 'fidelity and loyalty' was passed down to seonbis in King Seongjong's era. Among those seonbis, some stayed out of government service throughout their lives, while others became conscientious public officials. The representative seonbis who served as government officials were Kim Jong-jik (金宗直, 1431-1492), a successor of Gil Jae (吉再) in late Goryeo, and the literati influenced by him, namely—Kim Il-son (金馹孫), Kim Goeng-pil (金宏弼), and Jeong Yeo-chang (鄭汝昌), who were collectively dubbed 'sinjinsaryu' (新進士類, a group of promising scholars).

They consistently came into conflict with the established power 'hungupa' (勳舊派, a faction consisting of vassals of merit who were of assistance to King Sejo[20]), who included Yoo Ja-gwang (柳子光) and Yi Geuk-don (李克墩). This conflict was due to the breach of the injunction of '*bulsaigun*' (不事二君: not to serve two kings) on the part of those putatively meritorious vassals. 'Jeoleuipa' disregarded 'hungupa,' calling them petty and crafty men, while 'hungupa' disparaged 'jeoleuipa,' calling them wild nobility. Then one day, Kim Il-son, who later became a historiographer, recorded misconduct on the part of Yi Geuk-don, a member of 'hungupa,' in a 'sacho' (史草, a source material for *The Annals*). After learning of this, Yi Geuk-don decided to exact revenge on Kim. Later, when he became a senior official, he did this using the 'sacho,' which was confidential and unknown even to the king. This incident is described in detail below.

Kim Jong-jik wrote a 'jemun' (祭文: a funeral oration) for King Danjong, while grieving over his death caused by King Sejo, and the title of this oration was 'Joeuijemun' (弔義帝文). Since it was prohibited to use the name of King Danjong at that time, for the funeral oration Kim Jong-jik borrowed the name of a Chinese Emperor, Euije (義帝, Emperor of Yi of Chu), who was killed for the same reason. Kim Il-son, who had once served Kim Jong-jik, was aware of this, and included this funeral oration in a 'sacho' after he became a historiographer. But in 1498, his political opponent Yi Geuk-don discovered this and reported it as a slander on King Sejo to Yeonsangun, who loathed seonbis. Yeonsangun conducted the posthumous, symbolic execution of the deceased Kim Jong-jik, and put Kim Il-son, Gwon O-bok (權五福), Gwon Kyeong-yu (權景裕), Yi Mok (李穆), and Heo Ban (許盤) to death. In addition, dozens of people, including Jeong Yeo-chang and Kang Kyeong-seo (姜景敍) were banished, and historiographers, such as Yi Geuk-don, were relieved of their positions. This was the Muosahwa incident.

This was not the only calamity that seonbis experienced during the Joseon Dynasty. There were more calamities—including Gapjasahwa

20 They include Jeong In-ji (鄭麟趾), Shin Suk-ju (申叔舟), Yang Seong-ji (梁誠之), and Choi Hang (崔恒).

(甲子士禍, 1504, the 10th year of Yeonsangun's reign), Gimyosahwa (己卯士禍, 1519, the 14th year of King Jungjong's reign), Eulsasahwa (乙巳士禍, 1545, the 1st year of King Injong's reign). Among these, two were not committed for good reason. Gapjasahwa was caused by the tyrant Yeonsangun upon his learning (after coronation) of the reason for the death of his mother, and Eulsasahwa occurred due to the authoritarianism of Yoon Won-hyeong, a maternal relative of King Myeongjong. Only Gimyosahwa had the characteristic of a righteous act in the pursuit of just politics. The following is a description of Gimyosahwa. (It is also described at the end of the previous section "2. The Consequences of the Application of In")

The tyrant Yeonsangun was finally expelled through the restoration of King Jungjong. The meaning of restoration is 'returning something that is wrong to a state of rightness.' The restoration of King Jungjong was performed in the pursuit of renewal through reform that could remedy the misrule of Yeonsangun. The leading seonbis who participated in this renewal were Jo Gwang-jo and his followers.

Jo Gwang-jo was a student of Kim Goeng-pil, a renowned Confucian scholar. Because of his honesty and integrity, Jo gained the deep trust of the government and the people from the beginning of his career.[21] In order to meet the demands of the times, he actively promoted reform, advocating an ideal form of governance named utmost governance (至治). He initiated vigorous and radical reforms. Through the establishment of 'Hyeonryanggwa' (賢良科), an organization in charge of recommending talented people for important positions, he appointed many excellent seonbis. He also abolished 'Sogyeokseo' (昭格署), the chief temple of Taoism, under the pretext of overcoming superstitions. Since his reforms were radical and focused on the ideal rather than the practical, he had to face complaints from and conflicts with conservative adherents of 'hungupa,' such as Jeong Gwang-pil (鄭光弼). However, Jo Gwang-jo did not pay the slightest attention to

21 He was recommended by Minister of Interior Ahn Dang (安塘) and 200 Seonggyungwan scholars.

their complaints. In fact, he did not even hesitate to impeach 'hungupa' prime ministers.

Among his reforms, the negation of the 'wihun' (僞勳, undeserved accolades) granted upon 'meritorious retainers at the restoration of King Jungjong' (靖國功臣) was the most severe measure. Imposters to the status of meritorious vassal falsely listed as contributors to the restoration were detected and removed.[22] This was the form of the disclosure and punishment meted out to the adherents of 'hungupa' who had engaged in insidious attempt. 'Hungu' forces rose up in opposition, and fought back by any means. Unlike before, King Jungjong also became disgusted with the radical reforms of Jo Gwang-jo. Therefore, Hong Gyeong-ju (洪景舟), the father of a royal concubine called 'Hibin' (熙嬪), Nam Gon (南袞), Shim Jeong (沈貞), Kim Jeon (金銓), and Ko Hyeong-san (高荊山) formed a conspiracy against Jo at the palace. They slandered Jo, saying, "Jo Gwang-jo has formed a destructive faction and is undermining the government." King Jungjong, whose spirit was weakened, finally fell prey to the cunning trickery of 'hungupa.'

As a result, Jo Gwang-jo was exiled to Neungju and sentenced to death by poison in the Gimyo year (1519). Kim Jeong (金淨), Ki Jun (奇遵), Han Chung (韓忠), and Kim Shik (金湜) were also all exiled, and then were put to death or committed suicide. Kim Gu (金絿) and Bak Se-hee (朴世熹) also suffered the hardship of banishment. Ahn Dang (安塘, put to death two years later) and the brothers Kim An-guk (金安國) and Kim Jeong-guk (金正國), who defended them, were demoted, and the office of 'Hyeonryang' was abolished. In sum, reform efforts ceased. Those seonbis who lost their lives in this massacre were called 'Gimyomyeonghyeon' (己卯名賢).

Due to 'sahwas' (the calamities of the literati), many younger seonbis were sacrificed, and seonbi society became stagnant. However, the remaining seonbis did not surrender their *wimin*-oriented righteous

---

22 Almost three quarters of the meritorious vassals (76 people) were removed, including Sim Jeong, a figure of authority at that time.

philosophy, which increased people's admiration for them. Around this time, in the late 16th century, a collective name for seonbis, 'sarim' (士林) or 'sarimpa' (士林派) began to gain currency. Therefore, the righteous philosophy of seonbis also began to be called the 'sarim' spirit, especially when discussing Gimyosahwa. This is evidence that 'sahwa' significantly affected the formation and consolidation of 'sarim,' and Gimyosahwa was at the center of this evolution. Conscientious seonbis who pursued the realization of *wimin*-based *injeong* at the cost of their lives were seen as righteous people.

(4) The Righteous Attitudes of Seonbis Highlighted by the Righteous Army

The righteous acts of seonbis were not only motivated by domestic political situations, such as the realization of *injeong*. They actually performed more vigorous righteous acts in the face of foreign invasions. The rise of the righteous army around the period of late Joseon (1905-1910) and the nationwide battles of the righteous army during the Japanese Invasion of Korea (壬辰倭亂, 1592-1598) can serve as evidence of this.

The leaders of the righteous army were all seonbis without any political power who were engaged in study. They became righteous soldiers or generals because they believed that protecting the king, the country, and the people in a national crisis constituted the righteousness or fidelity of seonbis. The rise of the righteous army put into action their belief that righteous acts are the duty of seonbis.

After Seoul fell to the Japanese army in 1592, righteous armies were established throughout the country. The contribution of these armies to the defeat of the enemy was no less significant than that of the government army. Righteous soldiers played a crucial role in ending the conflict. There were so many righteous army generals who lost their lives in battle with the Japanese army that it is difficult to list their names here. Among them, the major figures are as follows:

Gwak Jae-woo (郭再祐), who established the first righteous army, Jeong In-hong (鄭仁弘), Bak Seong (朴惺), Gwak Jun (郭逡), Gwak Jeo (郭趄), Bak I-jang (朴而章), Kim Myeon (金沔) and Kim Hae (金垓) from Gyeongsang province; Jo Heon (趙憲), Shin Gan-su (申簡秀) and Jang Deok-gae (張德蓋) from Chungcheong province; Hong Eon-su (洪彦秀), Bak Chun-mu (朴春茂) and Woo Seong-jeon (禹性傳) from Gyeonggi province; Ko Gyeong-myeong (高敬命), Yoo Paeng-ro (柳彭老), Ko Jong-hu (高從厚), Kim Cheon-il (金千鎰), Yang San-ju (梁山璹), Im Gye-yeong (任啓英) and Kim Deok-ryeong (金德齡) from Jeolla province; Jo Deuk-in (趙得仁), Yi Jeong-am (李廷馣), Kim Man-su (金萬壽), and Kim Jin-su (金進壽) from Hwanghae province; and Yi Bung-su (李鵬壽) and Jeong Mun-bu (鄭文孚) from Hamgyeong province.

The activities of these righteous army generals were examples of the contribution of the seonbi spirit to the salvation of the country in the national crisis. This seonbi spirit of committment subsequently demonstrated its indefatigable power throughout Korean history. Seonbis in the 16th century lived up to the characterization of seonbi—"Seonbis are the premier energy in the country"—through their roles in righteous military activities. The righteous military activities of seonbis in national emergencies proved that the popular concept of the seonbi was wholly correct.

It is not an exaggeration to say that the righteous acts of seonbis was one of the driving forces that contributed to the historical progress of Korea. The 500-year-history of the Joseon Dynasty was not sustained through happenstance. A great part of the maintenance of the dynasty was attributable to seonbis who fought for the country at the risk of their lives.

In no other Confucian country, was there a case comparable to that in which seonbis saved the country and the people, being willing to sacrifice life and limb. In this light, the righteous acts of seonbis are regarded as a unique feature of Korean Confucianism. Today's rapid development of democracy in Korea may be somewhat related to the *wimin*-based affinity for joint governance pursued by seonbis. With their legacy in mind, it has become clearer that the Korean people have realized the principle of righteousness (義) throughout history.

4. Distinctive Aspects of the Practice of Propriety (禮)

(1) Propriety: The Basis of Pride as a Country Rich in Culture

A work of Chinese literature contained the following description of Koreans in ancient times prior to the Three Kingdoms Period: "Koreans are careful, have decency, and are not greedy."[23] The judicious and sincere attitude attributed to them implies a disciplined lifestyle, and their sense of decency suggests a courteous attitude. Even without relying on Mencius's statement, it is obvious that decency refers to courteous behavior that supports a kind of concession to others' feelings and needs. As can be seen from the above, Koreans have had a keen awareness of propriety since ancient times.

'Jecheon' (祭天, heaven worship) events, such as 'Yeonggo' (迎鼓) and 'Dongmaeng' (東盟), which were held at the national level during the Three Kingdoms Period, were rituals honoring the heaven. 'Dongmaeng,' known as a jecheon event, was also a rite of worship for King Dongmyeong, the founder of Goguryeo. In light of these traditions, it is evident that Koreans instinctively observed propriety even prior to the introduction, and its adoption merely strengthened this innate feature of Koreans.

In particular, during the reign of King Jinheung in Silla (540-579), beautiful maidens were selected as 'wonhwa' (原花) who would worship 'sinseon' (神仙, a supernatural being), and they learned the *hyoje* (filial piety and brotherly love) and *chungshin* (loyalty and fidelity) of Confucianism.[24] The principles of three religions (Confucianism, Buddhism,

---

23 'Yejo' (濊條), "Dongyijeon" (東夷傳) in *Samgukji* (三國志) and *Wiji* (魏志).
24 "Mireukseonhwa misirang jinjasa" (彌勒仙花 彌尸郞 眞慈師), *Samgukyusa*, Vol. 3. At that time, the trend of honoring a supernatural being called 'sinseon' (神仙) often referred to taste for 'poongryu' (風流). .

and Taoism) were proportionately taught, and the virtue of propriety was emphasized in the case of Confucianism. As these 'wonhwas' were later placed in 'Hwarangdo' (花郎徒), good deeds began to be pursued actively. Thus, the range of the maiden's study was expanded to include the five constant virtues (五常, *in/ ui/ ye/ ji/ shin*) and the six arts (六藝, rites/ music/ archery/ charioteering/ calligraphy/ mathematics), and the practice of propriety was stressed even more.[25]

During the Goryeo Dynasty (918-1392), a higher level of propriety was realized. In the 12th and 13th centuries, as noted above, early Confucianism (prior to Zhu Xi Confucianism) was introduced to Goryeo through exchange with the northern Song Dynasty. As described above, the *rigi*-based analysis of the creation of all things in the universe and the philosophical exploration of human nature began to be conducted.[26] In tandem with this, 'Yeuisangjeongso' (禮儀詳定所), a government organization, was founded in 1113 (the 8th year of King Yejong's reign). Around this time, Choi Yun-ui (崔允儀, 1102-1162) published *Sangjeonggogeumyemun* (詳定古今禮文), which is known as the world's first metal print book. If this is true, the consciousness of Confucian proprieties in Goryeo also blazed a trail in terms of publishing history. Although clear evidence is required, this allows us to hazard a guess as to the importance of propriety and their practice to Koreans at that time. Thus, there was also a significant improvement in 'yesok' (禮俗: customs of the proprieties) observed by ordinary people.

The increased emphasis on the customs related to the proprieties in Goryeo even to ordinary people can be seen in a record complied by Confucian scholar Kim Gu (金坵, 1211-1278). He wrote, "Every nook and corner of this country is subject to proprieties."[27] This proves that the practice of the proprieties was prevalent throughout the whole country, and thus, that the culture of proprieties had gained broad

25 "Mireukseonhwa misirang jinjasa" (彌勒仙花 彌尸郎 眞慈師), *Samgukyusa*, Vol. 3.

26 Chap. 10, "The Rise of Early Confucianism in Goryeo," *A History of Korean Confucianism* (Jisik Sanup Publications, 2012), pp. 141-157.

27 Kim Gu, "SangjwajuKimsangguk (yanggyeong) sajeoneuibalgye" (上座主金相國(良鏡)謝傳衣鉢啓), *Jipojip* (止浦集), Vol. 3.

acceptance. As a Chinese (Northern Song) envoy described Goryeo as a country of proprieties in his book *Goryeodogyeong* (高麗圖經) at that time, it is unlikely that Kim Gu's statement is an exaggeration. Kim also added the following description:

> "Although this country near the ocean has been located in a remote area since ancient times, people all called it 'sojunghwa' (小中華: small China)."[28]

This was a comparative description of Korea and China, taking into account the fact that the Chinese called their country 'junghwa' (中華), a country with a high level of culture. According to Kim, Goryeo could also be called 'junghwa' in terms of the level of the culture of proprieties. However, since the land of Goryeo was smaller than that of China, he used 'sojunghwa' instead of 'junghwa.' This 'sojunghwa' consciousness—Goryeo has a smaller land area but the same level of culture as China—shows the pride of Koreans that was maintained until the late Joseon Dynasty in the 20th century. Yi Hang-ro (李恒老, 1792-1868) in late Joseon also wrote that Joseon was the eastern country of courtesy (東方禮儀之國) and that it was also 'sojunghwa.'

(2) The Emergence of the 'Yehak' (禮學, Studies on Propriety) Period Caused by the Emphasis on Proprieties

In the 14th century, the principles of *The Family Rites of Zhu Xi* began to be observed by government officials who had studied Zhu Xi Confucianism since its adoption in the late Goryeo Dynasty. They eliminated Buddhist manners (which used to be observed) from customs, such as 'sangrye' (喪禮: funeral ritual). Jeong Mong-ju, who lost his life in the defense of the dynasty in late Goryeo and who was also known for his early insight into Zhu Xi Confucianism, especially *Saseojipju*

28 Ibid.

(四書集註, Notes on the Four Books of Confucianism), was among the first to observe the family rites.

In the early Joseon Dynasty (15th century), besides *The Family Rites of Zhu Xi*, the ideas contained in *Oryundo* (五倫圖), a book emphasizing the thorough practice of *oryun* (the five moral disciplines in human relations), and *Sohak* (小學), a basic Neo-Confucian educational guide, were actively promoted through various policies. Through the policy of using *oryun* as a topic of examinations for the recruitment and promotion of junior officials, Neo-Confucian emphasis on the customs of proprieties rapidly progressed, beginning in early Joseon.

The government promoted *yechi* (禮治: governing with courtesy), by creating *Gukjooryeui* (國朝五禮儀, The Five National Ceremonies) and *Joseongyeonggukjeon* (朝鮮經國典). This initiative stemmed from the fact that proprieties at that time, as they were derived from three books of proprieties—*The Boo\k of Rites* (禮記), *The Book of Etiquette and Ceremonial* (儀禮) and *The Rites of Zhou* (周禮)—included institutional and legal as well as moral characteristics. Policies prioritizing the customs surrounding the practice of proprieties and of courteous governance, which were similar to those of China, persisted until the 16th century.

However, at the start of the 17th century, the ruling class 'sadaebu' began to feel that *The Family Rites of Zhu Xi* and *Gukjooryeui* were inadequate texts in the effort to promote the practice of courteous acts. Therefore, they published even more detailed commentary on *The Family Rites* and on four kinds of rituals (四禮, coming of age, marriage, funeral and ancestral worship rituals). The scholar Jeong Gu (鄭逑, 1543-1620), well known for reorganizing and subdividing the past proprieties in his book *Oseonsaengyeseolbunryu* (五先生禮說分類), also wrote *Garyejipramboju* (家禮輯覽補註), *Saryemundaphwiryu* (四禮問答彙類), *Yegisangryebunryu* (禮記喪禮分類), *Obokyeonhyeokdo* (五服沿革圖), and *Simuijedo* (深衣制度). Kim Jang-saeng (金長生, 1548-1631), the author of *Garyejipram* (家禮輯覽) and *Sangryebiyo* (喪禮備要), also published *Euiryemunhae* (疑禮問解), which went beyond the limitations of the existing proprieties through dialogues with his disciples. Yi Jae's (李縡 1680-1746) *Saryepyeonram* (四禮便覽), which compendiously explained the four kinds of rituals: coming of age; marriage; funeral; and ancestral worship), was especially influential at that time.

Other prominent scholars and their publications included the following: Jeong Gyeong-se (鄭經世, 1563-1633) who wrote *Sangryechamgo* (喪禮參考) and *Samunrok* (思問錄); Kim Jip (金集, 1574-1656) who published *Euiryemunhaesok* (疑禮問解續); Bak Se-chae (朴世采, 1631-1695) who proved that he was one of the masters of 'yehak' by creating *Yukryeuijip* (六禮疑輯), *Namgyeyeseol* (南溪禮說), *Samryeui* (三禮儀) and *Beomhakjeonpyeon* (範學全篇); Kim Gan (金幹, 1646-1732) who wrote *Dongyuyeseol* (東儒禮說); and Kim Chang-jip (金昌集, 1648-1722) who published the unique book *Oryunjeonbieonhae* (五倫全備諺解).

This voluminous wave of texts dealing with proprieties finally brought about the golden era of 'yehak.' In the 17th century, the so-called 'yehak' era began. Among all the Confucian countries including China, only Korea uses the phrase 'the yehak era.' This hints at the fact that putting stress on proprieties and actively studying them was another distinctive feature of Korean Confucianism.

(3) Proprieties Used as a Tool of Factions

The active study of proprieties was conducted in order to practice 'yehaeng' (禮行, courteous acts), which are moral actions, and further to realize 'yechi' (governing with courtesy). In a place where 'yehaeng' is emphasized, individuals were evaluated in terms of their practice of proprieties. The titles of 'gunja' (君子,virtuous man) and 'soin' (小人, person who is petty and crafty) were the results of evaluations according to this standard. This is not a matter of guesswork, but a verified phenomenon that occurred at that time. In the late 16th century, the cliques or the factions (朋黨) of 'Dongin' (東人, the Easterners) and 'Seoin'

(西人, the Westerners) emerged. This was caused by one person calling another person 'soin' based on his conduct.[29] At the beginning of the 17th century, 'Dongin' and 'Seoin' were divided into 'Bukin' (北人, the Northerners) and 'Namin' (南人, the Southerners), and 'Soron' (少論) and 'Noron' (老論), respectively, and ultimately intense political disputes arouse. The fundamental context of this party strife in the 17th century was the debate over the proper practice of 'yehaeng.'[30] This is the reason for calling this dispute 'Yesong' (禮訟, disputes on the observance of propriety).

The 'Yesong' centered around two disputes over the wearing of mourning dress (服喪). The first dispute occurred in 1659 (the 1st year of King Hyeonjong's reign). Upon the death of King Hyojong (孝宗), a debate arose about the appropriate duration of the wearing of a mourning dress by Queen-Dowager Jaui (趙氏: Queen Jo), the stepmother of King Hyojong and a concubine of King Injo (仁祖). Song Si-yeol (宋時烈, 1606-1684) and Song Jun-gil (宋浚吉, 1606-1672) from the 'Seoin' side proposed wearing it for one year, whereas Yun Hyu (尹鑴, 1617-1680) and Heo Mok (許穆, 1594-1682) from the 'Namin' side insisted that it be worn for three years. The king and the royal court adopted the one-year proposal. However, 'Namin' did not agree with the king's decision, and the two sides conducted an argument over the issue for approximately 20 years. This was the first 'Yesong,' or in other words the first mourning dress dispute.

---

29 The reason for the emergence of 'Dongin' (東人) and 'Seoin' (西人) was as follows. Kim Hyo-won (金孝元, 1532-1590), who was already well known, and who was later designated 'Seoin,' stayed at Prime Minister Yoon Won-hyeong's (尹元衡,?-1565) residence for a period of time before passing the state examination. After learning this, Shim Eui-gyeom (沈義謙, 1535-1587) criticized Kim, saying that visiting an influential family was uncouth behavior that should be engaged in only by 'soin.' Later, when Kim Hyo-won became 'ijo jeongrang' (吏曹銓郎), he rejected the idea of recommending Shim Chung-gyeom (沈忠謙, 1545-1594), Shim Eui-gyeong's younger brother, for the position of 'jeongrang' on the grounds that the Shims were the maternal relatives of the king. Thus, the two sides ('Dongin' and 'Seoin') became political opponents.

30 Hyeon Sang-yun (玄相允, 1893-?) pointed out that the strengthening of the consciousness of proprieties would bring about division.

One of the reasons for this conflict was the desire on the part of both sides to seize power. Another reason can be found in literary sources that supported the claim of each side. One reference book, *Gukjooryeui* (國朝五禮儀), which is a text that details royal proprieties, said, "Mothers should wear a mourning dress for a year (朞年)." *The Book of Rites* also included the same opinion, and 'Seoin' made an argument based on these books. However, *The Book of Etiquette and Ceremonial* said that mourning dresses should be worn for three years (斬衰章), and 'Namin' quoted this passage.

There is one more point to note, which made this issue more complicated. The commentary by Gagongeon (賈公彦) on the quoted page in *The Book of Etiquette and Ceremonial*, wherein the three-year wearing of mourning dress was described, proposed that "If the second son of the legal wife becomes the king due to the death of the eldest son, he should also be called the eldest son." Because this rule was applied to King Hyojong, 'Namin' did not retreat from their claim. 'Seoin' (including Song Si-yeol) also reviewed this commentary in *The Book of Etiquette and Ceremonial*, and argued that there were also four other theories. As disputes between the two sides continued, the topic of their argument moved to the interpretation of the letter *seo* (庶).[31] The argument over this interpretation grew so intense that Yoon Seon-do (尹善道, 1587-1671) from 'Namin' even mentioned King Hyojong's right to succeed to the throne.[32] The ferocity of the debate finally diminished when it was decided to banish Yoon Seon-do. Therefore, the first 'Yesong' or 'Boksangron' ('Gihaeboksangron': argument on wearing mourning dress) was all but concluded.[33]

The second 'Yesong' (二次禮訟) was also an argument over the du-

31 *Hyeonjongsilrok* (顯宗實錄), Vol. 2, March, the 1st year of King Hyeonjong's reign.

32 "Yoonseondosangso" (尹善道上疏), ibid., April, the 1st year of King Hyeonjong's reign.

33 "...all but concluded" means that there were still some debates even after Yoon's banishment. This book provides only a brief description of this incident. Please refer to Chapter 22 in *A History of Korean Confucianism* (Jisik Sanup Publications, 2012) for more details.

ration of the wearing of mourning dress. Upon the death of the wife of King Hyojong, Queen Inseon (Queen-Dowager Jang), in 1674 (the 15th year of King Hyeonjong's reign), the issue of the mourning dress of Queen Jaui (Queen-Dowager Jo), King Injo's wife, was raised again.

Yejo (the Ministry of Rites) tentatively decided to promulgate the one-year wearing of mourning dress based on *Gukjooryeui* and *Gyeong-gukdaejeon*. However, as the ruling authorities such as Song Si-yeol from 'Seoin' advocated a nine-month period (大功服), Yejo altered its original decision and reported the nine-month wearing rule to the king. This decision was made pursuant to the ancient proprieties in *The Book of Etiquette and Ceremonial*, which fixed the duration of this period differently for the wife of the first son and the wife of the second son. Thus, in this decision, the wife of King Hyojong, Queen Inseon, was considered the wife of the second.

After learning this, 'Namin' stood in opposition to this rule, criticizing 'Seoin.' According to 'Namin,' 'Seoin' considered King Hyojong the firstborn son when the king died. As support for their opinion, 'Seoin' pointed to new texts on the proprieties, *Gukjooryeui* and *Gyeonggukdaejeon*, instead of the ancient text on proprieties, *The Book of Etiquette and Ceremonial*. However, they later ignored the one-year rule prescribed in their reference books, and 'Namin' saw this as irrational. The nine-month wearing of mourning dress that 'Seoin' advocated was a rule to be applied not to the death of the eldest son's wife but to the death of the second son's wife. Therefore, 'Namin' argued that the one-year rule should be applied in order to treat Queen Inseon, wife of King Hyojong, as the wife of the eldest son.[34]

The king thought that 'Namin''s argument was reasonable, and thus, he ordered Prime Minister Kim Su-heung (金壽興) from 'Seoin' to provide a rational response to it. However, 'Seoin' including Kim only made poor excuses for their past position without providing

---

34 *Hyeonjongsilrok (*顯宗實錄), Vol. 2, July, the 15th year of King Hyeonjong's reign.

any clear answers. Later, they began to mention 'Obokjo' (五服條) in *Gyeonggukdaejon* (經國大典), and maintained that 'jungjabu' (衆子婦) in 'Obokjo' contained a nine-month rule.[35]

Yoon Hu from 'Namin' once again pointed out the contradiction of 'Seoin''s mourning dress duration rule. He said that 'Seoin' only pretended to refer to annotations in *The Book of Etiquette and Ceremonial*, but were not arguing in good faith. He did not hesitate to criticize 'Seoin' for promoting the nine-month rule, pointing out that it was in their interest to regard the wife of King Hyojong not as the wife of the eldest son but the wife of the second.

The king was outraged and decided to observe the one-year rule pursuant to the rule established by the national institution. Prime Minister Kim Su-heung was exiled to Chuncheon, and other officials, including Minister of Rites Jo Hyeong (趙珩), were also punished. This was the end of the second 'Yesong' or the second 'Boksangron' (甲寅服喪論). The second 'Yesong' resulted in the fall of 'Seoin' and the rise of 'Namin.' The reason for saying that 'Yesong' had factional characteristics was because it caused a change in the ruling power structure.

(4) Issues Relevant to the Understanding of 'Yesong' (Disputes on the Observance of Propriety)

'Yesong,' which persisted for 16 years from 1659, was an extreme case of the exploration and practice of various theories of propriety during the 'yehak' period in the 17th century. This demonstrates that the prioritization of a philosophy of courtesy and the observance of proprieties in order to promote the practice of proprieties and to ensure courteous governance was in tune with the spirit of the times. 'Yesong' enables us to confirm that the issues that arose during the 'yehak' period constituted one of the major characteristics of Korean Confucianism.

35 Ibid.

Due to its significance in Korean Confucianism, various approaches have been taken to understand and evaluate 'Yesong.' It has tended to be understood from political, sociological, and economic perspectives in the academic world. Among these, the sociological approach to understanding it was taken first. According to this approach, 'Yesong' was caused by a mass increase in the population of the nobility (兩班層) who completely relied on government positions despite their limited availability. This was a reasonable argument, but it was one-dimensional in nature.

There is a more rigorous sociological understanding of 'Yesong.' According to this perspective, taking into account the fact that both the Japanese Invasion of Korea in 1952 and the Manchu War in 1636, the 'Yesong' phenomenon stemmed from the thoroughgoing promotion of Confucian proprieties in the process of restoring social order in the wake of the social chaos unleashed by these wars. The two wars had brought about impoverishment and significant changes in the social hierarchy. In particular, it became possible to alter one's social status, which was previously unheard of. All people, including even those of the lowest class or slaves, could become noblemen depending on their military exploits. The strict hierarchy centering on the nobility, which was notorious for its discrimination among the four social classes (士農工商, scholars of the gentry, peasant farmers, artisans, and merchants) and even between legitimate and illegitimate children, collapsed overnight due to the wars. Because a system of proprieties has the innate tendency to create social order, the scholars of the gentry began to put more stress on it than before. Their ardent interest in and indulgence of the study of proprieties and the governance with courtesy led to the emergence of 'Yesong.' This explanation is convincing to some extent. However, considering that Neo-Confucianism was applied as a governing principle during the 17th century, the close relationship between 'Yesong' and Neo-Confucianism should also be factored in.

There is another, quite distinct understanding of 'Yesong,' which needs to be mentioned prior to examining its relationship with

Neo-Confucianism. This was proposed by a Japanese government-patronized scholar during the Japanese colonial era. Takahashi Doru (高橋亨) understood 'Yesong' from the perspective of Korean ethnicity. According to him, 'Yesong' was caused by the inherent disruptiveness of the people of Joseon. What made him link mere political or factional disputes to ethnic disruptiveness? This is actually an easy question to answer. Japanese government-patronized scholars, such as Takahashi, with malicious intent or prejudice always emphasized the anarchic nature of Koreans to justify the colonization of Korea. By stressing that the people of Joseon inherently lacked the capacity to cooperate and to maintain a country, they were able to justify colonization, claiming that imperial Japan was attempting to aid and protect Joseon. Therefore, Takahashi's understanding of 'Yesong' was nothing more than a deliberate distortion of facts. The fact that this was so becomes clearer in light of the following understanding of 'Yesong' based on its association with Neo-Confucianism.

As mentioned several times above, as of the 17th century, it had been more than two centuries since Zhu Xi Confucianism had been adopted as a governing principle. The ruling class already had extensive knowledge of Neo-Confucianism, and a long history of its practice through the pursuit of idealist politics. The idealist political theory of Confucius associated with *yechi* (禮治) was originally based on the theory of *jeongmyeong* (正名, adjustments to names), which states, "The king must be a king, and the vassals must be vassals." This theory displayed a strong sense of moral justification. Thus, Neo-Confucianism had a keener sense of moral justification than original Confucianism and a firm command of formal and logical speculation. This had already been confirmed through the development of the argument of *sadanchiljeong* in the 16th century. Theories of propriety constituted arguments for the application of Neo-Confucian reasoning to Confucian proprieties, which were considered an attempt to elevate the concept of fidelity. In other words, this fidelity-based reasoning of Neo-Confucian scholars influenced the practice of the proprieties, and this led to 'Yesong' in the 17th century.

Thus, although 'Yesong' had a factional character, it seems to have been a highly sophisticated form of political action in that it prioritized rationality. This sophistication can be confirmed when comparing 'Yesong' with the political developments of other countries in the same period. In the Ming Dynasty of China, while the country was falling to the Qing Dynasty, eunuchs (宦官) monopolized the government and promoted the collapse of the dynasty. In Japan, samurai controlled the government through force during the Edo period. It was difficult to find rational, moderate, and sophisticated political practices in these countries. 'Yesong' in Joseon was a form of political dispute that differed from political conflicts in other countries in that it was based on a rational and reasonable and consensus-seeking argument. Factions at that time were not fundamentally different from those of today. Thus, it is apparent that the Japanese view on 'Yesong' including the prejudiced understanding of 'the disruptive nature of Koreans' was simply derived from a malicious distortion.

The next topic that needs to be discussed is *ji* (智 or 知, wisdom or knowledge), one of the principles of Confucianism realized in Korea. This topic will be described in the next chapters in terms of 'the doctrines of Wang Yang-ming' (Yangmingism), Neo-Confucian research, and 'Silhak' in the late Joseon Dynasty.

Chapter IV.

An Underdeveloped Aspect of Korean Confucianism: Wang Shou-ren's Study of the Mind

1. The Outstanding Scholar of Wang Shou-ren's Study of the Mind: Jeong Je-du

The field of Lu-Wang study (陸王學), especially Wang Shou-ren's study of the mind (心學, 'Simhak'), also known as Yangmingism (陽明學), emerged to oppose Zhu Xi Confucianism. It has already been pointed out that Yangmingism was introduced into Korea in the late 15th century, but there was no further development of this doctrine. Along with Lu Jiu-yuan (陸九淵), Wang criticized and rejected Cheng-Chu Neo-Confucianism for its objective attitude towards the pursuit of principles. Initially, Wang stated, "*Ri* (principle) is not outside (of our mind), but inside of our mind (理在此心)." This belief led him to focus on the study of the mind, a study of our controlling thoughts and will, without recourse to external principles.

The proposition Wang Shou-ren presented based on this belief was "The mind is *ri* (心卽理)." The reason his work was seen as the study of the mind is because he sought to realize and practice *yangji* (良知, innate knowledge of the good), a principle of our mind, while refusing to arrive at principles objectively or empirically. This constituted Wang Shou-ren's study of the mind, which was more popular and influential than Zhu Xi Neo-Confucianism in the Ming Dynasty in China.

Wang Shou-ren's study of the mind was completely and offhandedly rejected by prominent Korean Neo-Confucian scholars in the 16th century such as Yi Hwang (李滉). After reading Wang Shou-ren's *Jeonseuprok* (傳習錄), Yi Hwang spearheaded the criticism and rejection of Wang's major ideas. Yi's criticism of the theory of *jihaenghapil* (知行合一, unity of knowledge and action), Wang's core philosophy, is a good example. Earlier, Wang mentioned a phrase in *The Great Learning*, "caring for beautiful colors (好好色)," to explain his *jihaenghapil*. According to him, "knowing (知: knowledge)" and "caring for (行: action)" the beautiful colors occur simultaneously, and this is *jihaenghapil*. However, Yi Hwang pointed out that this philosophy was not applicable to the dimension of rationality which included fidelity, but only to the dimension of formal materials (形氣) which included the senses and instinct. Yi argued that "knowing and caring for virtue (善)" is different from "knowing and caring for beautiful colors." In order to support his argument, he cited the fact that there are people who have no propensity for virtue despite their knowledge of it. According to Yi Hwang, people should learn how to practice filial piety and strive to achieve it even if their desire for it is lacking. Therefore, Yi could not accept Wang Shou-ren's theory of *jihaenghapil* as a universal truth.[1]

Despite Yi Hwang's rejection, if Yangmingism had been actively supported by the ruling class of Joseon, it may have spread and developed. However, this did not happen. Some 'Soron' scholars were interested in Wang Shou-ren's work in the 17th and 18th centuries, but their period of rule was not long enough to popularize it. Even among 'Soron' scholars, there was a deep prejudice against Wang Shou-ren's work. At that time, it was not even imaginable to oppose or refuse to accept Zhu Xi Neo-Confucianism, the governing principle that set the terms of reference for politics and scholarly work. One's simple rejection of or refusal to accept Zhu Xi Neo-Confucianism could lead

1 Yi Hwang (李滉), "Jeonseuprokronbyeon" (傳習錄論辯), *Toegyejeonseo* (退溪全書, *The Complete Works of Toegye*), Vol. 1, p.924, (Daedong Institute for Korean Studies, Sungkyunkwan University).

to one's death as a *samunnanjeok* (斯文亂賊, a subversive who undermines the orthodox Confucianism). (Such rejection will be seen in the next chapter, with the emergence of 'Silhak' with the characteristics of De-Neo-Confucianism). As a result, during the 17th and 18th centuries, the academic world in Joseon was utterly dominated by Neo-Confucianism.

Nevertheless, there was a scholar who strove to explore Wang Shou-ren's study of the mind, which was considered to be a cult, ignoring the demands of the intellectual milieu. His name was Jeong Je-du (鄭齊斗, 霞谷, 1649-1736). More scholars pursued this field of study later, but only in the 20th century after the collapse of the Joseon Dynasty. Hence, those cases are not included in the history of Joseon philosophy. Here, Jeong Je-du's view on Wang Shou-ren's work will be described briefly. His theories have significance because they represent the contemporary level and characteristics of research into Wang Shou-ren's work in Korea.

2. Jeong Je-du's Stance on the Major Ideas of Wang Shou-ren's Study of the Mind

Jeong Je-du enjoyed a long life of 87 years, but he was in extremely fragile health when he was young. His health was so poor that he even sent his will to his teacher Bak Se-chae (朴世采) at the age of 34. Due to such poor health, he had to give up his aspiration for a government position, which guaranteed wealth and honor, at an early age. Later, his health suddenly improved, and he was able to serve as a government official in his later years. However, the difficulties that Jeong experienced in his youth seem to have given him the courage to withstand the academic and social marginalization caused by his adherence to what was viewed as a cult. After being fascinated by Wang Shou-ren's work at around the age of 23, he devoted a lifetime to it exploration. Ultimately he became an unrivaled expert in Wang Shou-ren's work in Joseon.

The fundamental feature of Wang Shou-ren's study of the mind is its proposition, "*Sim* is *ri* (心卽理, the mind is principle)." The theory of *jihaenghapil*, which emphasized *yangji* (innate knowledge of the good) corresponding to *ri*, is the second major feature. Therefore, whether Jeong Je-du's work is in a direct line of descent from Wang Shou-ren's work or not depends on Jeong's position on these two issues, which can be seen in his writing below:

> "If there is no *yong* (用, function or use) in *sim* (mind), there is no *che* (體, body), either. If *ri* lacks *che*, *sim* also lacks *yong*. *Ri* is *sim* (理卽心), and *sim* is *ri* (心卽理)."[2] "If *sari* (事理, the reasoning of things) is widely taught in terms of the division between *sim* and *ri*, and between *ji* (知, knowledge) and *haeng* (行, action), the concept of *ri* will break apart."[3]

Jeong proposed that "*Sim* is *ri*," and "*Ri* is *sim*" here, as Wang Shou-ren had. He also argued, "Knowledge and action should not be considered separately." These propositions clearly indicate the agenda Jeong pursued through his work. In this light, it is apparent that Jeong Je-du was not a Zhu Xi Neo-Confucian scholar but a scholar immersed in Wang Shou-ren's work.

Initially, Lu-Wang began to criticize Zhu Xi Neo-Confucianism due to its contrasting understanding of *The Great Learning*. Besides the aforementioned propositions, the Lu-Wang and Cheng-Zhu philosophies are differentiated in their views on *The Great Learning*. Thus, in order to examine whether Jeong Je-du in fact sought to extend Wang Shou-ren's philosophy, his interpretation of *The Great Learning* should also be considered.

Jeong Je-du's view on *The Great Learning* can be explored through the following strands of argument. While Jeong evaluated *The Great Learning* as a perfectly coherent book, he rejected

---

2 Jeong Je-du, "Joneon" (存言), *Hagokjeonjip* (霞谷全集), Vol. 1, p. 296.
3 Ibid., p. 319.

"Bomangjang" (補忘章) which was created by Zhu Xi, believing that the book was disorganized. Jeong divided *The Great Learning* into seven chapters, ignoring the 'gyeong' (經) and 'jeon' (傳) sections. He also had a different understanding of each chapter from that of Zhu Xi. For example, he validated only *myeongmyeongdeok* (明明德, to illustrate illustrious virtue) and *chinmin* (親民, to revitalize the people) as creeds, refusing to accept Zhu Xi's theory of the three fundamental principles (三綱領, to illustrate illustrious virtue, to revitalize the people and to remain in the state of highest excellence). He also rejected Zhu Xi's *sinmin* (新民, the creation of new people), instead preferring *chinmin*. Jeong said, "The only doctrine in *The Great Learning* is *hyojeja* (孝悌慈, filial piety, civility, and love). *Myeongdeok* (明德, illustrious virtue) is *hyojeja* or *hyojeingyeong* (孝悌仁敬, filial piety, civility, benevolence, and respect)."[4] In light of this statement, it is certain that Jeong Jedu was an acolyte of Wang Shou-ren.

A clearer method of identifying Jeong Je-du's affiliation can be devised by examining the difference between Zhu Xi and Wang Shou-ren in terms of their interpretation of *gyeokmul* (格物, the investigation of things), one of the eight essential conceptual imperatives (八條目) in *The Great Learning*. Jeong's position on *gyeokmul* can be ascertained in the following quotation:

> "The illustration of illustrious virtue depends upon the investigation of things. In the sentence 'Things having been investigated, knowledge became complete (致知在格物),' *chi* (致, to complete) connotes *to embody the utmost* or *to be the pinnacle of excellence* (至) and *ji* (知, knowledge) refers to the realization of *utmost* or *supreme virtue* (至善), the true nature of the mind. *Gyeok* (格, to investigate) connotes *to rectify* or *straighten* (正), and *mul* (物, things) refers to *states of affair containing meaning* (意所在之事). To achieve *yangji* in fact means to straighten things. To make something truly excellent (至) is nothing more than to allow it to play its natural role (實)."[5]

4 "seol" (大學說), ibid., p. 421.
5 Ibid., p. 399.

Jeong Je-du stated that *gyeok* (格) refers to 'straightening' (正), and *mul* (物) refers to 'things,' especially, 'states of affair containing meaning' (意所在之事). Thus, he interpreted *gyeokmul* as 'the straightening of apprehensions growing in the mind' (正意). Needless to say, this was also Wang Shou-ren's view. It is noteworthy that, although his interpretation of *chi* (致) in *chiji* (致知) as *ji* (至) is apparently similar to that of Cheng-Zhu, the meaning is not 'achieving with effort' but 'making excellent.' It becomes apparent once again that Jeong had affinity for Wang Shou-ren's work in that he viewed *ji* (知) not as objective knowledge but as innate *yangji* (良知). There is no doubt that Jeong Je-du embraced Wang Shou-ren's work, including such specific theories.

3. The Derivation of Jeong Je-du's Theories from Wang Shou-ren's Work

Jeong Je-du left multiple publications that owed to Wang Shou-ren's work. They include *Saseoseol* (四書說), *Munjip* (文集), in addition to "Hakbyeon" (學辨), "Joneon" (存言), "Jeongseongseohae" (定性書解), "Gyeonghakjiprok" (經學集錄), and "Shimgyeongjipui" (心經集義).

Wang Shou-ren belittled the study of theories or scriptures, that is, 'gyeonghak' (經學). He did so because he thought that the exercise of control over innate desire was more important than the acquisition of theoretical knowledge. Jeong Je-du also tended to disregard the pursuit of objective knowledge. However, it is also true that he left behind a large number of publications, paradoxically so given his negative attitude towards textual study.

Once, he mentioned his publishing activity. The following is his explanation for his book about 'yukkyeong' (六經, six Confucian classics).

> "The writings in 'yukkyeong' are as bright as the sun and the stars, and thus, people who read them all become well versed in them for

> themselves. (However) upon Zhu Xi's annotating of 'yukkyeong' using *mulli* (物理, objective *ri*), others also felt they had to annotate them. Because Zhu Xi's interpretation deviated from the original meaning of the ancient scriptures, another interpretation was needed for its correction. This is why I wrote this book."[6]

According to Jeong, 'yukkyeong' originally do not need annotations, but due to the manufacture of inaccurate interpretation by Zhu Xi, Jeong was compelled to also annotate 'yukkyeong' in order to promote their correct interpretation.

Among his aforementioned texts, his annotations on *The Book of Mencius, Jeongseongseo, Shimgyeong*, and *The Great Learning* were especially notable. They were important classics containing abundant materials for 'the cultivation of mind and heart' (心性修養), which were considered very important by Zhu Xi as well as Lu Jiu-yuan and Wang Shou-ren. The fact that Jeong Je-du valued them also demonstrates that his academic interests tended toward the study of the mind ('Simhak').

Although he sometimes denied it, it is apparent that Jeong Je-du was immersed in the annotation of scriptures related to mind and heart training. This suggests that Jeong actively engaged in scriptural or textual study to a great degree than any other scholars following Wang Shou-ren, and that he paradoxically also endeavored to obtain sufficient theoretical knowledge to support his work. In light of this, his academic character is revealed. Wang Shou-ren's work informed Jeong's profoundly, but Jeong was not slavish in his acceptance of it. He had his own theory and his work had its own qualities. Jeong actively sought theoretical knowledge and developed his own distinctive ideas, as delineated below.

Jeong Je-du grasped past Confucian history from the perspective of 'Simhak' (study of the mind). According to him, Confucian history, especially Confucianism in the ancient times and the Song Dynasty,

---

6 Ibid., p. 397.

was the history of successive theories of mind and heart training and discipline. The theory of *inshimdosim* (人心道心, *the human mind and the moral mind*), contained in *The Book of History* and given by King Shun to King Yu argues that, "*Insim* is at stake and *dosim* is invisible. Thus, focus on one thing and expend every effort to maintain your equilibrium." The key idea of Confucius, *in* (benevolence), emphasizes the ascetic rejection of selfish desire and the restoration of propriety (克己復禮), while *myeongdeok* (illustrious virtue) in *The Great Learning* stresses the absence of self-deception. According to *The Doctrine of the Mean*, the unity of heaven and humanity (天人合一) leads to the ideal state. All of these goals can be achieved through mental training performed on the basis of *gyesin* (戒愼, precaution and restraint) and *gongu* (恐懼, fear).

The following is the case of *The Book of Mencius,* which Jeong Je-du focused on by writing more copiously than any other scholar about it. According to Jeong, Mencius' work seeks *in* (benevolence), and this is practiced simply by walling the mind off distraction (救放心). Jeong also pointed out the statement of Mencius, "If one dedicates oneself to plumbing human nature (盡心知性), one will be able to understand Heaven (知天). Preserving the full capacities of the mind (存心) and developing the core of human nature (養性) is the path to serving Heaven (事天)." Jeong praised Mencius highly, saying, "This is how the great person (大人) discussed the study of the Way of Heaven (天道之學)."

Jeong also applied this perspective to Confucian scholars in the Song Dynasty. He reminded people of the fact that Zhou Dunyi (周敦頤) discussed *mugeuk* (無極, infinities) and *taegeuk* (太極, the great ultimate), and then established the exemplary standard of humanity, *ingeuk* (人極, the acme of humanity) by focusing on tranquility (主靜). Jeong greatly appreciated Zhou Dunyi's achievement, stating that it teaches us about the sage (聖人). In the case of Cheng Hao (程顥), Jeong wrote *Jeongseongseohae* (定性書解: annotations on Jeongseongseo written by Cheng Hao), which shows that Jeong regarded the *jeongseong* (定性, the determination of human nature) training as important.[7]

These publications of Jeong Je-du are significant in that they proved that Wang Shou-ren's study of the mind also descended from original Confucian traditions without deviating from them. This also justified Jeong's affinity for Wang Shou-ren's study of mind. In other words, it can be said that Jeong took these positions in order to defend his dedication to Wang Shou-ren's work.

Jeong Je-du was interested in various texts on the mind and heart training as mentioned above, and was especially attracted to Wang Shou-ren's work in *Jeonseuprok*. However, it is noteworthy that Jeong also proposed his own unique theories. One instructive example is his view on the relationship between *seong* (human nature) and *ri* (principle). Originally, the proposition "*Seong* is *ri* (性卽理)" was a basic component of the philosophy of Cheng-Zhu, but Wang Shou-ren did not reject it, stating "*Sim* is *ri* (心卽理)." This was the corresponding feature between Zhu Xi Neo-Confucianism and Wang Shou-ren's work. Jeong Je-du had a similar correspondence with Cheng-Zhu philosophy. However, he stated, "*Seong* is the *che* (體, substance) of *ri*"[8] and "*seong* is *chung* (衷, inner mind) with *che*, that is, *myeongdeok* (illustrious virtue)."[9] In Cheng-Zhu Neo-Confucianism, human nature is the phenomenal substance of the mind (心) and emotion (情), while Jeong regarded human nature as the substance of the mind (心) and principle (理). He equated human nature (*seong*) and principle (*ri*), but categorized them differently. Thus, his principle (*ri*) became the substance of the mind and the function (*yong*) of human nature (*seong*).

Although Jeong Je-du agreed with Wang Shou-ren's concept of innate knowledge of the good (*yangji*) and the unity of knowledge and action (*jihaenghapil*), he did not emphasize them to a great degree. This may have been because Jeong was familiar with Yi Hwang's theory, which pointed out the limitations of the theory of *jihaenghapil*. How-

7 Cf. Part 5, Chap. 26, *A History of Korean Confucianism (*Jisik Sanup Publications, 2012).
8 Jeong Je-du, "Joneon" (存言), *Hagokjeonjip*, Vol. 3, p. 298.
9 Ibid., p. 306.

ever, it is more convincing to argue that Jeong did not stress these two theories because he realized the shortcomings of Wang Shou-ren's work. This speculation is based on the fact that Jeong pointed out both the merits and shortcomings of Wang Shou-ren's work.

> "When I learned Yangmingism, I was highly pleased at the brevity and profundity of its philosophical tenets. While I was sleeping at Dongho (東湖) in June in the year of *sinhae*, in my dream, I suddenly realized that there is doubt about Wang's theory of *chiyangji* (致良知, ultimate knowledge of the good) based on emotion and desire, despite its sincerity."[10]

Jeong Je-du was aware of not only the merits but also the deficiencies of Wang Shou-ren's philosophy. Its most significant shortcoming was the great possibility it entailed of following the dictates of desire without limitation, due to the primacy it assigned to emotion. Needless to say, his concern was absolutely justified, and it became clear that Jeong did not slavishly echo every element of Wang Shou-ren's work. He engaged with Wang Shou-ren's philosophy through the prism of his own critical faculties.

Jeong explored some fields more profoundly than Wang Shou-ren. When agreeing with the proposition that "*Sim* is *ri* (心卽理)," he frequently elaborated on the terms *saenggi* (生氣, biological force) or *saengri* (生理, the biological principles) as follows: "One *hwalche* (活體, lively body) of the spirit (神) in the human mind, is *saengri*, and *jeongsinsaenggi* (精神生氣, biological force of the spirit in the human mind) is the *saengri* of the body"[11]; "The body of principle (*ri*) is in *saenggi*"[12]; and "The basis of *saenggi* is both *yeongmyeongjijeong* (靈明之精, the numinous and luminous force) and *saengri*."[13] Wang Shou-ren mentioned *saenggi* and *saengri* only very rarely to explain *in* (benevolence) in his book *Jeonseuprok,*

10 Ibid., Vol. 2, p. 315.
11 Ibid., Vol. 2, p. 285.
12 Ibid., Vol. 1, p. 287.
13 Ibid., Vol. 1, p. 285.

but Jeong Je-du used these concepts several times. This fact can be interpreted as suggesting that Jeong had a more vivid conception of the philosophy of life and was more absorbed in the exploration of *ri-gi* than Wang Shou-ren.

Ultimately, Jeong mentioned *saenggi* to emphasize the vitality of the mind. He also regarded *ri*, which is the body of the mind (*simche*), as *saengri*, and said that *saengri* is the basis of *saenggi*. In this regard, he lost the balance between *ri* and *gi*, and began to reach *ri*-oriented conclusions, displaying a tendency to focus on *juriron* (主理論, the *ri*-principal theory). In addition, by saying, "The biological force of the spirit in the human mind is the *saengri* of the body," he even ploblemitized the distinction between *ri* and *gi*. However, it is possible to see coherence on this statement. Considering that *sim* (mind) and *ri* (principle) are the same and that *sim* actually became *gi*, the theory that *gi* and *ri* are the same could be established on firm foundations. However, his theory entailed the serious problems of losing the distinction between *ri* and *gi*, and making the essential existence of *sim* impossible by stressing only *ri*, which is the body of *sim*, while ignoring *gi*.

These are the features and depth of Jeong Je-du's work in relation to Wang Shou-ren's philosophy (Yangmingism). Although even more serious problems with Jeong's ideas can be anticipated upon their further examination, it should also be understood that the depth of his exploration was comparable to that of other scholars.

Chapter V.

A Revaluation of Neo-Confucian Theories

1. The Initiation of the Neo-Confucian Theory of the Just Consequences for Good and Evil

(1) The Rejection of Buddhism and the Substitution of Neo-Confucian for Buddhist Concepts

Although Wang Shou-ren (王守仁, 1472-1528)'s 'simhak (心學, the study of the mind)' was unpopular in Korea, his Simhak was the first product of the study of wisdom (智) in Korea, which is a fundamental principle of Confucianism. The Neo-Confucian theories of the Joseon Dynasty were also products of this field of study. In this section I will examine chronologically the Neo-Confucian theories formulated on the basis of the intelligence and wisdom of Korean scholars.

The rejection of Buddhism which had started at the end of the Goryeo Dynasty, when Zhu Xi's Neo-Confucianism had begun to be introduced to Korea, intensified as Neo-Confucianism was adopted as the governing ideology of the Joseon Dynasty. The scholar who was in the vanguard of this rejection was Jeong Do-jeon (鄭道傳, 1342-1398) who took the central role in the dynastic revolution. He wrote *Joseongyeonggukjeon* (朝鮮經國典) and *Gyeongjemungam* (經濟文鑑), and then devoted himself to the establishment of moral codes based on the principles of Neo-Confucianism. He also actively promoted the observance of 'the proprieties of a family (家禮)' and the practice of 'the three fundamental principles and the five moral disciplines in human relations (三綱五倫)'. Jeong Do-jeon assiduously rejected Buddhism because he thought that it was the greatest obstacle to the establishment of social order based on Neo-Confucian manners and morals.

Bulssijapbyeon (佛氏雜辨) is his representative critical work on Buddhism. In this book, he compiled in accordance with his own viewpoint the criticisms of Buddhism by Chinese scholars from Han Yu (韓愈, 768-824) to Zhu Xi. Here he enumerated 19 cases of Buddhist abuses and weakness such as the misdeeds of Buddhist monks, the fictitiousness of Buddhist beliefs, and its views of karma and transmigration. Though all the critical views on Buddhism introduced in this book cannot be said to have been based on rational ground, it was a monumental work that illuminated why Neo-Confucian scholars rejected Buddhism.

Jeong Do-jeon also wrote *Simgiripyeon* (心氣理篇) with similar intention. In this book he linked Buddhism with '*sim* (心, heart or mind)', Taoism to '*gi* (氣, material force)', and Neo-Confucianism to '*ri* (理, principle)', and maintained that Neo-Confucianism based on the core idea of *ri* was more fruitful belief system than Taoism and Buddhism. However, as he interpreted the concepts of *sim, gi* and *ri* solely from the Neo-Confucian point of view, his ultimate view of the supremacy of Neo-Confucianism can be evaluated as a self-serving one. Such a prejudiced evaluation, however, was intended to facilitate the rejection of Buddhism by emphasizing its lack of merit. In other words, this book aimed to successfully substitute Neo-Confucianism for Buddhism.

In a similar context Jeong Do-jeon wrote another book entitled *Simmuncheondap* (心問天答). This text dealt with a concept similar to the Buddhist concept of retribution for evil and reward for good, that is, the concept that good deeds are rewarded with blessing and good fortune while evil deeds meet with disaster and misfortune. In *Bulssijapbyeon* he criticized the whole gamut of Buddhist thought, but he did not do so in this book because Confucians also encouraged good deeds and punished evil deeds and believed that good deeds would necessarily be accompanied by good fortune. He wrote *Simmuncheondap* simply to propagate the concept of retribution and reward not in Buddhist but in Neo-Confucian terms.

(2) Jeong Do-jeon's Fundamental Attitude toward Good and Evil

In *Simmuncheondap* Jeong Do-jeon explains the good deeds of humans in connection with '*Cheon* (天, Heaven or Heavenly God)'.

> "*Cheon* can naturally bestow *ri* on humans, but cannot make humans perform only good deeds."[1]

Jeong's above remark on *Cheon* entails Neo-Confucian ideas as follows. 1) The Confucian view of *Cheon* originates from that of '*sangje* (上帝, Heavenly God)'who is not an almighty being but a supervisor of the lives, motions and changes of all things. 2) Humans are born with 'the original nature (本性)' owing to *Cheon* (which is internalized as this original nature) as recorded in *The Doctrine of the Mean*, which stipulates that "What *Sangje* (Cheon) instills in the human being is called '*seong* (性, nature)'" 3) In Neo-Confucianism '*Seong* is *ri*. (性卽理)'. 4) Just as *seong* bestowed by Heavenly God is *ri*, '*Cheon* is *ri* (天卽理)'. Jeong Do-jeon's concept of retribution and reward are based on these ideas.[2]

Jeong's view that humans may do good deeds is based on the idea that, "Humans are born with 'the original nature (本性)' of benevolence, righteousness, propriety and wisdom."[3] Conversely, according to him, humans may also commit evil deeds for greed hinders the manifestation of this original nature. On the basis of 'the theory of *ri-gi* (理氣論)', he explains, the function of *gi* as greed hinders the issuing

1 Jeong Do-jeon, "Simmuncheondap", *Sambongjip*, Vol. 10, p. 288.
2 Ibid. pp. 291-292.
3 Ibid.

forth of *ri* as goodness. Simply put, evil originates from the function of *gi*. So he emphasized that in order to do good deeds autonomously we should repel greed or desire originating from the function of *gi*. Quoting Mencius' remark, "A general is to a soldier what will is to *gi*," he advised people to combat the impulse toward evil deeds by strengthening their will.[4]

(3) Jeong Do-jeon's Neo-Confucian View of the Just Consequences for Good and Evil

Jeong Do-jeon explained the consequences for good and evil, "If humans do good deeds, Heaven will respond to them with good fortune and if humans do evil deeds,[5] Heaven will respond to them with misfortune." Adhering to the concept of consequences for good and evil, he said:

> "It is 'the immutable principle of *ri* (理之常)' that good deeds are followed by good fortune and evil deeds by misfortune."[6]

Jeong Do-jeon, who firmly believed in the immutable principle of *ri,* also called it 'the justice of principle (義理之公)'.[7] He believed that the concept of consequences for good and evil is an indispensable principle that cannot and should not change.

However, a problem arises here. Is a good deed always followed by good fortune and an evil deed by misfortune? Frequently, we experience that the reverse is the case. Good deeds may actually lead to misfortune and evil deeds to fortune. This is the very problem implied in the concept of consequences that must be overcome in order to validate it.

Jeong Do-jeon also knew that consequences do not always follow

4 Ibid., p. 288.
5 Ibid., p. 290.
6 Ibid., p. 291.
7 Ibid., p. 288.

in accordance with the unchangeable principle of *ri* or the justice of principle. He called the case in which consequences are incompatible with action 'the irregularity of Heaven (天之不定)'[8] or the irregularity of *ri*'. Confronted with such cases, he did not surrender the concept of consequences for good and evil, but rather, he pondered over this problem and thought that just consequences depend only on humans themselves not on Heaven (Heavenly God), and so he maintained that humans should not complain to Heaven about unjust consequences.

> "Disaster and auspiciousness in the universe depend on the right and wrong of human deeds... How do humans come to complain to Heaven without reflecting on themselves and doing what they should?"[9]

> "If one's mind is righteous and one has a gentle '*gi* (氣, material force or spirit)', the mind and *gi* of the universe (天 地) also become gentle."[10]

Jeong Do-jeon did not concretely explain the mind of the universe. It may refer to the personification of nature (自然) derived from the thought of 'the identity of all things (萬物一體)' or of 'the identity of man and nature'. So Jeong Do-jeon's thoughts above may be summarized in the principle that "Human deeds may have influence on nature" or "If humans do good deeds, the *gi* of the universe and nature also becomes purified and creates a propitious environment." Then, the consequences through which the principle of *ri* or the justice of *ri* is applied are after all the natural result of human deeds or 'the function of *gi* (氣作用)'.

However, after such a reasoning process, there still remains a problem, for natural disasters occur regardless of man's good deeds and moreover, cruel human deeds may go unpunished.

---

8 Ibid.
9 Ibid., p. 292.
10 Ibid., p. 292.

Jeong Do-jeon attempted to resolve this problem, and suggested an idea he called 'more properly applicable thought'. This idea was based on 'the presence of the functional characteristics' implied in the concept of *ri* and *gi*.

> "'*Cheon* is *ri* (天卽理)'... *Ri* essentially has 'no function (無爲, non-doing)' while *gi* has function. A being without function is immovable and permanent, while a being with function is movable and easily changeable. 'Unjust consequences (災祥之不正)' are due to the function of *gi*..."
>
> "*Gi* functions by expanding or contracting, but *ri* is unchangeable. After aeons of time (when Heaven is firmly ordered), *ri* will surely return to its normal state of unchangeability and *gi*, complying with *ri*, will become orderly. So how could the reward of good with fortune and the punishment of evil with misfortune be gainsaid?"[11]

Furthermore, Jeong Do-jeon tried to solve the problem in accordance with 'regular and perfect *ri*' instead of 'irregular and imperfect Heaven'. *Ri* without any function does not change while *gi* with function always changes. *Gi*'s characteristic of constant changeability sometimes runs counter to the principle of *ri* and actually causes unjust consequences. However, after a lapse of time *gi*'s function complies with 'the principle of *ri*', and even 'unjust consequences become just'. So he maintained that the concept of the just consequences for good and evil become tenable in this way.

However, such a view is lacking in that we must 'wait' until 'the function of *gi*' complies with the principle of *ri*, in addition to the possibility that unjust consequences may actually occur. In other words, his view is akin to a confession that the consequences for good and evil are not realized in accordance with the indispensable law of cause and effect. So it may be said that his attempt to valorize the

---

11 Ibid., p. 291.

concept of just consequences ended in failure. The weak reasoning upon which his ideas were based might have been the result of his wholesale criticism, denial and rejection of the Buddhist 'doctrine of causation (緣起說, pratityasamutpada)' in his earlier work, *Bulssijapbyeon* (佛氏雜辨)[12]. Jeong Do-jeon's approach should have been more logical because the concept of just consequences itself entailed a kind of the logic of cause and effect.

However, his Neo-Confucian concept of consequences for good and evil was accepted by contemporary scholars, and it may have been a great impetus behind the rejection of Buddhism. Though his concept seems deficient, as we have seen, considering the contemporary ethical consciousness of the promotion of virtue and the reproof of vice, we may evaluate highly his intention of formulating the concept of just consequences. In short, we may conclude that Jeong Do-jeon's Neo-Confucian concept of just consequences ultimately contributed to the establishment of ethical politics in the Joseon Dynasty.

2. Studies on Cheonmyeong (天命) in the 16th Century

(1) The Publication of *Iphakdoseol* (入學圖說)

Neo-Confucianism could not but become the governing ideology of the Joseon Dynasty because the nobility were unable to become officials or belong to the governing class without some considerable knowledge of it. As a result, the nobility in this period displayed much enthusiasm for learning and studying Neo-Confucianism.

Gwon Geun (權近, 1352-1409), who was one of the representative Neo-Confucian scholars in the early period (the 14th century) of the Joseon Dynasty, wrote a primer on Neo-Confucianism entitled *Iphakdoseol* (入學圖說) in 1397. As writing a primer on any field of study

12 He took as an example of rejecting the theory of causation (緣起論, pratityasamutpada) the sowing of seeds: "Isn't the theory of causation tenable only when sowing a seed produces a grain?"

requires a profound knowledge of that field, Gwon Geun might well have had pride in his comprehensive knowledge of Neo-Confucianism.

In fact, the two volumes of *Iphakdoseol* display this knowledge, as they comprise a variety of 40 diagrams and commentaries on these diagrams. Concretely speaking, the book deals with the concepts of Heaven (天), the human being (人), mind (心), nature (性); the characteristics of 'The Four Books and The Five Classics (四書五經)'; Neo-Confucian ideas such as 'the Great Ultimate (太極)', 'the doctrine of the five elements of the positive and the negative (陰陽五行)', 'the co-existence of the five elements (河圖)', 'the incompatibility of the five elements (洛書)', 'the original source of the doctrine of the five elements (弘範九疇)', and 'the harmonization of Heaven and the human being (天人合一)'. These contents may be said to cover most of the fundamental bases of Neo-Confucianism,[13] as is supported by the fact that this book was republished several times.[14]

Gwon Geun structured *Iphakdoseol* in a unique way. He interpreted the concepts of 'Heaven, the human being, mind and nature (天人心性)' in a chapter entitled "The Diagram for the Analysis of Heaven, the Human Being, Mind and Nature (天人心性分釋之圖)"; he suggested the possibility of the harmonization of Heaven and the human being through the understanding and the cultivation of mind and nature (性) in a chapter entitled "The Diagram of the Harmonization of Heaven, the Human Being, Mind and Nature (天人心性合一之圖)"; he expressed his own view of the learning of the Five Classics on the basis of 'substance and function (體用)'. In addition, the chapter entitled "Commentary on The Five Classics (五經淺見錄)" reveals his extraordinary level of Neo-Confucian learning.

His interpretation of the concept of Cheon (Heaven) is an example

13 When he wrote this book Gwon Geun might not have read *Jujadaejeon.* So, though he followed Cheng-Zhu's theory, some of his views were still tied to Chinese Yuan's Neo-Confucianism.

14 Since this collection had bee first published in 1397 (the 1st year of King Taejo's reign) in Jinju, it was published several times in several places including the one published in Jinju in 1425 (the 7th year of King Sejong's reign).

The Diagram for the Analysis of Heaven, the Human Being, Mind and Nature (天人心性分釋之圖)

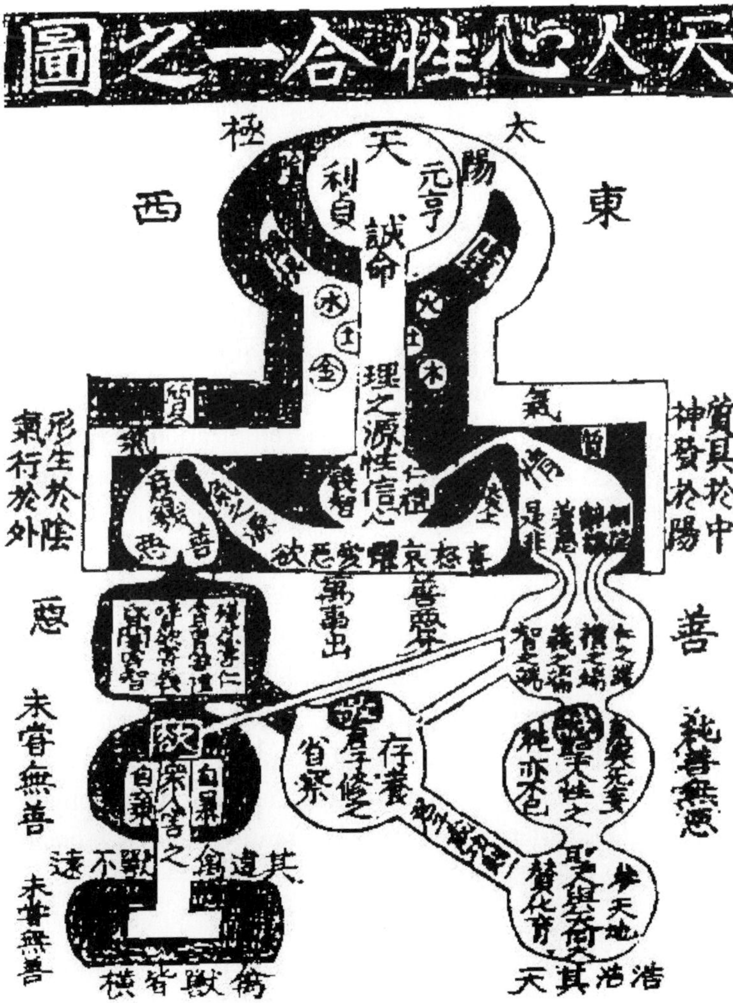

The Diagram of the Harmonization of Heaven, the Human Being, Mind and Nature(天人心性合一之圖)

of his unique understanding. He introduced the polysemy of the concepts of Cheon: entailing the empty void, Heavenly God, the *ri* of the universe and nature (自然). He thought that the letter '天 (Heaven)' is composed of '一 (one)' and '大 (largeness)' and accordingly explained that 天 denotes 'infinity (無限)', 'eternity (無窮)', 'peerlessness (無對)', and 'endlessness (無息)'. With these variegated meanings of '天' he uniquely 'identified '天 with *ri* (天卽理)'.

Gwon Geun's interpretation of 'the human being as benevolence (人卽仁)' is also distinctive for he reversed the interpretation of 'The Original Confucianism (本源儒學)', which stipulated that, "Benevolence is the facet of nature (性) that makes 'a human being like human (仁卽人)'." His "The Diagram of the Harmonization of Heaven, the Human Being, Mind and Nature (性)," which interpreted the close relationship of these four entities, was the first diagram of Neo-Confucian theories in the Joseon Dynasty, and had great influence on later scholars. The diagrams of 'Cheonmyeong (天命, The Mandate of Heaven)' drawn by 16th century Neo-Confucian scholars also revealed his influence. In particular, the very fact that he inserted the letter '心 (mind or heart)' between 'the four beginnings (四端)' and 'the seven feelings (七情)' influenced the interpretation of the four beginnings and the seven feelings on the basis of *ri* and *gi* in the diagrams of Cheonmyeong drawn by later scholars. These are only a few examples demonstrating the influence of *Iphakdoseol*.

(2) Studies on Cheonmyeong and "The Diagram of Cheonmyeong"

In the 16th century *Seonghaksipdo* (聖學十圖, *Ten Diagrams of Sages' Learning*) edited by Yi Hwang attracted the attention of the academic circles. The book is composed of Zhou Dunyi (周敦頤)'s "Taegeukdo (太極圖)", Zhang Zai (張載)'s "Seomyeongdo (西銘圖)", Yi Hwang's "Sohakdo (小學圖)", Gwon Geun's "Daehakdo (大學圖)", Yi Hwang's "Baeknokdonggyudo (白鹿洞規圖)", Jeong Bok-sim (程復心) and Yi Hwang's "Simtongseongjeongdo (心統性情圖)", Zhu Xi (朱熹)'s "Inseoldo (仁說圖)", Jeong Bok-sim's "Simhakdo (心學圖)", Wangbaek (王柏)'s "Gyeongjejamdo (敬齋箴圖)", and Yi Hwang's "Sukheungyamaejamdo (夙興夜寐箴圖)".

Among these, Yi Hwang's 'theory of the four beginnings and the seven feelings (四端七情說)' delineated in his "Simtongseongjeongdo" is most famous for it triggered the scholarly disputes between Yi Hwang and Ki Dae-seung (奇大升, 1527-1572). The theory originated from studies on Cheonmyeong, especially from diagrams of Cheonmyeong.

Jeong Ji-un (鄭之雲, 1509-1561) was the first scholar that studied Cheonmyeong. Jeong stated that he drew 'The Diagram of Cheonmyeong', with reference to *The Doctrine of the Mean* and Zhou Dunyi (周敦頤)'s *Taegeukdoseol* (太極圖說), for the instruction of newcomers to Neo-Confucianism.[15] He also wrote *Cheonmyeongdohae* (天命圖解), that is, a commentary on "*Cheonmyeongdo* (天命圖)." Yi Hwang, having consulted with Jeong, revised the diagram, and called it "The New Diagram of Cheonmyeong (天命新圖)". Kim In-hu (金麟厚, 1510-1560), who was acquainted with Jeong Ji-un, drew his own diagram of Cheonmyeong. In this way representative Neo-Confucian scholars at that time devoted themselves to the study of this area.[16]

The concept of Cheonmyeong (天命) is not easy to grasp, for *Cheon* (天), which has multiple-meanings, is added to *myeong* (命), containing equivocal meanings. However, some scholars including Jeong Ji-un simply regarded 'Cheonmyeong as *ri* (天命卽理)', for both Heaven and 'The Great Ultimate (太極)' are *ri*, and in this light *myeong* comes to have no special meaning.

The concept of Cheonmyeong which was introduced in *The Doctrine of the Mean* embodied the idea of 'endowing all things

15 Jeong Ji-un, "Preface", *Cheonmyeongdohae*.
16 Jeong Ji-un's "Diagram of Cheonmyeong" seems to have been leaked out from the beginning of its drawing. Yi Hwang happened to have obtained one of the leaked copy. Later Jeong gave him in person a copy for correction, and he drew "the New Diagram of Cheonmyeong" consulting Jeong. Kim In-hu, an acquaintance with Jeong, drew his own "Diagram of Cheonmyeong". Ki Dae-seung also drew his own diagram.

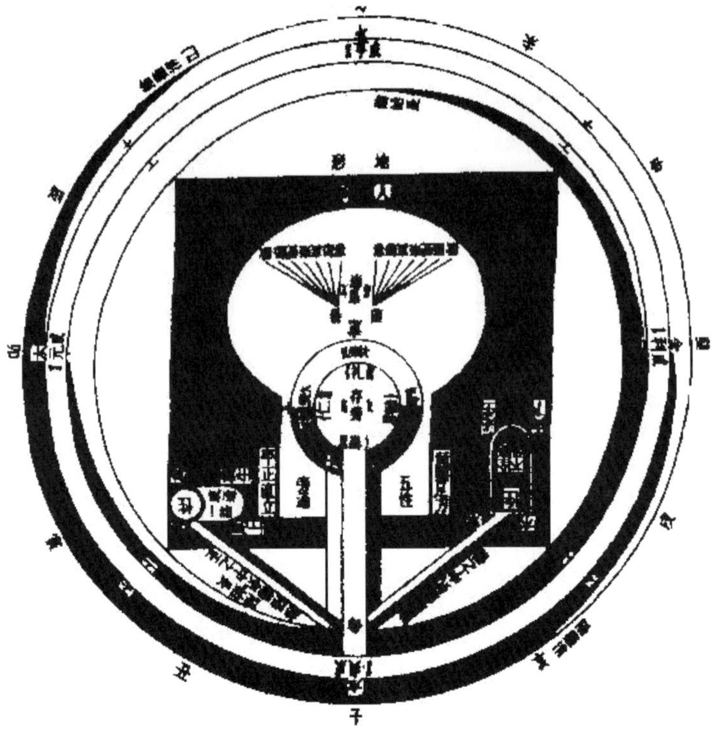

Cheonmyeongdo(天命圖) of Jeong Ji-un

with nature (天命之謂性)'[17] and Cheonmyeong as 'Taegeuk (太極, the Great Ultimate or the origin of the universe)' signified 'Taegeuk's ability to create all things (太極生兩義)' and the living significance of all things. Therefore, the content of "The Diagram of Cheongmyeong" can be said to encompass the whole gamut of Neo-Confucian metaphysics ranging over Neo-Confucian views on the universe, nature (自然), the human being, and ethics.

(3) The Characteristic Content of Cheonmyeongdo

"Cheonmyeongdo" is a diagram illustrating '*sim* (心, mind/heart)',

17 The concept of The Mandate of Heaven began to be frequently mentioned in *The Book of History*. Here the usages of the book were not introduced.

'*seong* (性, nature)', '*jeong* (情, feeling)' and the status of the human being living between heaven and earth in relation to the Cheonmyeong that is *ri*. The diagram is based on the Neo-Confucian view that the universe is composed of '*samjae* (三才, Heaven, earth, and human being)', so its content is different from that of Zhou Dunyi's Taegeukdo[18] (太極圖, the Diagram of the Great Ultimate), which is concerned only with 'the formation of the universe (宇宙生成觀)'.[19]

As contemporary Neo-Confucian scholars believed in 'Gaecheonseol (蓋天說, the view that Heaven is shaped like a shell and earth like the yolk of an egg)' and 'Honcheonseol (渾天說, the view that Heaven is shaped like an umbrella and earth is flat)', Heaven is drawn as a circle while the earth is flat in their "Cheonmyeongdo". Concretely speaking, in the diagram a tetragon corresponding to earth is drawn inside a circle denoting Heaven, and a human being is drawn inside the tetragon. And inside the human being there is a heart (心), within which are letters denoting *seong·jeong* (性, 情). That the head of a human being is round while the foot is rectangular shows that the human race is 'the combination of Heaven and earth' or 'the product of Heaven and earth'. Such a point of view, originating from *Chou-i* (周易, *The Book of Changes*), led to the view of human being as the lord of all creation, which implies that the human being is the only progeny of Heaven and earth.

This view is also explained by the right living posture of the human race. Jeong Ji-un and other Neo-Confucian scholars, in their diagrams of Cheonmyeong, demonstrated that the erect posture of the human being, unlike the plant and the animal, is the noblest. This thought is also related to the belief that the human being is the lord of all creation. So diagrams of Cheonmyeong may be said to have been drawn on the basis of a human-centered view of the universe.

---

18 Jeong Ji-un said that he drew his "Tageukdo" referring to *The Doctrine of the Mean* and Zhou Dunyi's "Tageukdo", but his diagram was different from the works he referred to.

19 Zhou Dunyi's "Taegeukdo", as is well-known, mainly deals with the formation of the universe--yangui (yin·yang) are formed by Taegeuk, the five elements (water, fire, metal, wood, and earth) are formed by yangui, and all things are created by the variation of the five elements.

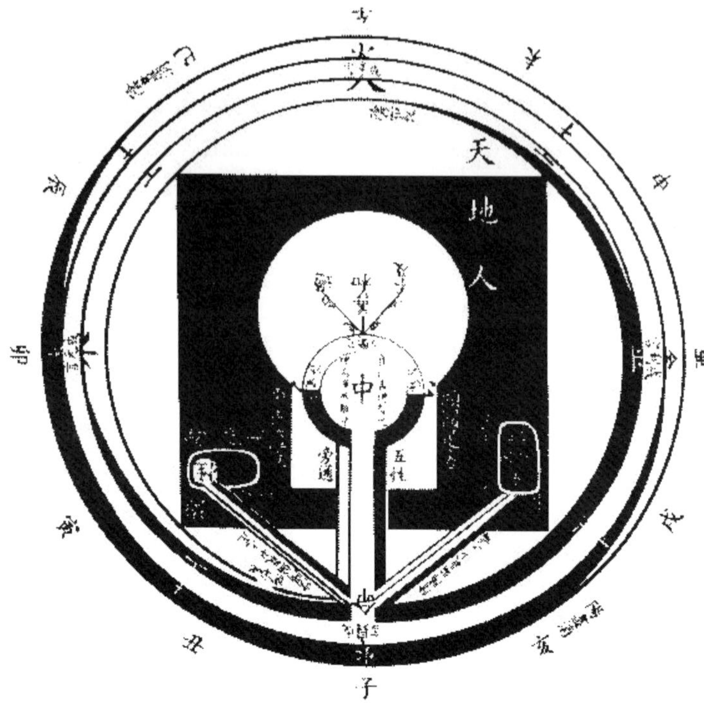

Cheonmyeongdo(天命圖) of Kim In-hu

The view of the human being as the lord of all creation was also based on the inner characteristics of all living beings. According to "Cheonmyeongdo", in the case of the plant the five constant virtues (五常 or 五性: benevolence, righteousness, propriety, wisdom, and fidelity) are completely absent and in the case of the animal one of the constant virtues may sometimes be revealed; however, the human being is endowed with each of the five constant virtues. So it may safely be said that the human being is the lord of all creation.

The five constant virtues constitute the good, original nature shaping human morality. "Cheonmyeongdo" illustrated in a diagram that Cheonmyeong (天命) is *seong* (性), which refers to the five constant virtues'. To compare the plant and animal with the human being on the basis of the five constant virtues is to compare the three on the basis of morals. The tendency of Neo-Confucian scholars to attach importance to morals and to argue that the human being as the lord of all creation through the practice of moral behavior is also a characteristic of their view of Cheonmyeong. Ultimately, it may be said that they attempted to locate the *raison d'être* of the human being in the realization of morals.

Jeong Ji-un and others connected the *myeong* (命, mandate) of Cheonmyeong directly to the heart. In the section of the diagram illustrating *sim* (心, mind/heart) the Chinese letters denoting the five constant virtues (五性: 仁義禮智信, benevolence, righteousness, propriety, wisdom, and fidelity) are written. The Chinese letters denoting *jonyang* (存養, cultivation of mind) are written among the disjointed strokes of *gyeong* (敬, reverence) occupying the center of the section of the diagram illustrating *sim*, and then the Chinese letters denoting joy, anger, sorrow, pleasure, and lust (喜怒哀樂欲) are written around the letters signifying the five constant virtues. 'Good and evil' are separated from the section of the diagram illustrating *ui* (意, volition), which is situated outside the section of *sim* and connected with the seven feelings of joy, anger, love, fear, sorrow, hate, and lust (喜怒愛懼哀惡欲). Such an arrangement suggests that both the five constant virtues and associated feelings wait inside *sim* until they issue forth in the section of *ui* (意) and determine what is good and evil. In other words, the arrangement suggests 'the source of the determination of moral behavior'. The emphasis on morals is also found in the letters denoting *seongchal* (省察, introspection) written above the disjointed strokes of *gyeong* situated between the letters signifying good (善) and evil (惡), which are below the letter denoting *ui* (意) situated outside the section of *sim*.

The intention of placing the disjointed strokes of *gyeong* (敬) and *jonyang* (存養) in the center of the section of *sim* and the aim of writing *seongchal* (省察) beside the disjointed strokes of *gyeong* below *ui* (意) outside the section of *sim* are also related to the cultivation of mind. These aspects of the diagram mean that one should cultivate and plumb the depths of one's mind on the basis of *gyeong* before and after *sim* issues forth. Such a comprehensive cultivation of mind will facilitate moral behavior or the practice of 'the innate mode of the human being (人道)'.

The contrast between 'The Way of Heaven (天道)' and the innate mode of the human being is also mentioned in "Cheonmyeongdo". Jeong Ji-un and others drew the increase and decrease of '*yin* and *yang* (陰陽, negative and positive elements)' in the largest round section of Heaven (天圈). Inside the section entitled 'The Principle of Heaven' or 'The Way of Heaven' comprising '*seong* (誠, sincerity)' and '*won, hyeong, ri, jeong* (元亨利貞, origination, flourish, advantage, firmness)' are also written. Such an arrangement implies that human beings seem to live under the influence of *yin* and *yang* but that the practice of being human should be focused on the Way of Heaven. It also implies the ideal of 'the harmonization of Heaven and the human being (天人合一)', or that the Way of Heaven and the mode of the human being may be united via principles such as sincerity (誠) and fidelity (誠實).

There is one more characteristic of Jeong Ji-un's "Cheonmyeongdo". We have already seen that Heaven is *ri* (理) and *ri* is '*seong* (性, nature)', which is stated in his *Commentary on Cheonmyeongdo* (天命圖解). Such concepts which are the fundamentals of Cheng-Zhu's philosophy were derived from conceptualizing 'the view of identifying Heaven with the Heavenly King (上帝天觀)'. Therefore, unlike Yi Hwang who drew Cheonmyeong in an upward direction, Jeong Ji-un and Kim In-hu drew it in a downward direction. These directions reveal these scholars' philosophical understanding of everything on the basis of *ri* and constitute an aspect of their thorough study of Cheonmyeong.

It is also remarkable that Jeong Ji-un interpreted 'the four beginnings and the seven feelings (四端七情)' on the basis of *ri-gi* (理氣) on both sides of the diagram as follows: "The four beginnings issue from *ri* while the seven feelings issue from *gi*."[20] He showed Yi Hwang

20 Yi Hwang, "Cheonmyeongdohae", *Toegyejeonseo* (Daedong Cultural Institution), Vol. 41-1, p. 915.

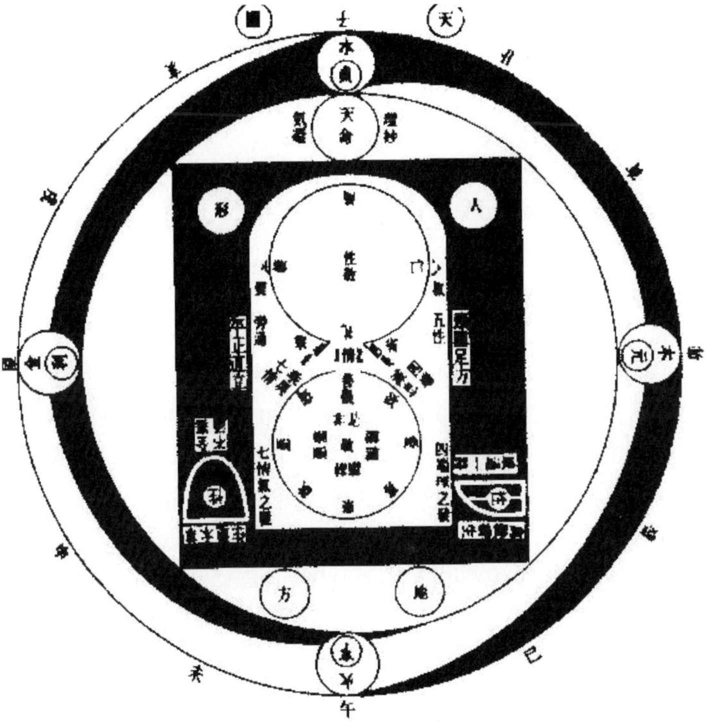

Cheonmyeongdo(天命圖) of Yi Hwang

his interpretation together with his "Cheonmyeongdo". Yi Hwang revised the interpretation a little, and this revision initiated the 18-year long controversy on the four beginnings and the seven feelings between him and Ki Dae-seung.

3. The Controversy over the Four-Seven on the Basis of *Ri-Gi*

(1) The Beginning of the Controversy over the Four-Seven

Being asked by Jeong Ji-un to revise his "Cheonmyeongdo", Yi Hwang corrected Jeong's statement, "The four beginnings issue from *ri* while the seven feelings issue from *gi*" as follows.

> "The four beginnings are the issuance of *ri* while the seven feelings are the issuance of *gi*."[21]

The above statement is called 'Yi Hwang's first interpretation on the four beginnings and the seven feeling (four-seven)'. Ki Dae-seung (奇大升, 1527-1572) was one of the scholars who had read Yi Hwang's revision of Jeong Ji-un's position. He was a 33-year-old budding scholar who had passed the State Examination and become a high official. He found something equivocal in Yi Hwang's revision and politely asked him about 'the ground of his revision', and Yi Hwang wrote a brief answer to Ki Dae-seung quoted below.

> "The issuance of the four beginnings is goodness itself because it is the genuine *ri*, while that of the seven feelings may be good or bad because it has the dual property of *ri* and *gi*."[22]

Ki Dae-seung, not satisfied with this revised interpretation, sent a letter to Yi Hwang, in which he expressed his own critical opinion of Yi Hwang's view. This was the beginning of a series of controversy between the two scholars.[23]

(2) Ki Dae-seung's Critical Opposition and Yi Hwang's Apology

First of all, Ki Dae-seung asserted that the difference between the four beginnings and the seven feelings lies in their different 'implications (所指而言)': the seven feelings imply the whole gamut of human feelings while the four beginnings imply only good feelings.

21 Ibid., "Cheonmyeongsindo", p. 916.
22 Vol. 16, "Yeogimyeongeon" (gimi), p. 402.
23 The footnotes on quotations from now on will be omitted, for they were quoted from Ibid. volumes 16-11, or "Yangseonsaengnonsadanchiljeongnon" in *Gobongjip*.

According to him, when human nature manifests itself and becomes feelings, the four beginnings refer to the feelings that fulfill the original goodness of human nature without the hindrance of *gi*. In other words, of the seven feelings, only the feelings complying with 'moderation (中節)' comprise the four beginnings. So, fundamentally, the four beginnings and the seven feelings are not different from each other, and it is not reasonable to distinguish the four from the seven by applying such words as 'genuine *ri* (純理)' and 'the combination of *ri* with *gi* (兼理氣)'.

According to Ki Dae-seung, *ri* and *gi* can 'conceptually' be distinguished. In reality, however, they are inseparable and what functions is not *ri* but only *gi*. Nevertheless, to say that both *ri* and *gi* issue forth does not conform to the concept of *ri-gi*. It is also unreasonable to say that the four beginnings comprise goodness itself and that the seven feelings may be good or bad because they are constituted by the combination of *ri* and *gi*. All kinds of feeling are constituted by the combination of *ri* and *gi*. So if the function of the *gi* of a feeling complies with moderation the feeling is good and if not the feeling is evil. Seen in this light, the four beginnings and the seven feelings are not different. Therefore, Yi Hwang's view of the difference of four beginnings and the seven feelings is not convincing.

Upon receiving a letter from Ki Dae-seung criticizing his view, Yi Hwang sent 'a detailed reply'[24] to him. He conceded Ki Dae-seung's point that the difference of the four from the seven lies in 'the difference of their implications', which means that the four beginnings are good while the seven feelings are in the state in which good or evil are not yet settled. (Yi Hwang also called the four beginnings good feelings or 'genuine goodness without evil [純善無惡]', adopting Mencius term. This means that he referred only to the aspect of ri of the four beginnings, which is the combination of *ri* and *gi*.) Therefore, according to Yi Hwang, the difference between the four beginnings and the seven feelings is like that between 'original nature (本然之性)', which is not related to 'physical quality (氣質)',

24 This is usually called 'the first reply'. In fact, it was the 'second reply'.

and 'physical nature (氣質之性)' which is related to 'physical quality'.

Yi Hwang clarified that the four beginnings are different from the seven feelings not only in their implications but also in their origins. That is, the four beginnings originate from the fundamental aspects of human nature such as benevolence, righteousness, propriety and wisdom, while the seven feelings derive from the perception of external phenomena. So, according to Yi Hwang, it can be concluded that the four beginnings are the issuance of *ri* and the seven feelings are the issuance of *gi*.

Moreover, Yi Hwang regarded it as contradictory for Ki Dae-seung to have asserted, "The difference of the four from the seven lies in the difference of their implications" and "The four and the seven do not have different meanings." At this time Yi Hwang seems to have been encouraged after finding in *Zhuzi yulei* (朱子語類) that Zhu Xi (朱熹)'s interpretation of the four-seven ("The four beginnings are the issuance of *ri*," "The seven feelings are the issuance of *gi*") was the same as his, and so he said, "Neither my own nor Jeong Ji-un's interpretations need be revised."

(3) Ki Dae-seung's Repeated Criticism and Yi Hwang's Revision

In response to Yi Hwang's answer, Ki Dae-seung sent a long letter to him. Here he again emphasized that the four beginnings and the seven feelings refer to the same feeling composed of the combination of *ri* and *gi*, and criticized Yi Hwang's view that the four and the seven are comparable to original nature and physical nature respectively. He agreed that the four beginnings may be analogous to original nature for the latter refers only to *ri*. However, he argued that Yi Hwang's identification of physical nature with the seven feelings was wrong for physical nature is equipped with both *ri* and *gi* while the seven feelings, according to Yi Hwang, are composed of only *gi*. In short, Ki Dae-seung maintained that Yi Hwang's mistake lay in his view of the seven feelings only as *gi,* not as the combination of *ri* and *gi*.

Bearing in mind that only *gi* has function, Ki Dae-seung asserted that the four and the seven have 'a common substance and different names (同實異名)'. In addition, based on the remark, "Feeling is the issuance of human nature (情性所發)," he asserted that not only the four but also the seven issue from the innate human characteristics of benevolence, righteousness, propriety and wisdom. Repeating that feeling is the combination of *ri-gi* and that not *ri* but *gi* actually issues, he pointed out that *ri* may spread only by riding on *gi*. And he added that his view was applicable not only to the seven feelings but also to the four beginnings. In this context he said, "The four beginnings are also *gi* (四端亦氣)."

Emphasizing the function of *gi*, Ki Dae-seung rejected Yi Hwang's view that the substance of *ri* exists apart from *gi*, and maintained that the substance of *ri* is no other than *gi* complying with moderation. In this context he said, "The seven feelings of the sages cannot but be the substance of *ri*," and "The cases that can be called the issuance of the *ri* of Heaven may be found even in the seven feelings of ordinary people." So he rejected Yi Hwang's view that the seven feelings refer to the state in which good or evil are not yet settled and said that the four beginnings as well as the seven feelings may deviate from moderation.

Upon receiving Ki Dae-seung's criticism, Yi Hwang examined his own view and amended some of his positions. He concurred with Ki Dae-seung's opinion that the four beginnings also issue from external sources, and corrected his remark on the seven feelings, "They are in the state in which good and evil are not yet settled," saying, "Though originally good, they are liable to fall into evil." However, he clung to what he thought was right. For example, he firmly opposed Ki Dae-seung's view that the four and the seven have a common substance and different names, and said, "Sometimes the *ri*-principal (主理) may be different from the *gi*-principal (主氣) and the former corresponds to the four beginnings and the latter to the seven feelings. How could this proposition be wrong?" The *ri*-principal and *gi*-principal became the terms frequently used in the Neo-Confucian circle in the late

Joseon Dynasty.

In his second reply to Ki Dae-seung, Yi Hwang suggested his newly revised interpretation on the four beginnings and seven feelings.

> "The four beginnings are the issuance of *ri* followed by *gi* and the seven feelings are the issuance of *gi* on which *ri* rides."[25]

The above interpretation, unlike his previous theory, clearly suggests that both the four beginnings and the seven feelings comprise the combination of *ri* and *gi*. He repeatedly stated that his revised interpretation was based on the differences between the four and the seven in terms of their concepts and their origins and modes of issuances. And in order to justify this interpretation he proposed the theory of 'the mutual issuances of *ri* and *gi* (理氣互發說)', which supported his final interpretation of the concepts of the four and the seven, but more than that, his theory of the origins of issuance of the four-seven.

(4) The Conclusion of the Controversy and Its Influence

Ki Dae-seung expressed his dissatisfaction at Yi Hwang's revised interpretation of the four-seven for it gave the impression that *ri* and *gi* seem to strive for priority inside feeling. He indirectly rejected Yi Hwang's interpretation through his criticism of Zhu Xi's view, which was almost indistinguishable from Yi Hwang's first interpretation. He asserted that it was wrong for Zhu Xi not to regard the four-seven as originating mainly from the functioning of *gi* or on the basis of the seven but to contrast, like Yi Hwang, the four with the seven. He also denied the mutual issuances of *ri* and *gi* for it seemed to encompass *ri*'s functioning or operation.

Yi Hwang had prepared his third reply to Ki Dae-seung but he didn't send it to Ki for he thought that there may be cases where the

25 Yi Hwang, Vol. 16-1, "Dapkimyeongeonnonsadanchiljeong 2seo".

four and the seven should be distinguished as the *ri*-principal and the *gi*-principal, though sometimes they should not.

The controversy between the two scholars were suspended for a while, and then ended with Ki's publication of *The Coda of the Four-Seven* (四端七情後書) and *An Outline of the Four-Seven* (四端七情總論). Here Ki agreed with Yi Hwang's first interpretation of the four-seven, especially what Yi meant by the four-seven. However, he clung to his assertion of the fundamental sameness of the four and the seven. Yi, pleased with Ki's final response, said that their controversy had been brought to a successful conclusion.

However, their debate had influence on the two-year disputes between Yi I (李珥, 1536-1584) and Seong Hon (成渾, 1535-1598). Yi I, accepting in general terms Ki Dae-seung's position, rejected Yi Hwang's interpretation and believed that only *gi* actually issues, though *gi's* issuance is caused by *ri*. So his interpretation of the four-seven on the basis of *ri-gi* could be summarized as '*gibalriseungildo* (氣發理乘一途, only gi issues and ri rides on gi)'. Seong Hon, on the other hand, advocated Yi Hwang's interpretation by quoting Cheng-Zhu's theory that the human mind (人心) originates from physical quality (氣質) while the moral mind (道心) derives from 'Heavenly Nature or The Mandate of Heaven (性命)'.[26] This controversy, after the formation of the schools of Yi Hwang and Yi I, continued intermittently until the end of the Joseon Dynasty (the early period of the 20th century).

(5) The Causes of the Continuation of the Controversy and Its Significance

The causes of the continuation of the controversy are as follows. From the beginning of the controversy, Yi Hwang, following Mencius view of human nature as fundamentally good, interpreted the four beginnings and seven feelings on the basis of their implication of the moral value of good and evil. According to his interpretation based on the implications of the four-seven, the four beginnings and

26 Refer to Vol. 10, "Dapseonghowon", Yi I's *Yulgokjeonseo*.

ri refer to goodness and the seven feelings and *gi* refer to the state in which good or evil are not yet settled. Therefore, connecting *ri* to the four beginnings and *gi* to seven feelings is completely legitimate.[27] Though the notion of 'issuance' of *ri,* which has no function, seems illogical, issuance in this case can be understood not as emergence but as revelation. Ki Daeseung's ultimate affirmation of Yi Hwang's interpretation may be said to have been based on such an understanding. Therefore, given the implications of the four-seven, Yi Hwang did not have to propose his revised interpretation, which retained some aspects that were inconsistent with his definitions of *ri* and *gi.*

The main issues in the controversy arose because the four beginnings and seven feelings were considered on the basis of their origin, which corresponded to the objective understanding of the four-seven. The debate on the moderation of joy, anger, sorrow and pleasure in *The Doctrine of the Mean* was a similar case. On the basis of objective understanding it would be correct to stipulate, as Ki Dae-seung and Yi I said, that both the four beginnings and the seven feelings are 'the motion or the issuance of *gi*' because only *gi* has the characteristics of function and mobility. Ki Dae-seung's argument that the seven feelings are the only valid object of consideration was based on this objective understanding. Nevertheless, Yi Hwang tried to interpret the four-seven on the basis of their implications as well as their objective status. Consequently, he proposed 'the mutual issuance of *ri* and *gi*' in order to provide a rationale for the actual motion or the issuance of *ri*. That is to say, he considered that *ri*, which is goodness itself, is an actual entity, and that *ri* even has the function of spontaneous issuance. Seen in this light, the fundamental reason why the controversy was interminable lay in the interpretation of the four-seven in terms of both their objective status and their implications.

27 Also in this context Yi Hwang said the distinction of the four and seven is like that of the original nature and physical nature. In this case the four refer to 'abstract feeling' or only good ri (principle) while the seven refers to 'concrete feelings' or the combination of *ri* and *gi*. He revised his theory in consideration of these standpoints.

Though there are some unsettled issues in the interpretation of the four-seven, their significance can be traced by referring to *The Book of Mencius* and *The Doctrine of the Mean* in which the theory of the four-seven is explicitly explored. Mencius' thought on the four beginnings (or the issuance of *ri*) is based on 'the ethics of virtuous character (德性倫理)' which discusses morals with the aim of the cultivation of the good in human nature. And the view on the seven feelings, based on Hsun-tzu (荀子)'s view that human nature, when left undisturbed, is prone to confusion caused by competition and struggle (性惡說), is based on 'the ethics of obligation (義務倫理)'. Therefore, it may safely be said that Korean Confucian scholars' interpretations of the four-seven on the bases of both *ri* and *gi* may reflect their attempts to holistically understand' the ethics of virtuous character and the ethics of obligation. I think that this is the significance of the interpretations of the four-seven on the basis of *ri-gi*.

The significance of the interpretation of the four-seven based on *ri* and *gi* can also be found in Jeong Ji-un's and Yi Hwang's works. Jeong Ji-un who designed "Cheonmyeongdo" maintained that 'the five constant virtues (五常)' of 'benevolence, righteousness, propriety, wisdom, and fidelity' are not only revealed as the four beginnings but also as the five cardinal human relations (五倫) such as the relation of father and son and that of lord and vassal,[28] Likewise, Yi Hwang's emphasis on the revelation or issuance of *ri* in spite of *ri*'s immobility revealed his intention to advocate and maintain the ethical basis of the contemporary social system through the five human relations. This is the central significance of the interpretation of the four beginnings on the basis of the issuance of *ri*.

On the other hand, Ki Dae-seung's interpretation of the seven feelings on the basis of the issuance of *gi* was characterized by his emphasis on goodness or the moderation of emotional desire. While Yi Hwang's interpretation, on the basis of *ri,* emphasized 'the maintenance of the social system' through the five desirable human

28 Jeong Ji-wun, Japhae, "Cheonmyeongdohae".

relations, Ki Dae-seung's interpretation of the seven feelings on the basis of emotional experience signified his deepseated intention to establish an ethical system *per se*. 'Kim In-hu, who is said to have sympathized with Ki Dae-seung's emphasis on the seven feelings',[29] underlined 'the excess or deficiency (good or evil) of the seven feelings in his "Cheonmyeongdo". He was also a scholar who was concerned with the establishment of an ethical system *per se*.

4. The View of the Unitary Origin of *Ri* and *Gi* Based on the Theories of *Cheyong* and *Gyeongwi*

(1) The Neo-Confucian Circles from the Late 16th Century to the Early 18th Century

The controversy that raged over the four beginnings and the seven feelings created a great sensation in the Neo-Confucian circles of Korea. Owing to the devoted studies of Yi Hwang and Yi I, who were the most eminent Neo-Confucian scholars in the 16th century, the controversy aroused nationwide interest. All the more so because, whenever it seemed to come to a standstill, a new spark of enthusiasm rekindled it.

One such instance occurred at the end of the 16th century among the followers of Yi Hwang and Yi I, who respectively advocated their own views on the four-seven based on the theory of *ri-gi*. Jeong Si-han (丁時翰, 1625-1707), Yi Hyeong-il (李玄逸, 1627-1704), and Yi Sang-jeong (李象靖, 1711-1781) belonged to Yi Hwang's school in the Yeongnam area while Kim Jang-saeng (金長生, 1548-1631), Song Si-yeol (宋時烈, 1607-1689), Gweon Sang-ha (權尙夏, 1641-1721), and Han Won-jin (韓元震) belonged to 'Yi I's school in the Hoseo area'. This alignment of intellectual forces ranged against each other was a characteristic situation of Korean Neo-Confucian circles from the

29 Refer to Yi I, "Dapseonghowon", *Yulgokjeonseo*, Vol. 10.

late 16th to the early 18th centuries.

Another characteristic of the Neo-Confucian circles of this period was that much importance was attached to the study of propriety (禮). In particular, the observance of the funeral rites of the royal family became a significant issue, resulting in partisan strife. From the 17th to the 18th centuries a trend called 'the courteous dialogues' of scholars arose, which has already been dealt with in Chapter 4 of Part III, and which it is unnecessary to review in detail here.

The two aforementioned characteristic situations suggest that Neo-Confucian scholars in this period focused their attention either on the study of the aspects of '*sim-seong* (心性, mind/heart and human nature)' such as the four-seven, or on propriety as moral behavior. However, there was a scholar who pursued his own branch of learning, in doing so standing aloof from the intellectual trend of the times. In the following section we will examine this scholar's work.

(2) The Inquiry into the Changes of the Universe and Nature

Jang Hyeon-gwang (張顯光, 1554-1637) was a Neo-Confucian scholar who did not neglect the study of *sim-seong* or behavioral norms. However, he is remembered as an extraordinary scholar for his profound inquiry into the changes manifest in the universe and nature.

His profundity is revealed simply by a glance at his representative works: *Yeokhakdoseol* (易學圖說, *A Diagrammatic Interpretation of the Science of Changes*), which was written over a 12-year period and was finished when Jang was 55, *Gyeongwiseol* (經緯說, *A Theory of Warp and Weft*) finished when he was 68, and *Manhakhoeyo* (晚學會要, *A Summary of My Late Learning*) written at the age of 75, *Yeokgwaechongnon* (易卦總說, *An Outline of the Divination Signs*) written at 77, *Ujuseol* (宇宙說, *A Theory of the Universe*) written at 78 and *Taegeukseol* (太極說, *A Theory of the Great Ultimate*) written at 79.

Jang Hyeon-gwang was a brother-in-law of a Neo-Confucian scholar named Bak Yeong (朴英, penname: 松堂 songdang, 1471-1540). As he was born after Bak died, his studies were not directly influenced by Bak. When he was young, he learned under the tutorship of an obscure scholar named Jang Sun (張峋). After Jang Hyeon-gwang in his late teens read the bulky Chinese classic *Xingli-daquan* (性理大典) comprising 70 volumes, he was engrossed in deep solitary contemplation and studied in isolation theories of Neo-Confucianism and the principle of '*xiangshu* (象數, images and numbers used for the divination of changes)', which falls under the rubric of 'the theory of changes (易說)' of the universe and human lives. According to his "Chronology", while reading *Xingli-daquan* , he was profoundly moved by the section on Shao-yung (邵雍)'s *Huangchi* (皇極, supreme principle, august and central) and began to immerse himself in the principle of *xiangshu,* in which he was deeply engrossed.

As is shown by his works, Jang Hyeon-gwang's studies took place mainly in the latter stages of his life. At that time scholars from the nobility usually sought and secured government positions, and Jang also held various government posts for 21 years from the age of 42. However, from the age of 60 until 84 when he died, though he was offered government posts over 20 times, he rejected them all[30] and engaged himself in learning in order to become a great scholar.

This was Jang Hyeon-gwang's goal from his teens. At the age of 18, he wrote, "The greatest vocation in the world is learning" and "Those who engage in the greatest vocation can become the most iconic figures in the world."[31] He also wrote, "A man born into the world should see the pursuit that is concerned with the universe as his duty"[32] These writings reveal his aspiration for learning. So it may be said that his dream of grasping the fundamental principles of the universe and nature and their philosophical systematization had already taken shape in his late teens.

Jang Hyeon-gwang's view of learning, as he himself expressed it, reveals his own direction and view of the purpose of learning.

---

30 Refer to "Yeonbo", *Yeoheonjeonseo*, Vol. 1.
31 Ibid., "Ujuyogwaljeom", *Sokjip*, Vol. 1, p. 345.
32 Ibid., "Pyojeyoeo", *Sokjip*, Vol. 1, P. 346.

> "*The Great Learning* and *The Doctrine of the Mean* were revised by Cheng Yi (程頤) and Zhu Xi (朱熹). However, they were reluctant to accept all the revisions of Cheng Hao (程顥 or 程明道) because the exercise of public righteousness entails stating one's view within one's own limits. I strove to perfect my work, but it is subject to later scholars' revisions. Would scholars who preceded me find fault with me? Certainly they may have forgiven me."[33]

Here Jang Hyeon-gwang defined the desirable method of learning as the pursuit of public righteousness. And he anticipated that though the practice of such a method might ultimately differ from the established views of Cheng-Zhu, scholars who adhered to that strand of thought may have accepted his work if his practice complied with the requirements of public righteousness. Here we may have a glimpse of his 'daring and unique conviction', his subjective consciousness, and his 'rationality' in pursuing the goal of public righteousness. To put it concisely, his works were the fruits of his subjective consciousness and rationality.

All of his 'views on changes (易說)' cannot be said to be original as they built upon preceding scholars' theories. However, it is evident that he tried to formulate a dynamic and lively 'theory of changes (易),' which had been neglected by preceding scholars, through his "Diagrammatic Interpretation of the Science of Changes." The following views on changes are examples of his philosophical attitude: There are two kinds of change, that is, change brought about by '*gyoyeok* (交易, interchange)' and by '*byeonyeok* (變易, mutation)'; the phenomena caused by change are brought about by the contrasting requirements of compliance to *yin·yang* (陰陽); the changes wrought by *yin·yang* on the basis of *xiangshu* (象數) arise in accordance with odd and even numbers; and the accumulation of odd and even numbers develops into 2 (yangui, 兩儀, *yin and yang*), 4 (sasang, 四象, four elements), 8 (palgoae, 八卦, eight signs), and 64 (六十四爻, sixty-four signs).

33 Ibid., "Nokuisajil", *Sokjip*, Vol. 1, p. 366.

Jang Hyeon-gwang differed from scholars who devoted themselves to the science of divination or fortunetellers who had been popular before the principle of *xiangshu* was prevalent. However, he did not cling to the principle of *xiangshu* or the theory of changes based on *xiangshu*. He was a Neo-Confucian scholar attempting to explicate all changes and beings on the bases of *ri* and *gi*. Moreover, his theories developed within the parameters of the doctrine of Cheng-Zhu, who interpreted changes on the basis of *ri* rather than *gi*. In his last books such as *A Theory of the Universe* and *A Theory of the Great Ultimate* he eventually interpreted the formation and change of the Universe in connection with 'the *ri* of Taegeuk (the ultimate source of the Universe)'.

(3) The Theory of *Ri* and *Gi* as Substance and Function or Warp and Weft

Jang Hyeon-gwang proposed 'a unique theory' in which *ri* and *gi* are understood respectively as *che* (體, substance) and *yong* (用, function) or warp (經) and weft (緯). It is a noteworthy theory which sublates the biased interpretations of the changes of nature on the basis of either 'the *ri*-principal (主理)' or 'the *gi*-principal (主氣)'.

There was a reason why either *ri* or *gi* was emphasized in the theory of *ri-gi*. Such unbalanced emphases were caused by divergent views on the relation of *ri* and *gi*. Since Zhu Xi, Neo-Confucian scholars had usually said, "In reality, *ri* and *gi* are not separated from each other," but also "Theoretically, they are separated from each other." In short, they thought that "*ri* and *gi* are inseparable and separable at the same time." This view, based on the assumption of the dualism of *ri* and *gi*, implied an insuperable contradiction, and sometimes resulted in advocacy for the *ri*-principal and at other times for the *gi*-principal. More precisely, the view of *ri-gi*'s inseparability resulted in the *gi*-principal and that of their separability in the *ri*-principal.

Nevertheless, Jang Hyeon-gwang wished to construct and actually pursued a theory of the dualism of *ri-gi* without tendentiousness, and in this connection he tried to understand the relation of *ri* and *gi* in view of the relation of substance and function or warp and weft, or of *ri* and *gi* as one with two aspects. Let's examine his own remarks beginning with his view on substance and function.

> "That *ri* becomes *gi* means the unity of *ri* and *gi*. In terms of the division of substance and function *ri* is substance and *gi* is function."[34]

According to Jang, to regard *ri* and *gi* as substance and function respectively was ultimately a way of 'combining *ri* and *gi*' which had been considered to be separated from each other. On the whole, Neo-Confucian scholars distinguished substance from function in various ways. Sometimes they were distinguished simply on the basis of their respective characteristics and at other times on the basis of their modes of application. In the former case, *ri* and *gi* referred to beginning (始) and end (終) or lightness (輕) and heaviness (重), while in the latter case, they referred to nature (性) and feeling (情), root (本) and branch (末) or concealment (隱) and manifestation (顯) respectively. However, he did not clarify his usage of substance and function, which is considered to be a limitation of his argument. He also applied the concepts of warp (經) and weft (緯) to *ri* and *gi* respectively. In his voluminous *A View on Warp and Weft* (經緯說) he compared the relation of *ri* and *gi* to that of warp and weft. It seems that 'the theory of *ri-gi* as warp and weft' rather than 'the theory of *ri-gi* as substance and function' represents his original theory of *ri-gi*, because there were precedents for assigning substance and function to *ri* and *gi*, while there was no precedent for assigning warp and weft to them.

Warp (經) and weft (緯) refer to the thread used in weaving cloth like silk. Though they are distinguished from each other as lengthwise and crosswise threads respectively, they combine to be woven into cloth. Without their combination cloth cannot be woven, and in this respect warp and weft are analogous to the concepts of substance and function. Jang Hyeon-gwang thought that like warp and weft, *ri* and

34 Ibid., Vol. 2, "Gyeongwiseolchongnon".

gi also combine to compose a given property.

In fact, Jang Hyeon-gwang was familiar with the theory that *ri* has the characteristic of immutability (不變) and *gi* that of mutability (變), and called *ri* 'immutable *ri* (理常)' and *gi* 'mutable *gi* (氣變)'. As warp is fixed and woof is mobile, he paired *ri* with warp and *gi* with weft. Moreover, as the relationship of *ri* and *gi* is based on 'mutual accompaniment (待對, 常須)', he considered that warp and weft 'combine by mutual accompaniment.'[35]

(4) The Characteristic and Significance of the Unitary Origin of *Ri-Gi* Implied in the View of Ri-Gi as Substance and Function

Ri and *gi* or warp and weft are often considered to be both contrary and symmetrical concepts. But Jang Hyeon-gwang, in his "Theory of the Great Ultimate (太極說)" wrote, "*Ri* generates *gi* (理生氣)," and "Warp precedes weft." In other words, he thought that *ri* and warp are entities that precede *gi* and weft. They are regarded as symmetrical or as being in a relation of mutual accompaniment only because of their inseparability in actuality. In his concept of *ri-gi*, however, *ri* and *gi* are obviously distinguished from each other:

> "*Ri* superintends *gi* and *gi* fulfills *ri*. Superintendency means the adoption of the role of root and hinge, and fulfillment means the realization of something beneficial and successful."[36]

Ri, which is compared to the root and hinge of all things in the universe, is in the position of superintending *gi*. *Gi* is in the position of fulfilling the principle of *ri* in actuality and securing the benefit resulting from the fulfillment of the principle. Jang Hyeon-gwang called the divergent positions of *ri* and *gi* 'the warp-principal becom-

---

35 His view of warp and weft is in fact implied in his view of human nature and principle suggested in "Nongyeongwigaiyuigi" and "Nonigiwigyeongwi".
36 "Gyeongwiseol", *Eoheonjeonseo*, Vol. 2, p. 96.,

ing weft (主經致緯).'[37]

What should be noted here is that Jang Hyeon-gwang applied the relation of warp-weft or substancc-function to that of *ri-gi* not to show the divergent positional distinctions of *ri-gi* but to demonstrate the actual circumstance in which *ri* and *gi* are regarded as inseparable or as displaying the relation of mutual accompaniment. In other words, he applied the relation of warp-weft or substance-function to that of *ri-gi* because immutability and mutability always accompany each other.

> "Without immutability substance cannot be formed while without mutability function cannot exist. The inevitable accompaniment of immutability and mutability or substance and function is really the principle of nature and the consistency of the Way."[38]

Jang Hyeon-gwang's view on substance-function and warp-weft is based on the premise that mutability and immutability are in accord with each other. What are the implications if mutual accompaniment is replaced simply by inseparability? Then, his view would become the same as or similar to Luo Chin-shun (羅欽順)'s view, "*Ri* and *gi* are one."

Luo Chin-shun's theory of *ri-gi* had been introduced into Korea before Jang Hyeon-gwang advanced his theories. Jang belonged to the school of Yi Hwang who criticized Luo's view that *ri* and *gi* are one. Seen in this light, his theories on substance and function and warp and weft may be said to be based on the mutual accompaniment of *ri-gi* and not on the view of '*ri* and *gi* as one and the same' or on 'the unity of *ri* and *gi*'. (Jang's view was based on 'the combination of *ri* and *gi*, not on their unity.) Therefore, his theories on warp-weft and substance-function were ultimately based on the composite meaning of 'both the inseparability and separability' of *ri* and *gi*. In this context he wrote

37 Ibid.
38 Ibid., "Gyeongwiseol", Vol. 2, p. 77.

the following:

> "*Ri* is the *ri* of *gi* and *gi* is the *gi* of *ri*. What does it mean that *gi* is inside *ri* when referring to *ri*? It means that *ri* implies *gi*. What does it mean that *ri* is inside *gi* when referring to *gi*? It means that *ri* becomes *gi*."[39]

The above quotation explains *ri* and *gi* in the light of both linguistic usage and in actuality. In terms of linguistic usage, while *ri* and *gi* are contrasted with each other, in their implication each comprises the other reciprocally. For example, when we refer to *ri* with respect to linguistic usage, *ri* comprises *gi* as the *ri* of *gi*. On the other hand, when we refer to *gi* with respect to their actual existence, *ri* becomes *gi* and is inside *gi*. In the former case, though *ri* and *gi* are distinguished from each other, the distinction is ignored. But in the latter case the distinction of *ri* and *gi* is made impossible as if 'they are one and the same'. We have to bear in mind that Jang Hyeon-gwang's 'mutual accompaniment' has been interpreted in these two ways.

Jang Hyeon-gwang's dicta that *ri* implies *gi*, and that *ri* becomes *gi* reveal that his view is mainly based on *ri*. On the other hand, Luo Chin-shun (羅欽順)'s doctrine that *ri* and *gi* are one, is biased toward *gi*. So it is clear that while Luo's view of the identity of *ri* and *gi* is based on the *gi*-principal, Jang's view of *ri* and *gi* as warp and weft or essence and function is based on the unitary origin of *ri-gi* based on *ri*.

Seen in this light, Jang's universe is a world where '*riilbunsu* (理一分殊, one principle and its instantiation in many manifestations)' is applicable. Therefore his universe corresponds to the system composed only of *ri*.' His view of the universe is also confirmed in his theory of 'the origin of the universe': "The *Ri* of Taegeuk (太極, the Great Ultimate) in essence implies all kinds of *ri* such as the *ri* of *yangui* (兩儀, *yin and yang*), *sasang* (四象, four elements) and *palgoae* (八卦, eight signs)."[40] As mentioned

39 Ibid., "Gyeongwiseolchongnon", p. 111.
40 Ibid., "Yeokguechongseol", Vol. 2, p. 40.

above, it is certain that Jang Hyeon-gwang argued for the unitary origin of *ri-gi* based on *ri* and the *ri*-oriented universe by applying the concepts of substance-function and warp-weft to *ri-gi*. In retrospect, his views as such are not dissimilar to Zhu Xi's or Yi Hwang's views on *ri-gi*--especially, *riilbunsu* and '*ri*'s generation of *gi* (理生氣說)'. His views are different from theirs only in that his unitary origin of *ri-gi*' and the universe based on *ri* were developed on the basis of his unique theories of substance and function and warp and weft.

Jang Hyeon-gwang's unique views may be evaluated highly. When we consider the intellectual climate of his lifetime, we cannot but form the impression that his views on *ri-gi* based on substance-function and warp-weft were aimed at refuting Luo Chin-shun's view, "*Ri* and *gi* are one." While Luo's view was an attempt to refute Zhu Xi's and Yi Hwang's views on *ri-gi*, Jang's views on *ri-gi* based on substance-function and warp-weft may be understood as 'a counterargument' to Luo's. So his views will be evaluated so far as they weakened, albeit in a circumlocuitous manner, Luo Chin-shun's rejection of Cheng-Zhu's Neo-Confucian views on *ri-gi*.

5. The Inquiry into the Status of Human Nature vis-a-vis the Thing's Nature

(1) The Comprehensive Study on the Status of Human Nature vis-a-vis the Thing's Nature

The inquiry into the status of human nature vis-a-vis the thing's nature was a representative achievement of Korean Neo-Confucian circles in the early 18th century. However, this inquiry can be traced back to 'The Original Confucianism'. For instance, Mencius maintained the difference between human nature and the thing's nature while the first chapter of *The Doctrine of the Mean* argues, "What Heaven orders is called nature", which suggests the identity of human nature and the thing's nature. And Zhu Xi, in his commentary, approved of these two opinions.

In Korea this issue had been debated sporadically among scholars before the 18th century. For instance, Jeong Si-han (丁時翰, 1625-1707), Bak Se-dang (朴世堂, 1629-1703), Kim Chang-hyeop (金昌協, 1651-1708), and Gwon Sang-yu (權尙游 1656-1724) set forth their opinions on this issue. In particular, Kim Chang-hyeop, having read the theory of the difference between human nature and the thing's nature in *Sabyeonrok* (思辨錄) written by Bak Se-dang, who belonged to Soron (小論, Young Doctrine) political party which was hostile to his own party of Noron (老論, Old Doctrine), caused a little agitation by criticizing Bak's view (1703).[41] His criticism went unanswered, for Bak had already died.

This issue had developed into wide-ranging debates between Han Won-jin (韓元震, 1682-1751) and Yi Gan (李柬, 1677-1727) since 1709. Since 1705 Han Won-jin had exchanged scholarly opinions via correspondence for about three years with his acquaintance Choi Jing-hu (崔徵厚, ?), and had argued for 'the difference between human nature and the thing's nature'. Han had also given his opinion on this issue to his master Gwon Sang-ha (權尙夏). In 1708 Choi informed Yi Gan of Han's view on the issue. In 1709 Yi Gan asked Choi to share with Han his view on 'the identity of human nature and the thing's nature'. With this impetus, Han Won-jin and Yi Gan, though they had never met before, started their debates on this issue via letters, and continued for about five years. As a result, their research into this issue can be said to be more profound than that of other scholars.

Their debates eventually became known to their masters, friends, and acquaintances who also expressed their own opinions on this issue. There was a group of eight famous scholars called Gangmunpalhaksa (江門八學士, eight scholars produced in the riverside private academy) under the tutorship of Gwon Sang-ha. They were: Han Won-jin, Yi Gan,

41 Kim Chang-hyeop, "Yeogwonyudoronsabyeonrokbyeon", *Nongamjip*, Vol. 15.

Choi Jing-hu, Yun Bong-gu (尹鳳九, 1681-1787), Chae Ji-hong (蔡之洪, 1683-1741), Yi Jae (李縡, 1680-1746), Bak Pil-ju (朴弼周, 1665-1748), and Eo Yu-bong (魚有鳳, 1672-1744). Sometimes Hyeon Sang-byeok (玄尙壁, ?-1731) was included in this groups. These scholars were divided into those who argued for the identity of human nature and the thing's nature and those who advocated the difference between them.

On the whole, those supporting Yi Gan's view on the primacy of identity lived in 'the capital area (Rakha, 洛下)' while those supporting Han Won-jin's view on the primacy of difference lived in 'the Chungcheong area (Hoseo, 湖西)'. Thus, the debates between them are called 'Horaknonbyeon (湖洛論辨)' as well as 'the debates on the identity of or difference between human nature and the thing's nature'. As the debates developed from the work of Han and Yi and the core ideas of the debates were based on their theories, we will focus on the views of these two scholars.

(2) The Different Approaches to Human Nature and the Thing's Nature and the Differing Views on Original Nature

Before the examination of Han Won-jin's and Yi Gan's views on the identity of or difference between human nature and the thing's nature, we should keep in mind that their approaches to this issue differed. Han Won-jin introduced the terms, '*chohyeonggi* (超形氣, transcendence of material form)' and '*ingijil* (因基質, causation by physical quality)',[42] while Yi Gan introduced '*ilwon* (一原, the One Origin)' and '*iche* (異體, various substances)' in place of Han's *chohyeonggi* and *ingijil*.[43]

The different application of these terms to this issue resulted in their divergent conclusions. If both Han and Yi had approached this issue on the basis of *chohyeonggi* and *ilwon*, they might have agreed on the identity of human nature and the thing's nature. Conversely, if both of them had emphasized *ingijil* and *iche*, they might have

42-Han Wonl-jin, *Namdangjip*, Vol. 10, p. 67
43 Yi gan, Vol., 7, *Oeamyugo*, p. 31.

agreed on the difference between human nature and the thing's nature. However, this was not the case, so their views differed.

Han Won-jin emphasized *ingijil* (corresponding to Yi's *iche*) while Yi Gan emphasized *ilwon* (corresponding to Han's *chogyeonggi*). Consequently, Han maintained the difference between human nature and the thing's nature while Yi maintained the identity of human nature and the thing's nature. Their divergent views, however, not only resulted from their differing emphases but also from their contrasting views on '*seong* (性, nature)'.

To both of them *seong* referred to 'original nature (本然之性)'. However, their concepts of original nature were at odds. That is, Han Won-jin's original nature referred to *osang* (五常, the five constant virtues) of benevolence, righteousness, propriety, wisdom and fidelity while Yi Gan's original nature referred to *Cheonmyeong* (天命, The Mandate of Heaven) or *Myeong* (命, Mandate). As they inherited Cheng-Zhu's principle "*Seong* is *ri* (性卽理)", Han did not deny that The Mandate of Heaven is the original nature and Yi sometimes agreed that the five constant virtues constitute it. However, in their discussion of human nature and the thing's nature, Han maintained their difference on the basis of the five constant virtues and Yi maintained it on the basis of The Mandate of Heaven.

First, let's examine Han Won-jin's case. According to him, ① with respect to '*ri* only' (or *chohyeonggi*, 超形氣), irrespective of *gi*, the *ri* of all things (and animals) and the virtues of benevolence, righteousness, propriety, wisdom and fidelity are all comprised of *ri*, and so human nature and the thing's nature cannot but be identical with each other. But ② with respect to 'the *ri* of *gi*' in the human mind (*seong*, or human nature, is *ri* in this case), *gi*, which human beings are endowed with, is perfect, as is human nature. However, as *gi*, with which things are endowed, is not perfect, the thing's nature is not perfect either. So human nature is different from the thing's nature but all human beings have an identical nature. ③ With respect to 'the inseparability of *ri* and *gi*', a variety of innate characteristics (such as sturdiness and gentleness and good and evil) may come into being. In this case human beings may have different natures from one another.[44]

This theory of Han Won-jin's is called 'The three grades of nature (性三品說)'. Han, basing his argument on the second grade, maintained that only the five constant virtues or the *ri* of *gi* in the human mind refer to the original nature of the human being, and so he argued for the difference between human nature and the thing's nature.

On the other hand, Yi Gan, in accordance with his approach to human nature and the thing's nature and the concept of original nature, maintained, "With respect to '*ilwon* (一原, the One Origin)', both The Mandate of Heaven and the five constant virtues can transcend '*hyeonggi* (形氣, material form)' and there is no difference of perfection and imperfection between human beings and things. This is the case of original nature. With respect to '*itche* (異體, various substances)', both The Mandate of Heaven and the five constant virtues are subjected to '*gijil* (氣質, physical nature)' and there is a difference of perfection and imperfection not only between the human being and thing but also between the saint and the ordinary person. This is the case of 'physical nature (氣質之性)'.[45] According to Yi Gan, with respect to '*itche* (異體)' or '*ingijil* (因器質, causation through physical quality)', human nature and the thing's nature are different from each other, and so he abandoned this approach, based on the characteristics of physical quality. Solely with respect to *Ilwon* or '*chohyeonggi* (超形氣, transcendence of material form)', and on the basis of The Mandate of Heaven and the five constant virtues which correspond to original nature, he argued for the identity of human nature and the thing's nature .

It was impossible for Han Won-jin and Yi Gan to agree with each other because of their divergent emphases and interpretations of original nature. Moreover, it was a weakness that Han neglected the identity of nature which was maintained in his theory of 'the three steps of nature (性三層說)' or that Yi maintained that the five constant

44 Han Won-jin,*Namdangjip*, Chap. 2-3, Vol. 7.
45 Yi Gan, *Oeamyugo*, Chap. 15, Vol. 7.

virtues together with The Mandate of Heaven belonged to the category of *ilwon* (*chohyeonggi*), not of *iche* (*ingijil*). As each of their views implied such unconvincing arguments, the two scholars could not help pitting themselves against each other's theory.

While continuing their debates they attempted to supplement their own theories. Therefore Han Won-jin stated, "The identity of the human being and the thing lies in the perception of the human mind," and Yi Gan argued, "The perception of the human mind is the source of the difference between the human being and the thing."

The motives behind their debates arose from the difference in their approaches, the difference in their concepts of original nature and the fact that they could locate the sources for their claims in classics such as *The Book of Mencius* or *The Doctrine of the Mean*. In addition to these motives, there were the incompatible meanings implied in the concept of original nature. That is, when original nature means essential nature, human nature and the thing's nature can be distinguished from each other. However, when original nature means the nature that has remained intact since the formation of the universe, it refers to the common nature of the human being and the thing.[46] Moreover, it should be noted that they were not satisfied merely with the inquiry into the difference in characteristics of the human being and the thing. Both of them accepted the five constant virtues with which the human being is endowed as their original nature, emphasized beneficent nature and aimed at the ethical realization of the good nature. To further this aim they also investigated through their debates whether or not goodness exists 'before the emergence or issuance (未發)' of the human mind.

---

46 I presented this view in "The Identity of or Difference between Human Nature and Thing's Nature" in *Philosophy* (Korean Society of Philosophy, 1982) Vol., 18. I also suggested this view in *The History of Korean Confucianism* (Jisiksaneopsa, 2012), Vol. 1, p. 518.

(3) The Inquiry into *Simche* and *Myeongdeok* before the Issuance of the Mind

The state 'before the issuance of the mind (未發)' (In the Yi Dynasty cerebration was called mind [心] because the science of anatomy had not yet been formed) refers to the state when mind is conscious of or perceptive of something though feeling or emotion has not yet been aroused. As mind in Neo-Confucianism is 'the combination of *ri* and *gi* (理氣之合)', it is also the source of original nature (本然之性) and physical nature (氣質之性). Therefore, it was a dilemma to Han Won-jin and Yi Gan whether original nature or the disposition to pursue goodness, that is, '*myeongdeok* (明德, illustrious virtue)' is internal to 'physical quality (氣質)' when they tried to locate the origin of good morality on the basis of mind. Moreover, in Neo-Confucianism the mind before issuance was considered to be 'the substance of mind (心之體)'. Therefore, Neo-Confucian scholars called the discussion on the state of mind before issuance the discussion of '*simche* (心體, the substance of mind)' and *myeongdeok*.

This discussion was related to the issue of the identity of or difference between human nature and the thing's nature. Han Won-jin's view on the difference between human nature and the thing's nature had a defect, as Yi Gan pointed out, in that physical nature and original nature are not clearly distinguished from each other. On the other hand, Yi's view on the identity that lays emphasis on The Mandate of Heaven, as Han pointed out, was quite alien to mental experience or morality and thus seemed somewhat empty of meaning. Therefore, in order to overcome their defects, they had to locate their theoretical bases in the fundamental dimension of the substance of mind before issuance rather than in the dimension of the physical phenomena comprising human beings and animals.

First, let me introduce Han Won-jin's view:

> "The original mind refers only to *ri* and physical nature refers to *ri* combined with *gi*... As in the state before issuance *gi* does not

function, only the extreme goodness of *ri* is revealed and the good or evil of *gi* is not revealed. Only after the issuance is the good or evil of *gi* revealed..."[47]

("I speak of consistency in tranquility because *gi*, which is sturdy or gentle, good or evil, does not function consistently in tranquility."[48]

Next, let me introduce Yi Gan's view.

"The so-called state before issuance refers to the state when *gi* does not function. In this state there are only consistent clearness, purity, and goodness without the combination of clearness and turbidness, purity and impurity, and without the combined operations of feeling and intention. It refers to the state of being neither biased nor inclined, that is, the state in which only righteous and apposite *ri* exists. Therefore, why do they speak of the state before issuance not with respect to solely *ri* but to the combination of *ri* and *gi* which does not function in this state?"[49]

Both of them agreed that goodness prevails before issuance. However, they differed over the reason why this is so. According to Han Won-jin, only the goodness of *ri* prevails in the state before issuance because *gi* has no function, though *ri* and *gi* coexist in this state. According to Yi Gan, goodness prevails not only because *gi* does not function but also because only *ri* needs be taken into account in the state before issuance.

They also differed in their views on the quality of *gi* in the state before issuance. Han defined the *gi* of mind in this state as *gi* sturdy and gentle, good and evil, while Yi defined it as *gi* pure, clean, and good.

It should also be noted that their usages of *simche* (心體, the substance

47 Han Won-jin, "Bonyeongijilsiseongseo", *Namdangjip*, Vol. 30.
48 Ibid., "Dapyigonggeo", Vol. 10.
49 Yi Gan, *Oeamyugo*, Vol. 12,

of mind) and *myeongdeok* were divergent. Han followed the usual definition of Neo-Confucian scholars and spoke of *myeongdeok* as original nature while Yi spoke of *myeongdeok* as another name of '*sim* (心, mind/heart)'. It is arguable that Yi Gan's usage obfuscated the distinction between *sim* and *simche* (心體).

In addition, Han said, "There are good and evil in the mind," and "'The empty and luminous (虛明)' original substance of mind before issuance is good regardless of its manifestation in sages or ordinary human beings." Here this 'empty and luminous' refers to the mind's perceptive quality. According to Han, with respect to the empty and luminous perception, sages, ordinary human beings, and animals are the same. I think that this view entails a problem, namely that Han, who had argued for the difference between human nature and the thing's nature, here seems to accept the identity of human nature and the thing's nature by saying that all entities enjoy the beneficent original substance of mind.

(4) The Significance of the Inquiry into the Identity of or Difference between Human Nature and the Thing's Nature

As we have seen, in the inquiry into the identity of or difference between human nature and the thing's nature '*seong* (性)' referred to original nature. Han Won-jin regarded original nature as consisting of the five constant virtues while Yi Gan saw it as composed of both The Mandate of Heaven (Taegeuk, or the Great Ultimate) and the five constant virtues. In anticipation of the consequences of their different theories of original nature, Han and Yi emphasized the following propositions in their debates.

Han Won-jin argued for the difference between human nature and the thing's nature, keeping in mind Yi Gan's work in which he maintained that human nature and the thing's nature were identical. Han proposed, "Human nature is more precious than the thing's nature,"[50]

50 Han Won-jin, *Namdangjip*, Chap. 24, Vol. 11.

for he judged that the superiority of human nature over the thing's nature can be ignored when their identity is maintained. Against this proposition Yi argued, "Not only the five constant virtues but also The Mandate of Heaven and the Great Ultimate are precious and good,"[51] and later wrote "The Exposition on the Five Constant Virtues (五常辨)" to further clarify his position. Their propositions suggest their views on the moral disposition implied in original nature. Han's view of the primacy of difference emphasizes the distinction of the human being from the animal on the basis of the ethical superiority of the human being, while Yi Gan's view of the centrality of identity emphasizes the originally absolute concept of the goodness of original nature. In order to bolster their positions they proceeded to investigate the good and evil characteristics of the substance of mind in the state before the issuance. Keeping in mind that the original nature, after all, refers to the innate good or virtuous nature of the human being, we may conclude that their sincere and serious thought constituted ethical inquiries focused on innate virtuous nature. I believe that their inquiries should be highly regarded from the standpoint of ethics.

Song Si-yeol (宋時烈, 1607-1689), who had been interested in this issue, thought that the ceaseless debates surrounding it originated from uncritical acceptance of Zhu Xi's theories (including interpretations of the concept of original nature) on the part of Korean scholars. As a result, Song began to collate discrepant usages, orthodox and unorthodox views, clerical errors, and mistranslations of Zhu Xi's works. As these texts were so voluminous Song's work of collation was continued by his disciples Gwon Sang-ha (權尙夏, 1641-1721), and then Han Won-jin. Their more than 50 years' work was crystallized into a book entitled *Jujaeonrondongigo* (朱子言論同異考, *A Bibliographical Study of Zhu Xi's Theories*). This book is a monumental work on Zhu Xi's Neo-Confucianism written by Korean scholars under the stimulus of the debates on the status of human nature vis-a-vis thing's nature.[52]

51 Yi Gan, *Oeamyugo*, Chap. 19, Vol. 7,
52 Yun Sa-soon, "A Study of the Identity of Difference between Human Nature and the Thing's Nature", *Philosophy* (The Society of Korean Philosophy, 1982),

The recondite Neo-Confucian learning of the Joseon Dynasty, which was superior to that of any other country in East Asia, may well be evidenced by this book alone.

Moreover, the debates had points of contact with the contemporary situations. In the early 17th century Song Si-yeol's 'Noron (老論, 'The Faction of the Old Doctrine: Scholars of this faction devoted themselves to the debates on human nature and the thing's nature.)' was the most powerful party. Though the Joseon Dynasty was under the influence of the Qing Dynasty, there was discord between the two dynasties, for the ruling party in Joseon was secretly groping for a way to fight against and conquer Qing. So it was important for the ruling party (Noron) to hold in check the opposing parties of Namin (南人, The Southerners) and Soron (The Faction of the Young Doctrine) and to maintain a seemingly friendly relationship with Qing.

The people of the Joseon Dynasty had long despised the Qing Dynasty as a barbarous country in the north. Moreover, during the invasion of Joseon by Qing (1636-1637), the Korean people suffered great hardship, and after the invasion they regarded Qing as a mortal enemy. When Prince Bongrim (鳳林大君) who had been held as hostage in Qing came back to Joseon and acceded to the throne and became King Hyojong, while maintaining a friendly relationship with Qing superficially, he devised a secret, improbable plan to conquer Qing. So the relationship of Joseon with Qing might well be compared to 'sharing the same bed with an enemy'.

Those who insisted on the conquest of Qing found justification in the theory of the difference between human nature and the thing's nature, while those who insisted on a friendly relationship with Qing found support in the theory of their identity. As both Han Won-jin and Yi Gan belonged to Noron, the ruling party at that time, Yi's view constituted the former pole, while Han's view supported the latter. Ultimately, they both contributed to the maintenance of Noron's rule like the two edges of a knife. Thus I think that the significance of the

---

Vol. 18.

debates between Han and Yi also encompassed the contemporary historical situation.

6. The Theory of *Seong-Ri* Biased toward the Unitary Origin of *Gi*

(1) Ihm Seong-ju's Scholarly Position

The core idea of Neo-Confucianism is the theory of *ri-gi*. As we have seen, theories of *ri-gi* were biased toward the centrality of either *ri* or *gi*. The cause of the bias can be attributed to the view of *ri* and *gi* either as in actuality 'inseparable (不離)' or as conceptually 'separable (不雜)'. It is difficult to bring the two views into balance with each other. In general, the former led to the theory of the *gi*-principal and the latter to that of the *ri*-principal. In the first half of the 17th century Jang Hyeon-gwang's view on *ri* and *gi* as substance and function and as warp and weft betrayed his intention to sublate the bias either toward *ri* or *gi,* though this project ended in failure. In the first half of the 18th century the debates on the status of human nature in comparison to or in contrast with the thing's nature were still based on such a pair of biases, toward one or the other, and Han Won-jin's view was biased toward the *gi*-principal while Yi Gan's view made the argument for the priority of the *ri*-principal.

In the 18th century Ihm Seong-ju (任聖周, 1711-1788) was a notable figure who was extremely biased toward the *gi*-principal. But he had not been so in the period of his elementary learning. When young, he learned under the tutorship of Yi Jae (李縡, 1680-1748) who argued for the identity of human nature and the thing's nature, so Ihm once held the viewpoint of the *ri*-principal. However, during the period of his self-education he gradually evolved in his scholarly positions and became more partial to the *gi*-principal.

The main figures who participated in the debates on human nature and the thing's nature, whatever viewpoints they might maintain, saw

Yi I's theory of *ri* and *gi* as the source of their debates. Yi I attached importance to the function of *gi* in his *simron* (心論, theory of mind) and insisted on the *gi*-principal by saying "mind is *gi* (心卽氣)." Ihm Seong-ju had an affinity for the *simron* of Yi I, who was the progenitor of his scholarly lineage. So Ihm turned against the teaching of Yi Jae who had been his master in his youth, and joined Han Won-jin and other scholars who advocated the *gi*-principal or the difference between human nature and the thing's nature. In his old age Ihm intensified his advocacy of the *gi*-principal and proposed a unique 'monistic theory of *gi* (唯氣論)', that is, a theory that expressed extreme bias toward *gi*.

(2) The Confirmation of the Monistic Theory of *Gi*

In accordance with the original theory of Neo-Confucianism, Ihm Seong-ju said that the universe and nature (自然) were generated by 'the *gi* of *yin·yang* (陰陽之氣, 太和之氣)'. Ihm, like Zhang Zai (張載) and Seo Gyeong-deok (徐敬德) enumerated as the characteristics of *gi* the concepts of heavy and cloudy (重濁), light and clear (輕淸), large and small (大小), rising and falling (昇降), gathering and scattering (聚散, 集散), sturdy and gentle (剛柔), and partial and impartial (正偏). Ihm called *gi,* that generates phenomena on the basis of these characteristics, '*yugi* (遊氣)', which corresponds to Zhang Zai's terms '*gaekhyeong* (客形)' or '*gihwa* (氣化)'.[53]

Gi-oriented scholars, in their discussions of *gi*, elucidated 'the phenomenal (spatio-temporal) *gi*' in contrast to 'the Primordial *Gi* (the gi of the primordial substance)'. Zhang Zai and Seo Gyeong-deok also assumed the existence of the two kinds of *gi*, and called the primordial substance of *gi* '*Taeheo* (太虛, Great Void)'. Ihm also called it *Taeheo*, and in addition, '*Cheon* (天, Heaven)', '*Wongi* (元氣, the Primordial *Gi*)', and '*Hogi* (浩氣, the Vast *Gi*)'.[54] And like Seo Gyeong-deok and other venerable *gi*-oriented scholars he called the primary characteristic of

53 Ihm Seong-ju, "Nokryeojapsik", 'Jabjeo', Vol. 19, p. 6.
54 Ibid., p. 6.

the Primordial *Gi* '*heo* (虛, void)', '*Taeheo* (太虛, Great Void)', or '*damil* (湛一, perfect purity)'.[55]

Elder scholars called the primordial substance of *gi* *Seoncheon* (先天, Ante-Heaven) and the phenomena generated by *gi* *Hucheon* (後天, Later Heaven). Though there is no specific evidence demonstrating that Ihm Seong-ju followed the views of the elder scholars, he seems to have been influenced by them. The distinction between the primordial substance of *gi* and the phenomena generated by *gi* did not refer to two kinds of *gi* with different qualities but only to 'the two states of the same *gi*'. This conceptualization was compatible with 'the monistic theory of *gi* (氣一元論)' that interpreted the universe on the basis of unitary *gi*. In this respect Ihm Seong-ju's theory was different from Cheng-Zhu's 'dualistic theory of *ri* and *gi* (理氣二元論)' that interpreted the universe on the basis of *ri-gi*.

Ihm Seong-ju had his own view of *ri*. His was different from Cheng-Zhu's but was very similar to Zhang Zai's and Seo Gyeong-deok's. According to Ihm, *ri* meant only the order (秩序), or logic (條理), or rule (法則) which is recognized during the functioning of *gi*. He regarded *ri* neither as actual being as Cheng-Zhu had nor as preceding *gi*, nor as the cause of *gi*'s functioning. He maintained, "*Ri* and *gi* are inseparable," and "*Ri* is in the midst of *gi*." His position is also confirmed by his remark, "The substance of *ri* and of *gi* are the same (理氣同實)."[56] According to him, "*Ri* is carried by *gi* and only follows 'the operation of *gi*' and does not have its own unique capability of superintendency."

Ihm Seong-ju rejected Cheng-Zhu's views on the universe and other issues based on the *ri*-principal, and superseded them with his own views based on the *gi*-principal. His remark below demonstrates this:

"*Riilbunsu* (理一分殊, one *ri* and its differentiation into numerous manifes-

55 Ibid.
56 Ibid., "Dapyibaeknul", Vol. 5, 'Seo', p. 6.

tations) is theorized on the basis of the *ri*-principal, and so it follows that '*bun* (分, differentiation)' should also be encompassed by *ri*. On the basis of the *gi*-principal, however, we may safely conceive of the existence of *giilbunsu* (氣 一分殊)."[57]

Cheng-Zhu explained that the universe is the system generated by '*riilbunsu*', that is, 'by one *ri*' for they believed that the universe was formed by 'the *ri* of the Great Ultimate (太極)'. Ihm Seong-ju criticized and rejected such a view and substitute '*giilbunsu* (氣一分殊)' for '*riilbunsu*'. In other words, he maintained that the universe was 'generated by *gi*'. His remark below is evidence that he rejected almost all of Cheng-Zhu's concepts.

"All kinds of *ri* (萬理) comprise all kinds of creation (萬象). The five constants (五常, benevolence, righteousness, propriety, wisdom, fidelity) are the five elements (五行: water, fire, wood, metal, and earth). *Geonsun* (健順, being sturdy and gentle) is *yangui* (兩儀, *yin and yang*), and Taegeuk (太極, the Great Ultimate) is *Wongi* (the Primordial Gi). All these are named on the basis of *gi*."[58]

Scholars belonging to Cheng-Zhu's intellectual lineage might have been greatly surprised to see that Ihm's interpretations of the main concepts were different from theirs. He defined Taegeuk or the ultimate source of the universe as the Primordial *Gi* (元氣) or the Great Void (太虛), and 'all kinds of *ri*' as 'all kinds of creation' generated by diverse instantiations of *gi*. In particular, his remark that the five constants are the five elements, though it seems illogical, corresponded to the proposition, "Human nature is *gi* (性卽氣)", which was in opposition to Cheng-Zhu's argument, "Human nature is *ri* (性卽理)." He defined '*geonsun*' as '*yangui* (兩儀, *yin-yang*)' for *geonsun* had referred to *yin·yang* in *The Book of Changes* (周易). In the last analysis, it becomes evident that his philosophy was based on the

57 Ibid., "Nokryeojapsik", Vol. 19, 'Jabjeo', p. 4.
58 Ibid., p. 4.

extreme *gi*-principal or the monistic theory of *gi*, which interprets all under the rubric of *gi*.

(3) The Theory of the Primordial Substance of *Gi* as the Generative Intention

We have seen that Ihm Seong-ju named the primordial substance of *gi* '*Taeheo* (太虛)', '*Cheon* (天)', '*Wongi* (元氣)', and '*Hogi* (浩氣)', and its characteristic qualities '*taeheo*' and '*damil* (湛一)'. Zhang Zai and the other *gi*-oriented scholars had also used the term, '*Taeheo*', but they had seldom spoken of the other terms Ihm proposed. *Cheon* (天) was usually regarded as the term denoting the primordial substance of *gi* because its conventional meaning was the source of the universe or the ultimate being. However, *Wongi* and *Hogi* were seldom used as substitutes for *Taeheo*. Since the Chinese Han Dynasty *Wongi* had meant the primordial element of the universe. As for *Hogi*, though it is the abbreviation of '*hoyeonjigi* (浩然之氣, vast tide of *gi*)' which had been conceptualized by Mencius, and means the *gi* suffusing the universe, it lacks the connotation of *Taeheo* which has the obvious implication of the existence of an objective primordial substance. In other words, *Hogi* is related to the characteristic nature of the human being, not to objective substance. For this reason, *gi*-oriented scholars did not regard '*Wongi*' and '*Hogi*' as the primordial substance of *gi*.

Wongi and *Hogi* are concepts denoting not only the fundamental *gi* but 'the vitality applicable to both nature and the human being'. Uniquely, Ihm Seong-ju regarded the concept of vitality as designating th e primordial substance, and to this extent, his view is worth noting. His views on *Wongi* and *Hogi* were connected with his theory of 'the characteristic of the Primordial *Gi*' as 'the generative intention (生意)'.

> "Inevitably there exists a being with the characteristics of 'void (虛), roundness (圓) and magnificence (盛大)'. It is vast and boundless, has no interior or exterior, no border, no beginning or end, and is altogether luminous and flexible—all these characteristics refer to

the generative intention. Its current has 'no action (無爲)' and its generation of things is unpredictable."[59]

According to the above argument, an entity with certain characteristics suffuses the natural phenomena brought into being by a constitutive cause. This being is called 'the generative intention (生意). Ihm Seong-ju understood that all natural phenomena are caused by the operation of the generative intention. To be more concrete, the generative intention running through natural phenomena is both the primordial substance generating things and its characteristics. Perhaps for this reason Ihm dubbed the generative intention 'virtue (德)', 'origination (元)', or 'the mind of Heaven and Earth (天地之心)'.[60]

Ihm Seong-ju's view on the universe originated from the theory of the life forms of the universe mentioned in *The Book of Changes,* which argues, "The innate characteristic of the universe is called life," and "The ceaseless flux of generation is called *yeok* (易, change)."[61] On the basis of this theory of the universe and life forms, Cheng Hao (程顥) called the characteristic of benevolence (仁), which belongs to original nature, 'the generative intention'. Ihm Seong-ju seems to have been influenced by such views. Nevertheless, it is Ihm's unique view that the primordial characteristic of *gi*, which is the fundamental formative element of the universe, is the generative intention and that he regarded this intention as the primordial substance of *gi*.

He anthropomorphized the universe and viewed the generative intention as 'the mind of Heaven and Earth'. In accordance with this view (concerning the disposition to generate the universe) he regarded all generations and changes caused by *gi* as the manifestations of 'the mind of the generative intention (生意之心)' or 'the mind of thing-generation (生物之心)'. In fact he viewed '*won* (元, origination)-*hyeong* (亨, flourish)-*ri* (利, advantage)-*jeong* (貞, firmness)', which was mentioned in *The Book*

59 "Simgyeong", Vol. 12, 'Jabjeo', pp. 19-20.
60 Ibid., "Nokryeojapsik", p. 1.
61-*The Book of Changes*, 'Gyesa'.

of Changes, as the principle of change of the universe, and as the circulating phenomena caused by the mind of thing-generation.[62] All these views represent his unique application of the philosophy of life and understanding on the basis of the philosophy of life, with which his *gi*-oriented philosophy may be said to have expressed itself most brilliantly.

(4) The Ethical Stance Based on the Monistic Theory of *Gi*

Seo Gyeong-deok who had advanced *gi*-oriented philosophy was not concerned with establishing the foundation of morality. On the other hand, Ihm Seong-ju was deeply concerned with ethical problems. While observing that the debates on human nature and the thing's nature were continuing with no end in sight, he judged that they failed in elucidating the ethical basis of the universe. So he devoted himself to illuminating the ethical basis of the debates with reference to his own theory of *gi*. Ihm Seong-ju, like Zhou Dunyi, thought that the innate *gi* of the human being is the most 'righteous *gi* (正氣)'. He said that although both sages and ordinary human beings are born of the pure primordial substance of *gi* and although the Primordial *Gi* of the human being is fundamentally righteous, ordinary human beings may nevertheless be wise or stupid because the spatio-temporal *gi* displays differences in terms of purity and impurity, and density and scarcity.[63] As for the *sim* (心, mind/heart) that is related to being wise or stupid, he seemed to believe that heart (心臟) is the site where the functioning of *sim* arises.[64] According to him, *sim* and *seong* (性, human nature) cannot be discussed without regard to *gi*. He argued, "*Sim* is the spirit (神明) of *gi* and *gi* is the foundation (質幹) of *sim*,"[65] and "*Sim* is the soul (靈) of *gi*, and *seong* is the virtue

62 Ihm Seong-ju, "Simgyeong," *Nokmunjip*, Vol. 12, 'Jabjeo'.
63 Ibid., "Dapyibaeknul", Vol. 5, 'Seo', p. 22.
64 Ibid., p. 22.
65 Ibid., "Daehak", Vol. 16, 'Japjeo', p. 2.

(德) of *gi*."[66] Such definitions are not very different from those of the other Neo-Confucian scholars.

His uniqueness is suggested in the following remarks: "*Sim* and *seong* are the same. When we speak of *sim*, *seong* is implied in it."[67] and "*Sim* and *seong* have 'the same substance (同實)'."[68] According to him, as *ri* and *gi* may be said to have the same content in that *ri* cannot be separated from *gi*, 'the identity of *sim* and *seong* is a definite rule'[69] for *seong* is in the midst of *sim*. Such a view is very different from Cheng-Zhu's definition of *sim·seong*.

Needless to say, theories of 'the good and evil' of human nature originated from the consciousness of autonomous moral behavior. Ihm Seong-ju concluded that 'human nature is good'.

> "Beneficent nature refers only to beneficent 'physical nature (氣質)'. Nothing corresponds to beneficent nature except beneficent physical nature."[70]

Ihm Seong-ju's statement that physical nature is itself beneficent or good reminds us of Gao-tzu (告者) who said, "The state of things at the time of birth is called nature (生之爲性)." Ihm had once read "The Chapter of Gao-zui (告子章)" and argued that the nature of the dog, cow, and human being is no other than 'the nature mentioned by Gao-zu (生之謂性)'.[71] To Ihm good denoted only the propensity one is endowed with at the time of one's birth.

However, here some problems arise. If the natural, instinctive propensity is good, does this mean that good ethical deeds can be performed without intentional endeavor? Isn't there anything like evil? How can it be that the confusion of struggle arises when the instinctive propensity is unattended to? Owing to such problems his

66 Ibid., p. 1.
67 Ihm Seong-ju, "Nokryeojapsik", *Nokmunjip*, Vol. 19, p. 20.
68 Ibid., "Dapgimbaekgo", Vol. 6, 'Seo', p. 12.
69 Ibid., "Dapyibaeknul", Vol. 5, 'Seo', p. 6.
70 Ibid., "Nokryeojapsik", Vol. 19, 'Japjeo', p. 5.
71 Ibid., "Dapyibaekgo", Vol. 6, pp. 2-3.

argument could not be unproblematically accepted. In response to these questions, however, Ihm Seong-ju said that evil can be attributed to the degradation of physical nature or the residue of *gi*. Thus, according to him, in order to do good deeds, as Yi I (李珥) once said, the recuperation of *gi* or physical nature, or the recovery of the primordial substance of *gi* called '*Hogi* (浩然之氣, vast tide of *gi*)' is necessary. In this context he proposed the utilization of 'the intention (志)' that Mencius called 'the commander of *gi*'.

> "If one has an intention one becomes upright when one moves or stands still. The uprightness when one stands still is the way (道) and the uprightness when one moves is righteousness. Righteousness and the way are the kernel of an intention, and if one maintains an intention, righteousness and the way are naturally in the midst of the intention."[72]

According to Mencius "*Hogi* (浩氣 or 浩然之氣, vast-tide of *gi*) is cultivated by uprightness and obtained by the accumulation of righteousness."[73] Uprightness and righteousness are the two axes along which the cultivation of *Hogi* takes place. However, Ihm Seong-ju in fact laid emphasis only on the maintenance of intention. Ultimately, he believed that *Hogi* is cultivated not only by the practice of uprightness and righteousness but also by the maintenance of good intention.

Moreover, Ihm Seong-ju emphasized the cultivation of '*gyeong* (敬, reverent mindfulness)'.[74] *Gyeong* is an attitude of the focused mind, and refers to reverent mindfulness even to the extent of piety. Ihm regarded gyeong as the basic condition for the maintenance of good intention, which comprises uprightness and righteousness. So his ethical view was that when one is acquainted with the way to maintain one's good intention one can perform ethical deeds based on

72 Ibid., "Maengjabudongsimjangseol", 'Vol. 21, 'Seol', P. 52.
73 "Gongsonchuk", *Maengja*, Vol. 1.
74 Kim Hyeon, "A Study of Reverent Mindfulness", *Ihm Seong-ju's Philosophy of Life*, (Hangilsa, 1995), pp. 170-173.

uprightness and altruism.

Ihm Seong-ju's ethical view, based on the philosophy of life, is completely different from that of the Neo-Confucian scholars in Cheng-Zhu's intellectual lineage, who tried to act morally by relying only on the recovery of original nature. As shown in the debates on the status of human nature with respect to the thing's nature, the Neo-Confucian followers of Cheng-Zhu attached great importance to original nature or innate 'illustrious virtue (明德)' for the dissemination of ethics and morals. Ihm, however, while believing that original nature is somehow related to physical nature, argued for the identity of *gi* or physical nature and 'mind (心)', and on the premise of this identity especially emphasized 'good intention (善意志)' which is the function of 'numinous and luminous (靈明)' mind with the characteristic not of original nature but of the 'mysterious and luminous (精爽)' *gi*. Simply put, Ihm's ethical view was based on the exercise of good intention. Though his ethical view was different from that of the scholars who upheld the *ri*-principal, as a *gi*-oriented scholar, he also attached importance to ethics and morals.

7. The Intensification of the View of the Universe Based on the Monistic Theory of *Ri*

(1) Ki Jeong-jin's Scholarly Attitude

Among Neo-Confucian scholars in the Joseon Dynasty Ihm Seong-ju was a very rare example of a thinker who was 'extremely biased toward *gi*'. During the dynasty's reign *ri*-oriented scholars far outnumbered *gi*-oriented scholars, for most scholars followed the theories of Cheng-Zhu, which served as the basis of the governing ideology of the dynasty. Moreover, in the 18th century when Ihm Seong-ju's *gi*-oriented view had been widely known for a long period, the number of *ri*-oriented scholars increased sharply, though it is not clear whether the increase should be ascribed to the reaction against Ihm's view or the inherent compatibility of this philosophical trend with the needs of the times.

From the late 18th century and into the 19th century the bias in favor of *ri* was intensified in the form of 'the monistic theory of *ri* (唯理論)'. Ki Jeong-jin (奇正鎭, 1798-1879)'s theory of *ri-gi* based on the unitary origin of *ri* was unprecedented in other countries as well as in Korea. He may be said to have been the sole originator of the monistic theory of *ri* in East Asia.

First, let's survey his career. He was a child prodigy who learned how to write at the age of four and immersed himself in the Confucian classics and history books at the age of eight or nine. At 34 he achieved first place in a state examination and was qualified for a junior government position. However, after a period he quit the position. At 45 he was appointed as an official called Byeolje (別提) of 'Jeonseolsa (典設司: an office responsible for the preparation of tents used for rituals)', a position he resigned from after only six days. Subsequently, he never again entered the government service until he died. Instead, as a scholar he devoted himself to the study of Neo-Confucianism.

Ki Jeong-jin seems to have thought himself unfit to be a government official. Moreover, as he lived in an age when Western imperialist countries had revealed their undisguised intention to invade the East, he might have labored under a heavy burden if he had been an official in such a situation. When he grew old, he was deeply concerned with 'defending orthodoxy and rejecting heterodoxy (衛正斥邪)', that is, with resisting foreign invasions while consolidating traditional Confucian culture.

As a scholar he did not dream of the prosperous life of a government official. Rather, he tried to be faithful to the contemporary view of where real influence resided, which was that the intellectuals are the primary power of a nation. Though he was from a rustic background and held no official position, he was always concerned with national affairs--especially with establishing a national policy designed to protect against the invasion of Western forces. For instance, he presented a Memorial to the Throne when Western warships made an incursion into the West Sea in 1866, the third year of King Gojong's reign.

In the memorial he wrote that complying with the request of Westerners to trade with the dynasty through an open-door policy might result in great loss rather than gain. According to him, the barbarous and bestial Westerners would fatally undermine Confucian ethical order, cause Koreans to waste gold, silver, and other goods by importing luxury items and consumer goods, and ultimately bring about the exhaustion of Korea's national resources. He asserted that to trade with Westerners would ultimately be to fall victim to their imperial designs. As a result, Ki Jeong-jin was seen as being in the party that advocated the defense of orthodoxy and the rejection of heterodoxy.[75]

Ki Jeong-jin's position in fact served as the spiritual foundation for the organization of 'righteous civilian soldiers (義兵)' who fought against the Japanese imperialists. At that time Yi Hang-ro (李恒老, 1846-1916) in Gyeonggi Province was a scholar who also asserted the need for resistance against foreign invaders. One of his followers, named Ryu In-seok (柳麟錫, 1842-1915) became a famous commander of the righteous civilian soldiers. Likewise, under the influence of Ki Jeong-jin, two commanders of the righteous army named Ki Wu-man (奇宇萬, 1846-1916) and Ki Sam-yeon (奇參衍, 1851-1908) appeared in Jeonnam Province. The former was Ki Jeong-jin's grandson, and the latter his cousin's grandson, who had lived in Ki Jeong-jin's hometown, Jangseong in Jeonnam Province. [76]

After the age of 40, Ki Jeong-jin devoted himself to writing many articles and books such as *Wugi* (偶記) (completed when he was 48), *Jeongjaseol* (定子說) (48), *Ritongseol* (理通說) (55), and *Oepil* (猥筆). *Oepil*, in which his other books including *Napryangsaui* (納凉私議) are bound together, contains the core ideas of his theory of *ri-gi*. *Napryangsaui* was conceived when he was 46.[77]

75 Ki Jeong-jin, "Chronology and Others", *Nosaseonsaengmunjip*.
76 Ibid.
77 Ibid.

He enthusiastically educated and produced many disciples, who were not exclusively from his hometown, Jangseong. It was an unusual situation in that era that his disciples came from distant districts such as the provinces of Gyeongnam, Chungcheong and Jeolla. They later became the protagonists of the Nosa (蘆沙) School. Though he lived in a village in Jangseong, Ki Jeong-jin was a scholar renowned throughout the nation.

(2) The Development of the Monistic Theory of *Ri*

Like the general characteristics of the theories of the *ri*-principal, Ki Jeong-jin's *ri* implied not only the importance of the law or orderly rule but also '*sodangyeon* (所當然, normative principle)' and '*soiyeon* (所以然, natural principle or cause)'. He advanced a *ri* that implies *soiyeon* or cause, saying "Oh, *ri*, *ri*, it is the seed of all beings."[78] The comparison of *ri* to seed reveals the understanding of '*ri* as actual being'. On the basis of this understanding he made affirmative propositions about *ri*: "*Ri* generates *gi* (理生氣)" and "*Ri* precedes and *gi* follows (理先氣後)." On the other hand, he rejected passive propositions about *ri* such as "*Ri* has no function but functions anywhere (無爲而無不爲)" and "*Ri* is weak while *gi* is strong (理弱氣强)."[79]

I have already explained that the definition of *ri* as *soiyeon* originated from Cheng Hao (程顥)'s and Cheng Yi's substitution of the supervision of Heaven or The Mandate of Heaven by the fundamental proposition, "Heaven is *ri* (天卽理)". Ki Jeong-jin underscored the supervision of *ri* and defined it as the command of *ri* to *gi*'[80] and *gi* as the recipient of *ri*'s command. In this context he said that to command means to make *gi* work.[81] Ki's definitions cannot be said to be unique for Yi Hang-ro, who was a contemporary, similarly defined the relation of *ri* and *gi* as that of host and guest.

78 Ki Jeong-jin, *Nosaseonsaengmunjip*, Vol. 16, p. 4.
79 Ibid., , *Oepil*, Vol. 16, p. 25.
80 Ibid., "Ritongseol", Vol. 16, p. 1.
81 Ibid., *Oepil*, Vol. 16, p. 25.

However, it should be noted that Ki Jeong-jin did not regarded the relation of *ri* and *gi* simply as that of host and guest. He grasped the relation in terms of the position of a more rigorous *ri*-principal. According to him, *ri* and *gi* correspond to 'host and servant' and further, 'body and limb'.

> "*Gi* issues and operates under the command of *ri*. So that which commands is host and that which obeys is servant."[82]

> "High and noble *ri* is unparalleled. How could *gi* rival *ri*!.... *Gi* is merely a function of *ri* and plays the role of hands and feet (limb) when *ri* prevails."[83]

The distinction between host and servant is like that between the noble and the base, but to regard *gi* as the limb of the body (*ri*) is a more extreme distinction than the theory of *ri* and *gi* as host and servant. To compare *gi* with the limbs is actually to obliterate the specificity of *gi* and to completely subordinate *gi* to *ri*, and clearly constitutes the monistic view of *ri* or the extreme bias toward *ri*. Needless to say, Ki Jeong-jin rejected the views based on the *gi*-principal suggested by Seo Gyeong-deok and Ihm Seong-ju. Moreover, he criticized the dualistic theory of *ri* and *gi* held by Yi Hwang, Yi I and other scholars, and their aim of maintaining the balance of *ri* and *gi* based on the *ri*-principal.

(3) The View on the Universe Based on the Monistic Theory of Ri and the Reinterpretation of ***Riilbunsu***

Ki Jeong-jin established the monistic theory of *ri* and applied it to his view on the universe. But the latter was influenced by Cheng Yi's theory of '*riilbunsu* (理一分殊, one principle and its instantiation in many manifestations)'. Originally *riilbunsu* was a theory of the source of the

82 Ibid., p. 26.
83 Ibid., p. 27.

universe as 'the *ri* of Taegeuk (太極, the Great Ultimate)'. This theory was elaborated by applying the propositions of Cheng Yi's propositions, "Heaven is *ri* (天卽理)," "Taegeuk is *ri* (太極卽理)," and Zhu Xi's 'view of Taegeuk (總體一太極 物物各有一太極, one Taegeuk for the whole universe and one taegeuk for each entity)' to the theory of 'the vital universe' mentioned in *The Book of Changes*. Simply plut, the One *Ri* of the whole universe is instantiated in numerous individual entities, each of which has its own *ri* (taegeuk). In a word, *riilbunsu* designates the universe as in the meshes of *ri*. As this theory complied with his monistic view of *ri*, Ki Jeong-jin accepted and theoretically elaborated it in devising his own view on the universe. He said:

> "Taegeuk is everywhere. This means that substance (體) is equipped with function (用)."[84]

Here he explains *riilbunsu* with respect to 'the theory of essence and function (體容觀)'. According to this explanation, the Taegeuk of the whole universe corresponds to substance (體) and that of each entity to function (用), and the One Substance of the Primordial Taegeuk is differentiated into the functions of numerous phenomenal entities. So Ki Jeong-jin accepted the original theory of *riilbunsu* and established his own view by elaborating and reinterpreting the theory.

It may not be a logical leap to say that his reinterpretation is centered around 'the differentiation (分) of *ri*'. According to Ki Jeong-jin, 'the differentiation', though it is related to 'the One *Ri*' (理一), does not remain subordinate to the One *Ri*. He said, "The differentiation is not manifested temporarily but is itself the way as it should be."[85] This remark implies 'the covert relation of the differentiation to the One *Ri* or the differentiation subsumed in the One *Ri*'. But the differentiated *ri*, in that it is qualified, is distinct from the Primordial One *Ri*.

---

84 Ki Jeong-jin, *Nosaseonsaengmunjip*, Vol. 1, "Dapmunryupyeon", p. 6.
85 Ibid., "Napryangsaui", p. 7.

> "Each differentiation..., as it is qualified, does not cross over its boundary... With respect to the fact that it is subsumed in the One *Ri*, it is extremely covert and deep *ri*, and with respect to the fact that it is a qualified entity, it must have *gi* as its basis."[86]

> "The *Ri* of Taegeuk ... neither allows this to be that nor allows that to be this. Therefore, each entity reveals its own differentiation."[87]

'The differentiation (分)' itself entails the state of 'being qualified', and so refers to *ri* within a certain boundary. In addition, the differentiation is ascribed to the phenomenal world of *gi*. According to Ki Jeong-jin, the formation of a certain thing in the phenomenal world of *gi* itself reveals 'the inevitability of *ri*' and so 'the differentiation is also the inevitable outcome'.

Ki Jeong-jin also called the world of *gi* the world where *ri* (Taegeuk) prevails. By nature the original Taegeuk or the One *Ri* (extremely covert and deep *ri*) is liable to become differentiated. And considering that the theory of 'substance and function (體用)' was applied to the One *Ri* (體) and 'its differentiation into many manifestations (用)', the One *Ri* and its differentiation should not be regarded as heterogeneous but as homogeneous concepts.

Ki Jeong-jin, attaching much importance to 'the differentiation (分)' manifested in substance, expressed his view of the differentiation as follows:

> "To the extent that we can perceive it, differentiation is 'the minute logic (條理)' of the One *Ri*, so there cannot be any severance between the One *Ri* and its differentiation. Not its differentiation but 'its differentiation into many manifestations (分殊)' is the counterpart of '*riil* (理一, the One *Ri*)'. *Riil* is so named for it alone subsumes numerous differentiations into concrete manifestations. In this sense *riil* may also be called '*ilmul* (一物, the One Thing)' because it alone

86 Ibid., p. 15.
87 163) Ibid., "Dapmunryupyeon", Vol. 1, pp. 2-3.

subsumes all things."[88]

> "My view implies the combination or reconciliation of *ri* and its differentiation. It is unnecessary to argue about their identity or difference because they can be compared to 'substance (體)' and 'function (用)' that have 'one and the same origin (體用一原)', the inseparable 'primordial world and the phenomenal world (顯微無間)', and 'the difference of sameness (同中有異)' and 'the sameness of difference (異中有同)'."[89]

Ki Jeong-jin regarded the differentiation as 'the minute logic (細條理)' belonging to *ri*. Therefore, according to him, there cannot be any severance between *ri* and its differentiation because the Primordial *Ri* is 'che (體, substance)' while the process of differentiation is its *yong* (用, function). So *ri* and its logic of differentiation are reconcilable with each other. Thus his view may be called 'the theory of the sole origin of *ri* and its differentiation (理分一原說)' or 'the theory of their reconciliation (理分圓融說)'. In this context he also called the relation of *ri* and its differentiation into many manifestations the inseparable relation or the relation of mutual accompaniment.[90] In conclusion, according to Ki Jeong-jin, the world of *gi* is the fulfillment of the logic of *ri* and is subsumed in and identified with *ri*. On this account his view on the universe can be said to have been based on an extremely monistic view of *ri*.

(4) The Extended Application and Significance of the Monistic View of *Ri*

Generally speaking, our given view on the universe may have some relevance to our views on the human being, 'mind and nature (心性)' and society, for there is an instinctive need to maintain compatibility

88 Ibid., "Napryangsaui", Vol. 16, p. 5.
89 Ibid., p. 14.
90 Refer to Bak Hak-rae, *A Study on Ki Jeong-jin's Philosophy* (Research Institute of Korean Studies, Korea University, 2003).

between our systems of thought. With respect to this imperative, the extremely *ri*-oriented view of *ri-gi*' is liable to impose its fundamental tenets on the universe and all subjects of philosophy within it.

Ki Jeong-jin tried to interpret the four beginnings and the seven feelings and the identity of or difference between human nature and the thing's nature on the basis of the monistic theory of *ri*. In the debates on four-seven he accepted only 'the issuance of *ri* (理發)', not 'the issuance of *gi* (氣發)'. He rejected not only Yi I (李珥)'s position on 'the issuance of *gi* alone (氣發一途說)' but also Yi Hwang (李滉)'s 'mutual issuance of *ri* and *gi* (理氣互發說)'. Ki even criticized Yi Hwang's contrast between the four beginnings and the seven feelings, for Yi mentioned 'the issuance of *gi*' as well as 'the issuance of *ri*'. Ki supported only 'the issuance of *ri* alone (理發一途說)'.[91]

Ki Jeong-jin's view on the status of human nature vis-a-vis the thing's nature was aligned with his view on the four-seven. It is tempting to suppose that Ki's insistence on their identity might have resulted from his inheritance of Yi Gan (李柬)'s view on their identity based on original nature and his disregard of *gi*. Ki's view, in fact, was different from Yi Gan's. Yi's original nature referred to The Mandate of Heaven, the Great Ultimate (太極, Taegeuk) and 'the five constant virtues (五常)' of benevolence, righteousness, propriety, wisdom and fidelity. Ki, however, consistently insisted that original nature refers only to the five constant virtues. He said, "Heaven endowed the human being and the thing with nothing other than the five constant virtues."[92] On the basis of this belief Ki insisted on the identity of human nature and the thing's nature. So it may be said that Ki's view of the five constant virtues as constitutive of original nature is more relevant to the field of ethics than that of Yi Gan.

Ki Jeong-jin's theories of the universe, mind and nature, and *ri-gi* were all formulated on the basis of the superintendency of *ri*. So in order to fundamentally grasp the tenets of Ki's philosophy we

91 Refer to Ki Jeong-jin, *Nosaseonsaengmunjip*, Vol. 16, 'Oepil'.
92 Ibid., "Napryangsaui," p. 11.

have to closely examine this aspect of his thought. We have seen that *ri*'s superintendency started from the substitution of *ri*'s 'natural principle (所以然)' for 'The Mandate of Heaven (天命)'. In other words, the concept of the superintendency of *ri* is formulated by replacing The Mandate of Heaven with the proposition, "Heaven is *ri* (天卽理)."

Neo-Confucian scholars usually compared the superintendency of *ri* over *gi* to horse riding. Ki Jeong-jin also said:

> "*Ri* naturally accompanies things. Though *ri* entrusts its authority to *gi*, *gi* receives orders from *ri*. The relation of *ri-gi* is like that of a rider and a horse. What actually runs is the horse but it runs quickly or slowly in accordance with the commands of the rider."[93]

Ki Jeong-jin understood that *gi*'s practical function is "what *ri* entrusts to *gi*." And he said that while *gi* like a horse has practical ability, *ri* like a rider has no such ability. However, he pointed out that the horse runs quickly or slowly in accordance with the commands of the rider. Likewise, 'the superintendency of *ri*' refers to *ri*'s orders to *gi*. Though *ri* has little or no actual function, it is intrinsically endowed with authority. In this context he said, "The issuance of *ri* means that *gi* follows the dictates of *ri* obediently."[94]

If the superintendency of *ri* is 'actually insubstantial, it may be of no practical use. But this is not always so, as there are times when such a superintendency can be of practical use. To make an analogy with the human world, even when a king is incompetent and cannot exercise his sovereign power, his existence itself can at least safely guarantee the succession of the throne to one of his descendants. In a similar way, *ri*'s superintendency reminds us of the phrase, 'Governance without governing (無爲而治)' [on the premise that there is a competent replacement for the king].

To understand all phenomena on the basis of *ri* alone is 'princi-

93 Ibid., "Dapgwonsineon", Vol. 4, p. 13.
94 Ibid., *Oepil*, Vol. 16, p. 26.

ple-oriented thinking'. However, it does not necessarily mean that all things are inevitable. Neo-Confucian scholars like Ki Jeong-jin thought that *ri* comprises 'soiyeon (所以然, natural principle)' and sodangyeon (所當然, normative principle). Ki attached more importance to sodangyeon or 'moral value'. Thus it may be said that his monistic view of *ri* was relevant to his aim of vindicating 'the existing moral order and system (the contemporary dynasty)'. Here we may confirm the conservatism of his thought.

His philosophy also seems to have been associated with the contemporary state of affairs, and he is presumed to have been deeply concerned with 'reforming obsolete systems'. During his lifetime high officials indulged in corrupting practices and reduced people to the greatest misery, while the Japanese imperialists were watching for an opportunity to invade Korea. Ki Jeong-jin and other scholars, who were active in the party dedicated to 'the defense of orthodoxy and the rejection of heterodoxy (衛正斥邪)', [95] tried to redress the damage caused by domestic corruption while defending Korea from unlawful foreign invasions. So it may be said that Ki's monistic theory of *ri* based on rationality ultimately pursued 'righteousness' which had to be rehabilitated urgently. I believe that in this focus lies the broader significance of his monistic theory of *ri*.

8. The Development of the Neo-Confucian Theory of *Simjeukri*

(1) The Conception of Ri-oriented *Simseol*

In the 19th century when Ki Jeong-jin elaborated his view of the universe on the basis of the monistic theory of *ri*, a scholar named Yi Jin-sang (李震相, pen name Hanju 寒州, 1818-1886) devoted himself to *simseol* (心說, the theory of mind/heart) or *simhak* (心學, the learning of mind/

95 Representative scholars included in this party are Ki Jeong-jin, Yi Hang-ro, Kim Pyeong-muk, Yu In-seok, and Yi Jin-sang.

heart). In his childhood Yi Jin-sang learned under the tutorship of his uncle Yi Won-jo (李源祚) who was a Neo-Confucian scholar. In accordance with the teaching of his uncle he attached much importance to the methodology of learning and understanding autonomously. He strove diligently to develop a methodology of learning and came to have a well-informed opinion on the kinds of form and logic' applicable to the development of Neo-Confucian theories. For instance, he regarded the concepts of the inseparability and the separability of *ri* and *gi* as 'the view of combination (合看)' and 'the view of separation (離看)' respectively, and classified the methods of developing theories or forms of understanding into 'the lengthwise view (竪看)', 'the crosswise view (橫看)', 'the inverted view (倒看)', 'the serial view (順看)', and 'the contrary view (逆看)'.[96] Such a methodological research was rarely found in the work of other Neo-Confucian scholars.

A Neo-Confucian scholar, Yi Jin-sang probed into the theory of *ri-gi* for he believed that it was 'the intellectual core (頭腦)' of learning.[97] Like Ki Jeong-jin he attached more importance to *ri* than to *gi* and he had an affinity for the *ri*-oriented *ri*-principal. He held that *simbeop* (心法) handed down by sages in ancient times was a theory based on the *ri*-principal.[98] *Simbeop* sometimes means the methodology of learning passed down from mind to mind but, more than that, it means the method of cultivating mind and the method of understanding mind. His theory of mind based on the primacy of the *ri*-principal was formed in this context. Yi Jin-sang wrote *Simjeukriseol* (心卽理說, *The Theory of Mind as Ri*) at the age of 44 (in 1861). At the age of 60 (1878) he composed his most representative work *Rihakjongyo* (理學綜要) on the basis of *Simjeukriseol*. Thus his theory of '*simjeukri* (Mind is *ri*)' based on the Neo-Confucian *ri*-principal achieved its fullest expression in *Rihakjongyo*.[99]

---

96 Refer to Song Chan-sik, "The Epistemology of Ri-oriented Scholars in the Late Period of Joseon", Vol. 18, *Dong Bang Hak Chi* (東方學志) (Yonse University, 1978).

97 Yi Jin-sang, "Dapyiginyeo", *Hanjuseonsaengmunjip*, Vol. 16, 'Seo'.

98 Ibid.

99 According to his "Jujaeoryuchauiseo", the motive of his initiation of such

When Confucian scholars talked about '*simhak* (心學, learning of mind)' or '*simjeukriseol*', they usually had in mind the works of Lu Chiu-yuan (陸九淵) and Wang Shou-ren (王守仁). Lu-Wang's *simhak* based on *simjeukriseol* is famous as the counterpart of Cheng-Zhu's theory of *seongriseol* (性理說, the theory of human nature and *ri*). Originally, however, Neo-Confucian scholars used the term '*simhak*' for the cultivation and understanding of *simseong* (心性, mind and human nature). The theory of the human mind and moral mind advanced in the Original Confucianism, and the vogue of cultivating *simseong* by Korean Neo-Confucian scholars such as Yi Hwang and Yi Jin-sang who devoted themselves to reading *Simgyeong* (心經) and *Simgyeong-buju* (心經附註) were all called *simhak*. Thus Neo-Confucian scholars belonging to the intellectual lineage of Cheng-Zhu were enthusiastic about developing their own concept of *simhak*. Nevertheless, Neo-Confucian scholars ascribed '*simjeukriseol*' to Lu-Wang's ideas and thoroughly rejected Lu-Wang's theories. Unexpectedly, however, Yi Jin-sang proposed *simjeukriseol* after his extensive inquiry into *simseong* (心性, mind and human nature). Both in Korea and in China, Yi Jin-sang was the only scholar that explored *simjeukriseol* from Cheng-Zhu's point of view. As a result, he was the sole source of Neo-Confucian *simjeukriseol*. His conception of *simjeukriseol* was unique to this extent.

(2) The Development of *Simjeukriseol* Based on the *Ri*-principal

As mentioned above, Yi Jin-sang wrote '*Simjeukriseol* (心卽理說, *The Theory of Mind as Ri*)' at the age of 44. He did not haphazardly mention '*simjeukri* (心卽理, "Mind is *ri*")', as it was a theory developed throughout his philosophical thinking. This theory, beginning with the proposition, "In the discussion of *sim* (mind) nothing is better than *simjeukri*",[100] was his central contribution. I will now summarize his

a theory was traced beck to his study of *Jujaeoryu* (朱子語類)for 11 years since he was 39 (1857-1867).

100 Yi Jin-sang, "Simjeukriseol", *Hanjuseonsaengmunjip*, Vol. 32, 'Japjeo',

concept of *simjeukriseol*.

First of all, Yi Jin-sang explained that he meant by '*sim* (心)' not the heart described in medical science but the object of discussion in Neo-Confucianism. He defined *sim* as the combination of *seong* (nature) and *jeong* (feeling)[101] or the combination of *ri* and *gi*.[102] He was influenced by Zhu Xi's and Yi Hwang's view and said that *seong* (性) is the substance of *sim* while *jeong* (情) is the function of *seong*.

He continued to explain the terms introduced in his theory. Though he defined *sim* as the combination of *ri* and *gi*, from time to time he stated, "*Sim* is *ri*." On such occasions he explained that he maintained this only with respect to *ri* or with respect to the *ri*-principal.[103] Moreover, he attempted to support his attitude of insisting on *simjeukri* as follows.

• He attempted to provide a basis for his view through a logical interpretation based on the composition of *sim*. According to him, *sim* is the combination of '*seong* (性, human nature)' and '*jeong* (情, feeling)'. As '*seong* is *ri* (性卽理)', the substance of *sim* is *seong*, and *jeong* is the *seong* that has already issued, *seong* and *jeong* refer only to one and the same *ri*, and therefore *sim* is evidently also *ri*.[104]

• In addition to the understanding based on the composition of *sim*, Yi Jin-sang discussed the subject of good and evil 'before the issuance (未發)' of *sim*. As his predecessors including Yi Hwang had pointed out, before the issuance of *sim gi* has no function, and *sim* is composed solely of *ri* and thus is in the state of goodness or beneficence. Thus, Yi Jin-sang concluded that '*simjeukriseol* (心卽理說)' is tenable before the issuance of *sim* when *gi* is absent and only *seong* or the substance of *sim* exists. [105]

• Yi Jin-sang also tried to support his theory by considering 'the

p. 677.
101 Ibid., p. 677.
102 Ibid., p. 679.
103 Ibid., p. 678.
104 Ibid., p. 677.
105 Ibid.. p. 678.

superintendency (主宰)' of *sim* after its issuance. The function of *sim* after its issuance is 'the superintendency of one body', and *sim* is mentioned with respect to the combination of *ri* and *gi*. As the function of *gi* seems to grow superior to that of *ri* after the issuance of *sim,* Yi even acknowledged 'the physical nature (氣質之性)' of *sim*. Here Yi maintained, "In the presence of *gi, seong* may incline toward evil and we cannot but say that *seong* is evil, and *sim* may become impudent and cunning. However, 'the real substance (眞體)' of *sim* is by no means confined to *gi*."[106] To this effect, Yi recalled Zhu Xi's remark, "The *seong* (the four virtues of benevolence, righteousness, propriety and wisdom) existing before the issuance of *sim* is manifested as *jeong* (the four beginnings of compassion, sense of shame, concession, and sense of right or wrong) after the issuance of *sim*."[107] So Yi distinguished the *sim* that manifests the four virtues and righteousness or justice from the *sim* that inclines toward *gi*, and called the former 'the true mind (眞心)' or 'the original mind (本心)'.[108] The true or original mind represents the real substance of mind. Yi recalled Zhu Xi's proposition again, "*Sim* is in fact the subject of superintendency and *ri* is responsible for superintendency."[109] According to Yi, as both *sim* and *ri* ultimately superintend, it is only rational to say, "*Sim* is *ri* (心卽理)."

• To this point we have summarized Yi Jin-sang's support for the theory of 'simjeukri (心卽理)'. Now we will evaluate Yi Jin-sang's fully developed theory. His explanation of the theory of *simjeukri* before the issuance of *sim* is conducted on the basis of the compositional capacity of *sim*, that is, only on the basis of *seong* (the substance of sim) without regard to the function of *gi*. In this respect, Yi's theory of *simjeukri* may be said to have been supported through the consideration of the two aspects of the composition and function (superintendency) of *sim*. And '*seong* (性)' as the substance of *sim* plays the key role in his theory. As *seong* is *ri* and *ri* implies moral obligation, the theory of

106 Ibid., p. 677.
107 Ibid., p. 677.
108 Ibid., p. 679.
109 Ibid., p. 677.

simjeukri is also characterized by its moral insight.

• Such a moral characteristic is clearly confirmed in Yi Jin-sang's theory of cultivation. We have seen that he distinguished ordinary *sim* that inclines toward *gi* from *sim* that does not, and called the latter 'the true mind (眞心)', 'the original mind (本心)', and 'the real substance (眞體)' of mind. So cultivation means the recovery of the true mind or the original mind. Yi Jin-sang meant by the original mind 'the mind of a sage (聖人之心)' or 'the Mind of Heaven and Earth (天地之心)'. What matters here is that Yi proposed the recovery of the original mind as the aim of cultivation. In order to free himself from 'the human mind (人心)' and achieve 'the moral mind (道心)' he said, "'The righteousness of the original mind (本心之正)' can be achieved if we maintain watchfulness consistently."[110]

• Yi Jin-sang regarded it as an example of '*simjeukri* (心卽理)' that Confucius said, "At the age of 70, one can follow whatever one's mind craves for without deviating from etiquette (從心所慾不踰矩)."[111] His quoting of Confucius implies that original nature, recovered through cultivation, functions in accordance with the principle of *ri*. It is also in this context that he said, "As my mind is the combination of *ri* and *gi,* only after achieving control over *gi*, instead of reinforcing *ri*, can the true mind achieve purity in any circumstance."[112]

As *ri* is identified with *sim* in Yi Jin-sang's view, he emphasized that the superintending *sim* should guide us to perform good deeds not in accordance with *gi* but *ri*. In other words, his meaning was that the quality of the true or the original mind that fosters the capacity in us to do good deeds is the superintendency of *sim,* which is identical to the normative principle of *ri*. Therefore, his theory of *simjeukri* implies that superintendency as the function of *sim* is identical to the superintendency of *ri*." I conclude that Yi Jin-sang's theory of *simjeukri*, based on the superintendency of *sim* and *ri*, was proposed for the facilitation of moral deeds.

110 Ibid., p. 677.
111 Ibid., p. 677.
112 Ibid., p. 679.

(3) The Purpose of the Establishment of *Simjeukriseol*

Before Yi Jin-sang elaborated his ideas, Yi Hang-ro (李恒老), had proposed the theory of '*simjeukri* (心卽理)' by associating the superintendency of *ri* with that of *sim*. However, Yi Hang-ro mentioned *simjeukri* only once while Yi Jing-sang theorized about it more extensively. In the 19th century the theory of the '*ri*-principal (主理)' was deeply rooted in Korean Neo-Confucianism, and the relation of *ri* and *sim* was intensively investigated. In particular, the study of the superintendency of *ri* reached a climax in the work of Ki Jeong-jin and Yi Jin-sang. Yi, keeping in mind that the superintendency of *ri* underlies that of Heaven, enumerated the implications of *ri* such as cause (所以然), capability (所能然), morality (所當然), inevitability (必然) and spontaneity (自然). He attempted to comprehensively grasp these implications by applying them to '*riilbunsuseol* (理一分殊說)', the four virtues (四德, benevolence, righteousness, propriety, wisdom) and the four beginnings (四端).[113]

We have seen that Yi Jin-sang attached much importance to the superintendency of *sim* and that of *ri* because of the ethical significance they entail. We have also examined the establishment of ethical order as the aim of the theory of *simjeukri* and the resultant significance of this theory in terms of its contribution to the establishment of righteous morals. Such an aim can be ascertained from Yi Jin-sang's criticism of Lu-Wang's theory of *simjeukri* which seemed superficially similar to his own theory. Yi criticized Lu-Wangs theory as follows.

Yi Jin-sang criticized the theories of Lu Chiu-yuan (陸九淵) and Wang Shou-ren (王守仁) for though they superficially advocated *simjeukri*, their theories were in reality similar to '*simjeukgi* (心卽氣, "Mind is *gi*")'. Referring to Lu Chiu-yuan he said, "He regarded *yin·yang* (陰陽) as the way (道) and spirit (精神) as *sim*,"[114] and recalled Zhu Xi's criticism of Lu: "He knows not the disorderliness of physical nature,

113 Youn Sa-soon, *The History of Korean Confucianism* (Jisiksaneopsa, 2012), Vol. 2, p. 243.
114 Yi Jin-sang, "Simjeukriseol", *Hanjuseonsaengmunjip*, Vol. 32, p. 678.

and regards the numerous functions of *gi* as the abstruse principles of *sim*, and absurd acts arising from intention and desire as the consummate expressions of *ri*."[115] According to Yi, Wang Shou-ren's theory was not dissimilar to Lu Chiu-yuan's theory for Wang's view was based on Lu's. Yi also criticized Wang, especially his view on *simjeukri* based on *yangji* (良知, the innate knowledge that distinguishes good from evil). Yi, assuming that *yangji* was the one and only principle of Wang's philosophy, quoted Wang's remark, "The mysterious function (of *yangji*) is spirit (神) and its prevalence is *gi* (氣)." And Yi claimed that Wang's view forsook Taegeuk (太極, the Great Ultimate) and instead regarded *yin·yang* (陰陽) as substance, and that his putative *ri* was indecent, 'not the clean and pure whole'.[116]

Yi Jin-sang thought that to effectively propose the theory of '*simjeukgi* (心卽氣)' by regarding *sim* as *gi* or *gijil* (physical nature) might bring about many immoral practices.

> "Why is it wrong to say, '*Sim* is *gi*'? *Sim* is the superintendent of a body. If the superintendency is under the control of *gi*, the Principle of Heaven (天理) may be subject to *hyeonggi* (形氣, material form), and numerous evils may arise in the mind. *Sim*, having no substance (體), takes *seong* (性) as its substance. However, to insist '*Sim* is *gi*' is to regard 'seong as *gi*.' This view of Kao-tzu's (告子) reduces the human being to the status of the animal."[117]

According to Yi Jin-sang, to regard '*sim* as *gi*' was to regard '*seong* (the substance of sim) as *gi*, and furthermore, 'the *Ri* of Heaven', which is identical to *seong*, as *gi*. In that case, the *Ri* of Heaven may be subject to *gi* or *hyeonggi* (形氣, material form). So Yi claimed that the theory of *simjeukgi* entrusted the superintendency of a body not to *sim* or *ri* but to *hyeonggi*, and that it might thus degrade the status of the human being to that of the animal that lacks the ability to judge

115 Ibid., p. 678.
116 Ibid., p. 678.
117 Ibid., p. 678.

right or wrong. As a matter of course, this criticism was considered to be the ground on which Lu-Wang's putative *simjeukriseol* was marginalized.

We have confirmed that Yi Jin-sang's theory of '*simjeukri* (心卽理)' was proposed in order to overcome the immoral practices entailed by Lu-Wang's theory of *simjeukri,* which had virtually the same characteristics as '*simjeukgi* (心卽氣)' and might diminish the status of the human being to that of the animal without moral consciousness. Evidently, Yi's theory of *simjeukri* was developed with the purpose of encouraging ethical behavior on the basis of the superintendency of *sim* and *ri*. Therefore, it may be said that his theory of *simjeukri* was established on the ground of moral necessity rather than in consideraion of the practical world.

Yi Jin-sang's work is highly evaluated throughout the Confucian bloc of East Asia for his achievement of superceding Lu-Wang's superficial theory of *simjeukri* with his own *simjeukriseol* which belonged to Cheng-Zhu's intellectual lineage. In addition, we should keep in mind that his theory together with the theories of other *ri*-oriented scholars such as Ki Jeong-jin, may well have reflected the spirit of the age and contemporary social circumstances, which made them active in the party dedicated to 'defending orthodoxy and rejecting heterodoxy (衛政斥邪波)'.

Chapter VI.

An Example of Neo-Confucian Silhak — Focused on Yi I's Silhak

1. The Concept of *Sil* and the Terms of Silhak

(1) The Reason for Choosing Yi I's Silhak as an Example

My original plan for the investigation of Korean Confucianism was to examine Neo-Confucian theories in the Joseon Dynasty, and then the De-Neo-Confucian Silhak (實學, Practical Learning) of scholars who were dissatisfied with and attempted to overcome the limits of Neo-Confucianism. However, I inserted the section on Neo-Confucian Silhak between the sections on Neo-Confucian theories and De-Neo-Confucian Silhak. My readers may be curious about the reason. You may also be curious about the meaning of Neo-Confucian Silhak for Neo-Confucianism and Silhak have usually been considered to encompass contrary concepts. So, first of all, I think I should quench your curiosity.

The first scholar who used the term Silhak (實學, Practical Learning) was Cheng Yi in the Chinese Sung Dynasty. He introduced the term 'silhak' to refer to the substantial contents of *The Doctrine of the Mean*. At that time Silhak meant Confucian or Neo-Confucian concepts such as being substantial, practical, pragmatic, and positive. Subsequently, Silhak came to mean a Confucianism inclining toward '*sil* (實, practicality)',[1] or Confucianism itself.

Neo-Confucian scholars in the early period of the Joseon Dynasty had used the term 'silhak' before the scholars of Practical Learning in the late period of the Dynasty. Jeong Do-jeon (鄭道傳) in the early period, Yi I (李珥) in the middle period, and after them Yun Jeung (尹拯) and Jeong Gu (鄭逑) referred to Neo-Confucianism as Silhak. So in order to fully understand Silhak in the late period of the Joseon Dynasty, we have to examine the original Neo-Confucian usage of 'silhak' in the early period.

I will investigate Silhak emerging from Neo-Confucianism before examining De-Neo-Confucian Silhak for the following reason. If I do not inquire into the practical thought implied in Neo-Confucianism after my investigation of the philosophy of Neo-Confucianism, I may cause the misunderstanding that Korean Neo-Confucianism is concerned only with philosophical subjects, and not with pragmatic and practical subjects such as politics, the economy, social studies and national defense. As I have discussed the application of the fundamental principles of Confucianism such as benevolence, righteousness, propriety and wisdom to the real world, there may be little chance of such a misunderstanding. However, I have not gone on to define the category of Neo-Confucianism in my investigation, so I have not classified theories according to whether or not they fall under the rubric of Neo-Confucianism. This is another reason why I will now investigate Silhak emerging from Neo-Confucianism or Neo-Confucian Silhak.

Yi I was one of the representative Korean Neo-Confucian scholars who studied Neo-Confucianism from the viewpoint of the centrality of Silhak. It may not be unsustainable to say that unlike Yi I who studied Silhak *per se*, most Neo-Confucian scholars (including those who were influenced by Yi I's Silhak) in the late Joseon Dynasty focused on partial aspects of Silhak such as the cultivation of self and courteous manners. However, Yi I's focus on '*sil*' had influence even on

1 I'm going to examine the meaning of '*sil*' in the next section.

De-Neo-Confucian scholars of Silhak in the late period of Joseon. Though the ramifications of Yi I's conception of Silhak were different from those of De-Neo-Confucian scholars, his vocation of exploring the *sil* of Silhak was not dissimilar to theirs. Most of the De-Neo-Confucian scholars highly evaluated his spirit of pursuing Silhak directed as it was toward 'timely reform'.[2] So it may be said that De-Neo-Confucian Silhak was related to Yi I's Neo-Confucian Silhak, and in this context Yi I's Neo-Confucian Silhak is regarded as an example of Korean Neo-Confucian Silhak.

(2) The Meaning of *Sil* and *Musil*

In order to grasp Yi I's concept of Silhak, we must first examine his usage of Silhak terms beforehand. He used some of the relevant terms in the following statements.

> "They say, 'A Learner's self-cultivation for the improvement of virtue (進德修業) depends only on maintaining the attitude of reverent mindfulness consistently.' If he does not maintain this attitude, the precept above becomes merely an empty statement. So he should maintain the attitude consistently and incessantly. Valuable precepts should shine through his speech, exemplary conducts through his action... His diligent endeavor should end only when he dies. This is the very essence of Silhak."[3]

> "Those who describe Cheng-Zhu and speak of *seongri* (性理) usually assume solemn airs and carefully select words, and try not to bring any disgrace upon the deceased. However, when they are confronted with the situations of choosing loss or gain, profit or loss, and what is important or what is not, though it is not a matter of life and death, feeling anxious and with glaring eyes, they abandon what

2 The Late De-Neo-Confucian scholars such as Yi Su-gwang, Yu Seong-won, Yi Ik, and then Hong Dae-yong, Bak Ji-won, Jeong Yak-yong, Choi Han-gi highly evaluated Yi I's practical spirit.
3 Yi I, "Japjeo·Hakgyomobeom", *Yulgokjeonseo*, Vol. 15.

> they have cherished. So, how many people could sustain '*samgang* (三綱, the three basic principles in the relations of king and vassal, father and son, and husband and wife)' and '*osang* (五常, the five virtues of benevolence, righteousness, propriety, wisdom, and fidelity)' in times of national crisis? Few people, if any, could do so. This can be ascribed to the fact that Silhak has not yet prevailed and '*sayu* (四維, the four general principles of propriety, righteousness, integrity, sense of shame) has not been unfolded yet."[4]

According to the first statement, one of the precepts of Silhak was to promote a serious attitude of mind for the cultivation of virtue, and on the basis of this attitude the attempt to be an exemplary person in speech and conduct. According to the second statement, it is essential to observe '*sayu* (四維)', '*samgang* (三綱)', and '*osang* (五常)', in order to strengthen national defense. In view of these statements it may be said that Yi I's Silhak was conceived in order to encourage moral conducts through self-cultivation and to strengthen national wealth and power through the abandonment of selfish interest and desire. In fact, Yi I's Silhak has focus and characteristics similar to those of Confucianism, and it corresponds to the typical Confucian view. In other words, with respect to the two statements quoted above, it may be said that Yi I's Silhak was not different from that of traditional Confucianism.

Until this point, the unique and distinctive aspects of Yi I's Silhak have not been unearthed. Only after we examine the meaning of '*sil* (實)' in his concept of Silhak and the contents of his learning to which the meaning was applied, might we fully grasp the intricacies of his Silhak.

---

4 Ibid., "Gi·Buyeohyeonuisagi", Vol. 13.

(3) The Concept of *Sil* and the Limits of Its Application

(A) The Meaning of *Sil* and the Attitude of *Musil*

Yi I frequently used the concept of '*sil* (實)' in works such as *Donghomundap* (東湖問答) and *Seonghakjibyo* (聖學輯要). His frequent use of the concept in itself suggests that he attached much importance to it.

Sil has many implications. It implies the antonyms of falsehood: 'truth (眞)', 'practical fact (事實)', 'practical substance (實質)', 'practical verification (實證)'; the antonyms of surface: inside, kernel, gist, 'substantiality (內實)'; the antonyms of 'voidness (虛)', and 'emptiness (空)': fullness; the antonyms of inefficiency: substance (*silsok*), 'practical efficiency (實效)', 'practical efficacy (實功)'. Occasionally, *sil* even implies existence as the antonym of non-existence. *Sil*, having such a wide range of implications cannot easily be grasped. However, it can be concluded that on the whole practicality present in both 'practical substance (實質)' and 'practical use (實用)' captures the numerous implications of '*sil*'. Yi I's use of *sil* is compatible with the above conclusion. In this context, he said:

> "Like the one who only sees the breakfast table without eating a spoonful of food until the late morning, what can you do with empty words without *sil*?"[5]

'*Sil*' here means substantiality. 'Empty words' without substantiality are like false words and false writings. Yi I also understood'empty words without substantiality' in the same way as 'false words without substantiality'.[6] As one should eat heartily when the table is set, the practical efficiency or the practical efficacy of a word or a project, according to Yi I, is the core meaning of '*sil*'. In this context he said:

---

5 Ibid, *Donghomundap*, Vol. 18.
6 Ibid., "Maneonbongsa", Vol. 5,

> "Now, if the King surely wants to recover 'the old way (古道)' through his reign he should keep in mind practical efficiency."[7]
> "If a politician does not devote himself to practical efficacy, despite his ardent wish, the practical efficiency of his governance will be difficult to achieve."[8]

Yi I meant by *sil* mainly the practical efficacy that is contrary to empty words and false writings. In the context of emphasizing *sil* he suggested the concept of '*musil* (務實, practical endeavor)'. His view was that *musil* was a prerequisite for supplementing his Confucianism with the elements of Silhak. In the beginning of this book I added *sil*, in addition to benevolence, righteousness, propriety, and wisdom, as a fundamental principle of Confucianism because I judged that the concept of *sil* has great importance in Confucianism.

Musil may be summarized as a concept that emphasizes 'practicality (實際性)' which constitutes the meaning of *sil*. Owing to such an emphasis, the spirit of *musil* has been seen as a standard characteristic of Silhak in Korea since Yi I. The reason for linking Silhak with Neo-Confucianism is due to the spirit of *musil* that was taken up in Neo-Confucianism. In this context Yi I's thought on *musil* contributed to the formulation of the view of Confucianism as Silhak.

(B) The Application of *Musil* and Its Intellectual Framework

Yi I suggested in *Donghomundap* (東湖問答) the following ten areas to which the concept of *musil* is applied:

> "The *sil* of '*gyeokchi* (格致, the extension of knowledge through the investigation of things)', the *sil* of '*seongui* (誠意, sincerity)', the *sil* of '*jeongsim* (正心, right mind)', the *sil* of '*susin* (修身, cultivation of mind and body)', the *sil* of '*hyochin* (孝親, filial piety)', the *sil* of '*chiga* (治家, the management of family)', the *sil* of '*yonghyeon* (用賢, the appointment

7 Ibid., *Donghomundap*, Vol. 15.
8 Ibid., "Maneonbongsa", Vol. 5.

of the wise)', the *sil* of '*geogan* (去姦, the removal of deceitful figures)', the *sil* of '*bomin* (保民, the protection of the people)', the *sil* of '*gyohwa* (教化, the enlightenment of the people)'."

The source of the above ten areas is 'The Eight Items' discussed in *The Great Learning* (大學), which comprise '*gyeokmul* (格物, the investigation of things)', '*chiji* (致知, the extension of knowledge)', '*seongui* (誠意, sincerity)', '*jeongsim* (正心, right mind)', '*susin* (修身, the cultivation of mind and body)', '*jega* (齊家, the management of family)', '*chiguk* (治國, statecraft)' and '*pyeongcheonha* (平天下, the governance of the world)'. The ten areas Yi I designated as the fields of application of *musil* take the eight items as their template. Originally, the eight items emerged in the process of teaching the realm and philosophical tenets of Confucianism according to their order of importance. Therefore, the methodology and ideals of Confucianism are implied in these eight items. Yi I's intention of taking the eight items as a model was formed in order to realize the methodology and ideal of *musil* he had suggested himself.

Yi I's ten areas are a little different from the original eight. Among the eight items *gyeokmul* and *chiji* are combined into *gyeokchi*, *jega* is divided into *hyochin* and *chiga*, *chiguk* is intricately divided into *yonghyeon*, *geogan*, *bomin*, *gyohwa* and *pyeongcheonha* is excluded. Though Yi I revised the eight items of *The Great Learning* a little, his intention of adopting them as the fundamental sources of the ten areas to which the concept of *musil* was applied allowed him to embrace the whole of Confucianism through his Silhak, which was based on *musil*.

The contents of Confucian learning were sometimes suggested not by the eight items but simply by '*sugi* (修己, self-cultivation)' and '*anin* (安人, devotion to achieving the comfortable lives of the people)' or *sugi* and '*chiin* (治人, the governance of the people)' or '*jeongdeok* (正德, righteous virtue)' and '*husaeng* (厚生, the welfare of the people)'. *Sugi* and *anin* were first suggested by Confucius and *jeongdeok* and *husaeng* refer only to an aspect of *sugi* and *anin*. Thus *sugi* and *anin* are used not only to distinguish among the contents of Confucianism itself but also to distinguish Neo-Confucianism from Silhak in the late Joseon period. I will now examine Yi I's Silhak on the basis of *sugi* and *anin*.

2. Self-cultivation on the Basis of *Musil*

In Confucianism '*sugi* (修己, self-cultivation)' is the requisite virtue to be practised before '*anin* (安人, devotion to achiving the comfortable lives of the people)', and Yi I's *musil* (務實, practical endeavor) must be applied to self-cultivation before *anin.* Yi I said, "*Musil* is the prerequisite of self-cultivation."[9] Even when he was not conscious of *musil*, Yi I considered self-cultivation the prerequisite of 'the learning to discover my true self (爲己之學)' and attached more importance to self-cultivation than any other scholar. For him self-cultivation should be practiced as follows:

> "The practice of *sugi* requires only *geogyeong* (居敬, attitude of reverent mindfulness), *gungri* (窮理, pursuit of principle), and *yeokhaeng* (力行, diligent practice)."[10]

According to Yi I, the prerequisites of self-cultivation are 'the attitude of reverent mindfulness (居敬)', 'the pursuit of principle (窮理)' and 'diligent practice (力行)'. Reverent mindfulness (敬) is the attitude of concentrating on one object. After assuming the attitude of reverent mindfulness, one should pursue the normative principle for righteous conduct, and then endeavor to put the acquired normative principle into practice. This is the content of Yi I's 'general view of self-cultivation'.

I said 'general view of self-cultivation' because it is the relevant view before the application of *musil*. However, Yi I, in addition to the

9 Ibid., *Donghomundap*.
10 "Nonsugijang, 1", *Yulgokjeonseo*, *Seonghakjipyo*, 2.

general view, had another view on self-cultivation based on *musil*. He said:

> "As the sought-after normative principle has already been illuminated, personal endeavor may be possible. But only after 'the true mind (實心)' arises, can one be endowed with 'practical efficacy (實功)'. Therefore, 'sincerity (誠實)' is the foundation of personal endeavor."[11]

In the above statement Yi I omitted the attitude of 'reverent mindfulness (敬)' and mentioned only the pursuit of the normative principle and personal endeavor, which he substituted for diligent endeavor. He pointed out that personal endeavor does not guarantee practical efficacy as soon as the normative principle is known. According to him, after gaining knowledge of the principle, one can access the true mind and promote the practical efficiency of one's endeavor. He also stated that the foundation of personal endeavor lies in the practice of the principle of 'sincerity (誠實)'. Now, he substituted 'the true mind (實心)' and sincerity for '*gyeong* (敬, reverent mindfulness)', which had been mentioned with respect to 'the general view of self-cultivation'.

What are '*silsim* (the true mind)' and '*seongsil* (sincerity)'? According to the above quotation they are the same in that both of them are related to gaining efficacy. Even in ancient times, *seongsil* meant 'the attitude of mind without falsehood', and so it is not different from *silsim*. At the same time, however, they are distinguished from each other in that '*seongsim* (誠心, sincere mind)' is the mind that may become *silsim*' while '*silsim* is the mind that has already become sincere. However, when the two states of mind are neither strictly distinguished from each other nor denote some characteristic aspect, they are considered to be the same.

The attitude of *gyeong* mentioned in the general view of self-cultivation and *seong* mentioned in the theory of self-cultivation based on

11 Ibid., "Seongsiljang, 5", *Seonghakjipyo*.

'*musil* (務實, practical endeavor)' are also distinguished from each other. Why did Yi I think that *gyeong* and *seong* are different though they usually seem to be the same? We have already seen that Yi I viewed '*geogyeong* (居敬, the attitude of reverent mindfulness)', '*gungri* (窮理, the pursuit of principle)', and '*yeokhaeng* (力行, diligent practice)' as the essential elements of his theory of self-cultivation. His view as such was merely a repetition of the position of preceding scholars including Zhu Xi, who said, "*Gyeong* (敬), which is the concentrated state of the serious mind, is also the alpha and omega of learning."

Yi I distinguished '*gyeong* (敬, reverent mindfulness)' from '*seong* (誠, sincerity)' in their strict senses. According to him, "*Gyeong* is the prerequisite of maintaining endeavor while *seong* is the basis of gaining efficiency."[12] Though *gyeong* and *seong* seem similar to each other, he distinguished them as motive and consequence. As he was conscious of practical efficacy, or '*musil* (務實, practical endeavor)', he used the term *seong* instead of *gyeong* in his consideration of self-cultivation based on *musil* (practical endeavor). [This is the difference between Yi I and Toegye (退溪), who attached more importance to *gyeong* than *seong*.]

So Yi I regarded sincerity as the essence of the true mind and as the prerequisite of self-cultivation. This is the primary characteristic of his theory of self-cultivation based on *musil*. This characteristic is also confirmed in his remarks on self-cultivation'.

> "What is naturally attained is the Way of Heaven and what is attained with endeavor is the way of the human being. Truth without falsehood is the Way of Heaven and trying to be true and not engaging in falsehood is the way of human being."[13]

> "The Way of Heaven is the practical principle and the way of the human being is the true mind."[14]

---

12 Ibid., "Sugi 2, Jeongsimjang 8", *Seonghakjipyo* 3.
13 "Sipyu", *Yulgokjeonseo*, Vol. 6.
14 Ibid.

> "Heaven, with its '*sili* (實理, practical principle)', achieves the efficacy of creation and cultivation. The Human being, with his '*silsim* (實心, the true mind)', achieves the efficiency of '*gamtong* (感通, emotional communication)'. The so-named *sili* and *silsim* refer to no other than '*seong* (誠, sincerity)'."[15]

Originally, *seong* was conceived as the prerequisite of self-cultivation in *The Doctrine of the Mean* : "Sincerity is itself the Way of Heaven and the attempt to be sincere is the way of the human being." So it may be said that Yi I's theory of self-cultivation based on *musil* (務實, practical endeavor) fundamentally developed from the theory of self-cultivation in *The Doctrine of the Mean*. Thus, his aims of self-cultivation were developed firstly to properly practice the way of the human being, and then 'to reconcile the way of the human being with the Way of Heaven'. In other words, his aims of self-cultivation were the pursuit of 'moral behavior' and ultimately the attainment of the Confucian ideal, 'the harmonization of Heaven and the human being (天人合一)' through moral behavior.

3. *Anin* Based on *Musil*

(1) Statecraft in View of Contemporary Circumstances

I have examined the ten areas to which the concept of *musil* was applied. Of them, 'the appointment of the wise (用賢)', 'the removal of deceitful figures (去姦)', 'the protection of the people (保民)' by strengthening the national defense, and 'the enlightenment of the people (教化)' are those that fall under the rubric of *anin* (安人, devotion to achieving the comfortable lives of the people) or *chiguk* (治國, statecraft).

However, Yi I did not leave a single, unified work dealing with the theory of *anin* based on *musil* by binding texts on the four areas

15 Ibid.

together. He only dealt with them separately in his works and in numerous Memorials to the Throne. In particular, as the two areas of 'the appointment of the wise' and 'the removal of deceitful figures' were like two sides of the same coin, he did not deal with them separately even in his Memorials to the Throne. He discussed them in isolation only when he introduced Jo Gwang-jo's (趙光祖, 靜庵, 1482-1519) idea of 'establishing Hyeonryanggwa (賢良科, a government examination for the recruitment of high officials)'.

Yi I emphasized the protection of the people by strengthening the national defense to the extent that he mentioned it in almost all of his Memorials to the Throne. He insisted on the improvement of military affairs and the strengthening of the army through military training. In his *Chronicle* (年譜), he proposed building up 'an army of a hundred thousand soldiers', which was logical in view of his extraordinary emphasis on the strengthening of the army.

As for the enlightenment of the people, Yi I advanced this objective not in a Memorial to the Throne but in his *Yeossihyangyak* (呂氏鄉約), and subsequently, in *Seowonhyangyak* (西原鄉約), *Haejuhyangyak* (海州鄉約), and *Sachanggyeyaksok* (社倉契約束), which were more befitting to the circumstances of Joseon (朝鮮) than *Yeossihangyak*. He also discussed the enlightenment of the people in books written as materials for elementary learning such as *Gyeokmongyogyeol* (擊蒙要訣) and *Hakgyomobeom* (學校模範).

The aforementioned four objectives are included in his 'scheme of reform (更張說)' proposed to advance 'people-oriented (民本)' statecraft and 'for the improvement of the lives of the people (爲民)'. So his view of '*anin* (安人)' based on *musil* should be considered in relation to his scheme of reform rather than with respect to the limited scope of the four objectives. His scheme of reform is summarized below.

First of all, Yi I regarded grasping the contemporary situations as the basis of reform'.

> "What is important in politics is the knowledge of the contemporary

> situations and what is essential in working is 'practical endeavor (務實)'. Politicians who are ignorant of the contemporary situations and workers who do not devote themselves to attaining practical efficacy will not attain the efficiency of good 'administration (治績)' even though there may be sages among them."[16]

According to Yi I, *musil* should be applied to politics in order to attain 'the efficiency of good administration', and the first requirement of politics is to grasp '*siui* (時宜, the contemporary situations)', without which no administrative efficiency can be expected.

Siui presupposes reasonable measures to counter difficult living conditions, and argues that appropriate measures and ideas can be devised by grasping siui comprehensively. To do so is to correctly evaluate contemporary circumstances, which requires a shrewd, keen and accurate sense of reality. Yi I's emphasis on *siui* is itself proof of his insightful sense of reality and practicality.

(2) The Theories and Objectives of Reform

The understanding that *siui* enables may be focused on the abuses and needs of a certain period. Thus the significance of grasping *siui* lies in correcting abuses and satisfying needs. Yi I diagnosed 'the period he lived in'.

> "From of old, when a country drew toward a '*jungsoegi* (中衰期, a period when a country is in decline), people's minds became accustomed to idle lives and the country was in decline... It is about 200 years since our country was founded. Now, it's time to attain The Mandate of Heaven again... If we do not resolutely rise up today, there will be no hope for the future of our country."[17]

> "If a baby falls into a well, even an enemy... will be amazed and

16 "Maneonbongsa", *Yulgikjeonseo*, Vol. 5.
17 Ibid., "July, the 9th Year of the Manryeok Era", *Gyeongyeonilgi*, Vol. 30.

> rescue it. How much more would the parents do? Now, it's long since our country became like the baby falling into the well... This is because the King, as the father of the people, does not devote himself to the betterment of people's lives."[18]

Yi I judged that he lived in an age (the 16th century) called '*jungsoegi* (中衰期)' when various deep-rooted abuses were prevalent. *Jungsoegi* refers to an age when people are helplessly reduced to great misery, like the baby of his parable falling into the well. It is a by-product for us that we realize that Yi I's sense of reality was all too correct. He diagnosed that 'reform (更張)' was the necessary countermeasure to the deep-rooted abuses inflicted upon the people, and to their distress. In fact, reform was an indispensable objective for the governance of the nation'.

> "The circumstances of a country vary in accordance with its age, but they may roughly be classified into the three stages of foundation, maintenance, and reform... To carry out reform in a situation needing maintenance is like giving a dose of a medicine to a healthy person and thereby making the person fall ill. To cling to an established legal system in a situation needing reform is like a sick child refusing to take medicine and lying in bed until he dies."[19]

According to Yi I, 'reform' is as important as 'foundation (創業)' and 'maintenance (守成)'. If it is not carried out when it is needed, a country may perish. So reform is indispensable.

Yi I proposed many schemes of reform in his Memorials to the Throne in the name of *so* (疏), *gye* (啓), *bongsa* (封事), and *chaek* (策). The most representative memorials were "Yukjogye (六條啓)", "Maneonbongsa (萬言封事)", "Uijinsipyeso (擬陣時弊疏)", "Jinsisaso (陳時事疏)", and "Donghomundap (東湖問答)."

The most important aspect of his schemes was 'the aim of reform',

18 Ibid., *Donghomundap*, Vol. 15.
19 Ibid., *Seonghakjipyo*, Vol. 25.

and his aim was to promote the welfare of the people. Here we can confirm 'his thought on people-oriented statecraft and his concern for the improvement of the lives of the people (民本, 爲民 思想)'.

> "Generally speaking, the substitution of the new for the old is based only on the judgment of 'right and wrong', and 'gain and loss', and its cause is to promote the comfortable lives of the people..."[20]

> "To say that there is no substance in the present policies refers to the fact that old laws have caused corrupt practices and have had injurious effects upon the people. So by establishing new policies and abolishing corrupt practices we can allow the people to live in comfort."[21]

According to him, reform should aim at achieving the comfortable lives of the people. The following statement shows that his concern for the improvement of the lives of the people was based on his people-oriented thought.

> "The people depends on food and the State depends on the people. Without food the people cannot live and without the people the State cannot exist."[22]

The above statement implies Yi I's people-oriented thought that echoed fundamental Confucian statecraft since Mencius. He also inherited Mencius' people-oriented thought, which was implied in Mencius' dictum, "The people is the most valuable element, the State is secondary, and the King is less valuable than the State."[23]

In his Memorial to the Throne called "Maneonbongsa (萬言封事)" Yi I proposed, under the title of 'Anminwigang (安民爲綱, The measures for

20 Ibid., "Dapseonghowon", Vol. 11.
21 Ibid., "Maneonbongsa", Vol. 5.
22 Ibid., "Uijinsipyeso", Vol. 4.
23 *Mencius*, Vol. 2,〈Jinsim〉.

the promotion of better lives for the people)', the following five items: ①The King should wholeheartedly attempt to secure allegiance from all the vassals. ②The King should revise the tax system so that the people may not suffer from unreasonably heavy tax. ③The King should eradicate a growing propensity for luxury by stimulating frugal and thrifty living. ④The King should alleviate the distress of the slaves belonging to the central government offices by revising the slave (or hostage) system. ⑤The King should reform military affairs to strengthen the national defense. It is not an exaggeration to say that these five proposals comprise the core ideas of his reform plans.

(3) Yi I's Central Reform Proposals: The Emancipation of Slaves and Freedom of Speech

I believe that the most novel of Yi I's reform proposals were those concerning illegitimate son and slave and 'the formation of free consensus (公論)'. He recommended that competent illegitimate sons be allowed to be qualified for government service and that slaves be given the status of commoners on condition that they completed military service or payed a fee to secure their freedom. He also recommended that the channels of open speech be extended to allow the formation of free 'consensus (公論)'.

Yi I proposed concrete ways of abolishing the system of discrimination against illegitimate sons and slaves, and of elevating their status as follows:

> "... recruit into the army illegitimate sons and public or private slaves who have some military accomplishments. Let them prepare their own dry food and defend the southern province for 20 months or the northern province for a year. After 'The Ministry of Military Affairs (兵曹)' dispatches selected volunteers to their posts, illegitimate sons should be qualified to enter government service and slaves should be qualified to be given the status of commoners... Those who are not

> qualified because they do not have military accomplishments should pay fee to the offices of the southern or northern province to obtain their qualifications... When Yi Si-ae (李施愛)'s revolt broke out long ago, the slaves who carried the military utensils of the government troops were granted the status of commoners and the illegitimate sons who participated in the war were permitted to apply for the government examination. This was the regulation Gwon Si (權時) enforced during the reign of King Sejo (世祖)."[24]

In the period when Yi I lived the discrimination inflicted on Ilegitimate sons was very severe. An illegitimate son, though he hails from the *yangban* (the upper class), could not apply for the government examination to become a public official. Slaves were listed like things so that they might be bought or sold. In that period illegitimate sons and slaves were completely estranged from society. In opposition to such a practise, based on the precedent of Yi Si-ae's revolt, and on the condition of their finishing military service or paying fee, Yi I proposed the reform of permitting illegitimate sons to be qualified to enter the government service and slaves to be qualified to be granted the status of commoner.

His proposals were surely an attempt to advance the fundamental human right'. Though they were not derived from his own ideas, they were epochal when we consider the contemporary social mores in which discrimination was regarded as a matter of course. Here lies the real aspects of 'his thought for the improvement of the lives of the people' that can also be found in his theory of '*anin* (安人, devotion to achieving the comfortable lives of the people)' based on *musil*.

The following is his view on the extension of the channels of open speech for the formation of free consensus:

> "The rise and fall of a country depends on the opening and closing of the channel of speech."[25]

24 "Jinsisaso", *Yulgokjeonseo*, Vol. 7.
25 Ibid., Vol. 3.

"Consensus is the primal force of a country. If consensus comes from the Court, the country may be well governed and when it comes from 'a certain middle class (閭巷)' the country may fall into confusion. If both the upper and middle classes reach no consensus, the country will perish.

... So how can it be right for us to prohibit the formation of consensus?"[26]

"Moreover, establishing 'national policy (國是)' is not a matter of lip-service. What the people is in agreement with is called consensus and the outcome of consensus is national policy. National policy is what the people of a country naturally agree with."[27]

According to Yi I, a consensus is an opinion which the people of a country agree with, and 'the primal force (元氣)' of a country. The closing of the channels of open speech or the prohibition of the formation of consensus, he thought, brings about the fall of a country. The opening of the channels of open speech or the free formation of consensus entails freedom of speech. Yi I also argued that the national policy derived from the ideology of a nation should be adopted through consensus which is derived from the agreement of the people. In this context he called national policy 'the outcome of consensus'.

Yi I did not think that a country is the King's possession or that the people are subject to the King. Actually, his view was similar to the principle that sovereignty rests with the people. Therefore, his people-oriented view was comparable to the democratic idea. In this context he said:

"In old days there was no 'office of advisors' to the King, instead, all retainers of the Court advised the King in accordance with their duties. Merchants debated in markets, passers-by criticized on the road — everyone was an advisor to the King. How wide the scope

26 Ibid., "Daebaeksaamchanso", Vol. 7.
27 Ibid., "Okdangnonwihuncha", Vol. 4.

of public speech might have been!"[28]

This shows that Yi I's people-oriented view even included the affinity for political engagement by the people, albeit in a relatively mild form. This can be called 'the democratic people-oriented view', so I believe that his view of statecraft focused on *anin* on the basis of *musil* was the consummation of the people-oriented view.

4. The Characteristics and Influence of Yi I's Thought on Silhak

Now, I will discuss the characteristics of Yi I's conception of Silhak. It should not be overlooked that its characteristics were derived from his attempt to be faithful, on the basis of *musil*, to the two axes of the original Confucian concepts of '*sugi* (修己, self-cultivation)' and '*anin* (安人, devotion to the comfortable lives of the people).' Given that his Confucianism was seen as Neo-Confucianism, the characteristics of his conception of Silhak should also be grasped in terms of contemporary Neo-Confucianism.

Before the discussion of Yi I's thought on Silhak, some knowledge of the usage of the terms of contemporary Silhak is required. The first Neo-Confucian scholar who regarded 'Neo-Confucianism as Silhak' in the Joseon Dynasty was Jeong Do-jeon. As a primary figure of the revolution that led to the establishment of the Joseon Dynasty, he put Joseon's politics on a solid foundation, and, as a part of his cultural position, rejected Buddhism, which had been the national religion of Goryeo, and promoted Neo-Confucianism as the governing ideology of the new dynasty. Substituting Neo-Confucianism for Buddhism, he compared them and called Neo-Confucianism 'Silhak (Practical Learning)'.

Jeong Do-jeon proclaimed, "Recently Buddhism has grown more

28 Ibid., "Okdangjinsipyeso", Vol. 3.

eccentric, dissolute, wicked, and impractical, while Neo-Confucianism is the Silhak aiming at the realization of old sages' 'illustrious virtue(明德)' and 'the renewal of the people(新民)'."[29] Here he maintained that Buddhism is a form of vacuous learning of no practical utility while Neo-Confucianism teaches people to cultivate the virtue of original nature and has a practical utility that is beneficial to people's lives.

To explain in more detail, Neo-Confucianism had been formulated in the process of reorganizing 'the Original Confucianism(本源儒學)' in order to overcome the limits of Buddhism. As Jeoeng pointed out, Neo-Confucian scholars laid emphasis on self-cultivation by illuminating illustrious virtue or the beneficent original nature, and on the basis of people-oriented thought they attempted again to enlighten the people by encouraging them to observe propriety. In this context Neo-Confucian scholars asserted that their learning was more 'substantial and practical' than that of Buddhist scholars. This was the background against which Neo-Confucianism began to be called Practical Learning'.

Since then Neo-Confucian scholars had devoted themselves to self-cultivation more thoroughly than their predecessors and called Neo-Confucianism a form of learning aimed at developing 'one's true self(爲己之學)'. And such a trend developed into the comprehensive practice of 'propriety and good morals'. Actually, while Buddhism had the tendency of 'escaping from reality', Neo-Confucianism had the practical tendency of 'emphasizing good morals', and for that reason it was natural for Neo-Confucianism to be called Silhak (Practical Learning). Moreover, as the emphasis on governance for the people could not be found in Buddhism it was quite reasonable for Neo-Confucianism to be associated with Practical Learning.

Moreover, Yi I's theory, in which he emphasized the true mind(實心) or sincerity by applying the concept of 'the *sil* of *musil* (務實, practical endeavor)', can safely be said to be a theory of 'Neo-Confucian

---

29 Ibid., "Okdangjinsipyeso", Vol. 3.

Practical Learning'. Like preceding Neo-Confucian scholars, he also advocated the governance of the people under the sway of people-oriented thought. However, he alone proposed practical schemes for social improvement based on *musil* in the name of '*gyeongjang* (更張, the reform of abuses that cause the distress of the people)'. His proposals may also be regarded as a characteristic of 'Neo-Confucian Practical Learning'. It was not accidental that De-Neo-Confucian as well as Neo-Confucian scholars in the late period of the Joseon Dynasty began their scholarly careers by learning Yi I's 'practicality-oriented thought' or being influenced by his practical spirit.

However, Neo-Confucian Silhak after Yi I, without undergoing any fundamental change, passed for Silhak only in opposition to Buddhism. Additions to the tenets of Silhak after the 17th century were seen only in Yun Jeung (尹拯, 1629-1714)'s Silhak which was focused on *silsim* (實心, true mind) and Jeong Gu (鄭逑, 1543-1620)'s Silhak, focused on 'the learning of propriety (禮學)'. Aspiring scholars of Neo-Confucian Silhak, without presenting any unique reform ideas as Yi I had, admitted the weakness of Joseon's social system and focused their attentions primarily on self-cultivation and propriety.

On the other hand, De-Neo-Confucian Silhak scholars since the 17th century had criticized Neo-Confucianism as well as Buddhism as vacuous or impractical fields of learning. Scholars of De-Neo-Confucian Silhak in the late period of Joseon, though they admitted the importance of self-cultivation just as the scholars of Neo-Confucian Silhak had, attached more importance to reforms aimed at the improvement of the lives of the people, and the reform measures they proposed were more far-reaching than those of Yi I. For instance, De-Neo-Confucian scholars such as Yu Hyeong-won (柳馨遠, 1622-1673), Yi Ik (李瀷, 1681-1763), Bak Ji-won (朴趾源, 1737-1805), and Jeong Yak-yong (丁若鏞, 1762-1836) even argued for 'the elimination and reorganization of the social system of the Joseon Dynasty'. In addition, they revised the terminological definitions of Silhak so that the renovated concepts might be adequate to the requirements of reform, and established, through new approaches to classical studies, De-Neo-Confucian philosophy which incorporated De-Neo-Confucian Silhak. The reason why Silhak is generally associated with De-Neo-Confucianism can be ascribed to the positive view of reform entailed by the De-Neo-Confucian or Anti-neo-confucian trend.

Chapter VII.

The Characteristics of De-Neo-Confucian Silhak

1. The Opposition to Self-professed Neo-Confucian Silhak

(1) The Impracticality of Neo-Confucian Silhak

The Silhak (實學) of the Chinese Qing Dynasty rejected both Zhu Xi's and Wang Shou-ren's learning — the latter more comprehensively than the former. The rejection was rooted in the fact that the propagation of Silhak had been facilitated by the Chinese Han ethnic group's affinity for it. When th'e Han were subordinated to the Manchurian ethnic group, there was an attempt to overcome the abuses of Wang Shou-ren's learning that had become similar to zen-Buddhism (禪佛教).

The De-Neo-Confucian Silhak of Korea formulated in the late period of Joseon (from the 17th century to the late 19th century) was similar to the Silhak of the Qing Dynasty. However, as Korean Silhak did not experience the abuses of Wang Shou-ren's learning, it did not forcefully reject Wang's learning, as was the case in the Qing Dynasty. Korean scholars of Silhak in the late period of Joseon generally tolerated Wang's learning and some of them like Hong Dae-yong thought rather favorably ot it. Korean Silhak in the late period of

Joseon arose as a reaction to Neo-Confucianism, which had brought about many abuses since the middle period of Joseon.

Korean politics based on Neo-Confucianism became disorderly from the 16th century on, and after the invasions of Japan (1592-1598) and Qing in the 17th century the Korean people lived in utmost distress. Korean Silhak emerged as a reaction to the incompetence of politicians, and aimed for the improvement of the impoverished lives of the people. Some Confucian scholars thought that the people, who had been driven into miserable circumstances, could not be helped without resolute reform measures. De-Neo-Confucian Silhak in the late period of Joseon rose as a consequence of such people-oriented thought. Therefore, Korean Silhak was more concerned with overcoming the limits of Cheng-Zhu's Neo-Confucianism rather than with rejecting Wang's learning. This is the difference between De-Neo-Confucian Silhak in the late period of Joseon and the Silhak of the Qing Dynasty.

The rise of De-Neo-Confucian Silhak was an inevitable outcome of the general trend of thought in the late period of Joseon, embodied in philosophies such as Neo-Confucian Silhak mentioned at the end of my review of Yi I's Silhak. For example, Yun Jeung (尹拯, 1629-1714) who was a Neo-Confucian scholar deeply versed in Yehak (禮學, the study of propriety) called his own learning Silhak (Practical Learning). However, his Silhak was biased toward self-cultivation or 'the true mind (實心)' — he was not concerned with the miserable lives of the people. Jeong Gu (鄭逑), who was also a scholar of Yehak, regarded Silhak only as a form of learning that pursues and practises propriety. The study of the true mind and propriety helped to cultivate personality and could be said to have its own practicality. It was true that such a practicality was highly evaluated by the 17th and 18th century Neo-Confucian scholars who specialized in the study of propriety. However, the value of their focus could not be said to be equal to the worth of the focus on the welfare of the people. In short, the true mind and propriety could not fill people's empty stomachs, whcih was the very decisive defect that plagued Neo-Confucian Silhak in the late period of Joseon. The attitude of regarding the study of propriety as Silhak might be said to have had practical efficacy only in comparison with the practice of Buddhism. The 'disputes on propriety (禮訟)' in the latter part of the 17th century (from 1659), which was a case of partisan strife, was not free from the criticism of vacant disputes seen from the perspective of people-oriented thought. What mattered was that governance through propriety could not solve the accumulated problems in the late period of Joseon (especially from the latter part of the 18th century to the 19th century). I will now examine these problems in detail.

(2) The Abuses of Governance and the Neo-Confucian Circle

In the late period of Joseon (from the 17th to the 19th centuries) most people were badly off because of the depravity of 'the three policies (三政)', which referred to the land, conscription and government grain loan repayment policies. The hardship inflicted by these three policies was the main cause of the outrage of ordinary people.

Land in the Joseon Dynasty was principally owned by the State. National revenue was primarily gathered through the taxes paid by the tenants of state-owned land. However, as large tracts of land had been exempt from taxation since the early period of Joseon, the nobility and wealthy landowners manipulated landownership and, with the passage of time, discreetly came into possession of such large tracts. Moreover, the Japanese invasion in 1592 caused the devastation of the agricultural system and brought about a marked decrease in national revenues, and as a consequence ordinary people had to bear a heavier burden of tax. In addition, corrupt officials levied, under various pretexts, additional taxes, various charges, and even taxes on unproductive land. The enforcement of the conscription policy also led to a confusion. Young men had to serve in the army, and in the event that they couldn't they had to pay a certain amount of cotton cloth or hemp cloth to the government. And the shortfall in revenue was met through new and unfamiliar taxes such as 'the fishery and salt tax' and 'the shipping tax'. Taking advantage of the original system under which the nobility, petit bourgeois town officials and slaves owned by government offices were exempt from military service, and of the progressive breakdown of public order, some ordinary people evaded their military service by currying favor with and bribing influential persons. Owing to this underhanded practice, it was necessary for public officials who had been bribed to exaggerate the number of soldiers in the army. Taxes were often levied on children who were falsely recorded as adults in tax registries, and even on dead men. Such unjust chicanery eventually forced people to leave their hometowns and move to unfamiliar places. The purport of the government grain loan system was to lend grain to poverty-stricken farmers and to recover from them the same amount of grain plus a little interest after harvest time. It was originally established for the relief of poor people. However, in the 17th century the system was transformed, and led to the offering of loans at onerous interest rates, which brought about the greatest abuses of the aforementioned three policies. Those who exploited farmers through unreasonably high interest rates were mostly 'petit bourgeois town officials (衙前)'. The fact that they were unpaid officials was a weakness in the system of government. Their lack of salary functioned as a signal for them to commit theft, and they exploited farmers in various ways. Magistrates of district offices who were in charge of petit bourgeois officials were also eager to satisfy their greeds. Many magistrates overlooked these officials' embezzlement of money and grain belonging to district offices, and in fact conspired in the theft with them. Though 'the secret royal inspectors (暗行御史)' dispatched by the central government checked on district offices from time to time, the inspectors could not eradicate the widespread illicit financial dealings and abuses of power. Consequently, the fraudulent burden accompanying the repayment of grain became the cause of nationwide insurrections of the people. In this way the abuses of the three policies put people into distress, and ultimately incurred the fall of the Joseon Dynasty.

Owing to such critical conditions that brought about the decline of the Joseon Dynasty, some Confucian scholars came to feel skepticism toward, discontent at the methods, capacities and tenets of Neol-Confucianism as a governing ideology. Some Confucian scholars who had mastered Neo-Confucianism as a form of elementary learning pursued the new Silhak, regarding Neo-Confucianism as anything but practical learning, in fact as impractical vacuous learning that had no capacity to overcome the ills of society.

At a minimum, the following scholars should be recognized as the main figures who pursued the New Silhak (De-Neo-Confucianism) from the 17th to the 19th centuries: Yi Su-gwang (李睟光, 1563-1628), Yu Hyeong-won (柳馨遠, 1622-1673), Bak Se-dang (朴世堂, 1629-1703), Yi Ik (李瀷, 1681-1763), Hong Dae-yong (洪大容, 1731-1783), Bak Ji-won (朴趾源, 1737-1805), Jeong Yak-yong (丁若鏞, 1762-1836), and Choi Han-gi (崔漢綺, 1803-1879). These were the representative De-Neo-Confucian scholars in the late period of the Joseon Dynasty.

These scholars thought that the social situations of the late period of Joseon, which we have already discussed reflected the actual limitations of Neo-Confuciansm as the governing ideology of Joseon. So they insisted on the vanquishing of political corruption and criticized the academic climate of Neo-Confucianism. For instance, Jeong Yak-yong wrote about 'the unsound and impractical academic traditions' of Neo-Confucianism:

> "Confucius' learning pursued only 'self-cultivation (修己)' and the righteous 'governance of people (治人)'. Now, scholars daily engage only in the debates on '*ri-gi* (理氣, principle and material force)', '*sa-chil* (四七, four beginnings and seven feelings)', the numbers of 'Hado-Nakseo (河圖-洛書, the coexistence of the five elements and their incompatibility)', and the theories of 'Taegeuk (太極, the Great Ultimate)' and 'Wonhoe (元會, the Unit of Time of the Universe)'. I doubt whether such subjects are relevant to the self-cultivation or renewal of the people."[1]

1 Jeong Yak-yong, "Wibansanjeongsuchiljeungeon", *Dasanjeonseo*, Book

"Now, Neo-Confucian scholars mention '*ri* (理, principle)', '*gi* (material force)', '*seong* (性, nature)', '*jeong* (情, feeling)', '*che* (體, substance)', '*yong* (用, function)', '*bonyeon* (本然, originality)', '*gijil* (氣質, physical nature)', '*gibal* (氣發, the issuance of *gi*)', '*ibal* (已發, the state after issuance', and 'mibal (未發, the state before issuance)'... and think that they diligently pursue the lofty and marvelous principle of Heaven and Earth... Each scholar hoists a banner; each scholar builds a rampart. However, during their whole lifetime the disputes at issue cannot be solved, and for generations they may not untie the knot. They uphold those belonging to their school and treat with contempt those who secede from their school. They revere those belonging to their party and censure those who leave their party. Nevertheless, they think that they stand on righteous ground. How absurd they are!"[2]

Neo-Confucian scholars since the middle period of Joseon devoted themselves to heated debates on nonproductive philosophical theories such as *ri-gi* and four beginnings-seven feelings, and as a result, they had no intellectual energy to expend on practical, real-life issues. Moreover, Neo-Confucian scholars were divided into schools in accordance with the theories they upheld. And the divergent schools, inciting troubles and conflicts among themselves, amplified the impracticality and nonproductiveness of their work.

According to Jeong Yak-yong, the disputes of Neo-Confucian scholars could not be concluded during the lifetime of the participants or even after several generations. The attitudes of scholars inquiring into vacuous issues lacking possible definitive conclusions were compatible with neither the self-cultivation nor the governance of the people mentioned in Confucius' Original Confucianism. Therefore, Jeong judged that such a trend of learning should be superceded. In this light, we can confirm his trajectory toward De-Neo-Confucian Silhak.

Jeong Yak-yong's above statements elucidated the reason why later

1, Vol. 17.
2 Ibid., "Ohakron".

scholars of Silhak believed that contemporary Neo-Confucianism was an impractical form of learning. And his denunciation of or 'opposition to Neo-Confucian scholars' was also the ground on which he formulated De-Neo-Confucian Silhak anew.

2. The Formulation of De-Neo-Confucian Silhak

(1) The Pursuit of Practicality by Making Use of the Spirit of the Original Confucianism

Scholars of De-Neo-Confucian Silhak (實學, Practical Learning) in the late period of Joseon studied Neo-Confucianism as their elementary stage of learning, and so they were very familiar with the strong and weak points of Neo-Confucianism. They also knew that a challenger to Neo-Confucianism, which was the reigning ideology of Joseon, would be stigmatized as 'samunnanjeok (斯文亂賊, those who think and act against orthodox Neo-Confucianism)'. In the 17th century Yun Hyu (尹鑴, 1617-1680) was the first scholar to be killed for broadly opposing Zhu Xi's Neo-Confucianism, based on his knowledge of Confucian classics. Bak Se-dang (朴世堂, 1620-1703) was the second scholar who was killed for a similar reason. These shocking incidents brought about the temporary congealing of the contemporary scholarly atmosphere.

Nevertheless, most scholars of Silhak in the late Joseon period criticized the abuses of the Neo-Confucian unworldly and impractical pursuit of learning and proposed reform plans based on people-oriented thought. Following in the footsteps of Yun Hyu and Bak Se-dang, scholars in the 18th and 19th centuries criticized and rejected Zhu Xi's Neo-Confucian theories. In order to overcome the limitations of Neo-Confucianism, Silhak scholars, first of all, advocated the slogans "Return to the Original Confucianism of Confucius and Mencius" and 'Recovery of the Practical Spirit' of the Original Confucianism. Silhak scholars in the late period tried to reevaluate the Original

Confucianism, just as the Neo-Confucian scholars of Chinese Sung had attempted to rehabilitate the Original Confucianism in order to overcome the limitations of Buddhism.

Like the Silhak scholars in the late period, the Neo-Confucian scholars of Joseon were also intent on the recovery of the Original Confucianism through study of classic texts such as *The Analects of Confucius, The Book of Mencius, The Doctrine of the Mean*, and *The Book of Changes* but for a different reason. Their aim was to discover some theoretical sources that were analogous to Buddhist metaphysical theories such as *seon* (禪) and *karma* and could be helpful to the strengthening of Confucian philosophy and self-cultivation. On the other hand, the Silhak scholar's aim was not to unearth profound philosophical theories but to acquire the wisdom of living in a period of turbulence and rapid changes. In addition, they studied the Original Confucianism, which was far more authoritative than Zhu Xi's Neo-Confucianism, to protect themselves from the oppression caused by their criticism of Zhu Xi's philosophy. The following quotations demonstrate the attitude of these Silhak scholars.

> "According to a classic, one has to pass through a nearby place first in order to arrive at a distant place..., Likewise, one has to enter shallow water first in order to enter deep water... Today, one studies the six classics with the intention of arriving at a far and deep stage of wisdom, neglecting the shallow and familiar stage... However, one should bear in mind that a journey of a thousand miles starts with but a single step."[3]

> "The Sage's speech and behavior are contained in *The Analects of Confucius*. The speech comprises easy and familiar terms and the behavior is also easy to understand and to practise. His behavior never demands a high and difficult standard."[4]

---

3 Bak Se-dang, *Sabyeonrok*, 'Seo'.
4 Ahn Jeong-bok, "Jehahakjinam", *Sunamjip*, Vol. 19, 'Jehu'.

> "In olden days children learned the Six Arts. Therefore, after they grew up, though they did not grasp the profound way, they did not fail to apply themselves to fundamental things. Today, people only try to study classics, abdicate and neglect the understanding of the fundamentals or the learning of the Six Arts."[5]

> "The profound study of the classics presupposes the future observance of their admonitions. To discuss a classic without practicing what it teaches is like only knowing how to read."[6]

> "... one has to daily step on the real ground with real mind and take part in actual worldly affairs. Only with such a true attitude may one foster a noble mind, the development of knowledge, self-cultivation, and the good governance of the people without empty words."[7]

The inability of Neo-Confucianism to deal with worldly matters resulted from its profound but empty theories which neglected the practicality needed in daily life. On the other hand, the methodology of the Original Confucianism was 'to begin from the near and low position' or 'to learn from elementary things'. Thus, sages in the period of the Original Confucianism, first of all, taught the Six Arts of etiquette, music, archery, horse-riding, calligraphy, and calculation. On the other hand, Neo-Confucian scholars, neglecting the Six Arts, were only concerned with the inquiry into the classics and self-cultivation based on reverent mindfulness. This attitude of Neo-Confucianism was the cause of its impracticality. So De-Neo-Confucian Silhak scholars believed that this attitude should be superceded in order to transform Confucianism into 'more truthful Silhak'.

Bak Se-dang, Yi Ik, and Hong Dae-yong thought it important to study the classics and to cultivate the self, and so they acknowledged

---

5 Hong Dae-yong, "Sohakmunjip", *Damheonjip*, Vol. 1, 'Naejip'.
6 Yi Ik, "Poems", *Seonghosaseol*, Book 1, 'Gyeongsapyeon', 'Gyeongsamun', Vol. 6.
7 Hong Dae-yong, "Dapbakrangjaemunhanseo", *Damheonjip*, Vol. 1, 'Oejib'.

the 'attitude of reverent mindfulness (居敬)' and the cultivation of true mind. However, Yi Ik maintained that this acknowledgement was premised on practical utility. According to Hong Dae-yong, study of the classics and self-cultivation should be concerned with actual facts. That is to say, scholars should attempt to 'seek truth grounded in concrete evidences (實事求是, *silsagusi*)'.[8] Hong Dae-yong also said, "One should daily step on the real ground while engaging in worldly affairs." Positive attitude came from attaching importance to worldly affairs and the terrain of reality, and practical utility, according to Bak Ji-won, burgeoned forth from the attachment of importance to practical use and advantage, which had been neglected and rejected by Neo-Confucian scholars. Here we should remember that the utilitarian tendency of Silhak scholars was in the service of achieving the happiness of all people.[9]

When we agglomerate the attitudes of Silhak scholars, we can grasp the intention implied in the maxim, 'the recovery of the spirit of the Original Confucianism'. That is, their intention was to formulate, by making tactical use of the Original Confucian spirit of pursuing practicality, Silhak (Practical Learning), which was appropriate for the situations of the late period of Joseon. Therefore, their fundamental tenet was advanced not as a retrospective echo of the past but as a methodology for eliminating the Neo-Confucian way of thinking. In fact, De-Neo-Confucian Silhak which was appropriate for the actual situations of the late period of Joseon, was not simply a restoration or revival of the Original Confucianism. This was demonstrated by the fact that the principle of 'the recovery of the spirit of the Original Confucianism' disappeared soon after the formulation of

8 Among Korean Confucian scholars, Yang Deuk-jung (1665-1742) and Kim Jeong-hui was the representative scholars who defined the meaning of '*Sil* (實)'. The former defined *Sil* as 'truth' and 'sincerity' while the latter defined *Sil* as 'the pursuit of truth' based on facts'. Hong Dae-yong complied with Kim's definition.

9 Refer to Bak Ji-won, Vol. 4, 'Gwanongsocho', *Yeonamjip*, This tendency can also be found in Neo-Confucian scholars. But it's far more stronger in the late Silhak scholars.

De-Neo-Confucian Silhak.

(2) The Pursuit of Erudite and 'Miscellaneous' Learning and the Evolution of the Theories of Silhak

'The pursuit of practicality' of the Late Silhak scholars was concretized, above all else, by the pursuit of 'erudite learning (博學)'. Contemporary Neo-Confucian scholars regarded Neo-Confucianism as a form of orthodox learning while despising erudite learning as paradoxically unsophisticated 'miscellaneous learning (雜學)'. However, the late Joseon Silhak scholars intentionally pursued erudite learning, indicating that the Original Confucianism also attached importance to this endeavor.

> "According to a classic, "One who is in command of erudite learning speaks and asks in detail." Erudite learning is for one's own sake not for another's. It's wrong to say that erudite learning is for another's sake."[10]

The above quotation is a statement of Yi Su-gwang (李睟光, 1563-1628) who was a predecessor of the late Joseon Silhak scholars. According to him, Neo-Confucian scholars highly respected only self-cultivation and the study of the Principle of Heaven, human nature, *ri*, and *gi* as 'the learning for self (爲己之學)', and neglected the pursuit of erudite learning as 'the learning for others (爲人之學)'. Conversely, Yi Su-gwang believed that erudite learning is 'the learning for self', as had been suggested in the Original Confucian texts such as *The Doctrine of the Mean*. Thus, he justified the value of the pursuit of erudite learning as a kind of the Original Confucian methodology.

His pursuit of erudite learning is represented by his encyclopedic work, *Jibongyuseol* (芝峯類說). Here he dealt with a variety of subjects, namely, astronomy, geography, almanacs, state examinations,

10 Yi Su-gwang, "Hakmun", *Jibongyuseol*, Vol. 5, 'Yudobu'.

education, bureaucratic systems, agriculture, tools, fruit growing, trees and plants, and floriculture. Though he also wrote an essay about Neo-Confucianism in this work, it was only an outline of his fundamental theories.

Even in the 16th century when Neo-Confucianism was prevalent, there were exceptionally a few encyclopedic books. However, in the late Joseon period they came into fashion. For instance, Yu Hyeong-won (柳馨遠, 1622-1673) who was regarded as a predecessor of the late Silhak scholars, together with Yi Su-gwang wrote *Bangyesurok* (磻溪隧錄) which discussed the necessity of reform in various spheres. In addition, Yi Ik (李瀷, 1681-1763)'s *Seonghosaseol* (星湖僿說), Ahn Jeong-bok (安鼎福, 1712-1791)'s *Japdongsani* (雜同散異) and Yi Gyu-gyeong (李圭景,1788-?)'s *Ojuyeonmunjangjeonsango* (五洲衍文長箋散稿) were all encyclopedic texts in that they compiled a wide variety of informations. Jeong Yak-yong (丁若鏞, 1762-1836), who is regarded as the compiler of the late Silhak corpus, wrote hundreds of books dealing with a variety of subjects. He was to his core a man of erudite learning.

Those scholars who highly regarded erudite or miscellaneous and eclectic learning intended to extend their sphere of learning more widely than Neo-Confucianism had, and such an intention led to the transition from the Neo-Confucian view of learning to Silhak scholars' view. In this context Bak Ji-won defined Silhak as follows.

> "In olden days people were classified into 'scholars, farmers, artisans, and tradesmen (士農工商)'. The work of farmers, artisans, and tradesmen as well as the work of scholars originated from sages' experiences and ways of thinking... As scholars' learning comprises the principles of the work of farmers, artisans, and tradesmen, the three kinds of works could not be performed without the contribution of scholars. Who else except scholars could guide farming, establish the channels of trade, and bestow benefits on people through devising new strategies for manufacturing? If farmers, artisans, and tradesmen make mistakes in the future, it is solely due to scholars

who are ignorant of Silhak."[11]

According to Bak Ji-won, Silhak should not only deal with theories of *seong-ri* (性理, human nature and fundamental principles, or Neo-Confucianism) but also illuminate and circulate the principles of agriculture, manufacturing industry and commerce, and in doing so it could ultimately bring benefits to people. Silhak scholars kept in mind this extended scope of Silhak, and thought that it might in the end help 'to make the people wealthy and the country affluent and powerful (裕民益國)'.[12] The practical pursuit of Silhak was ultimately directed toward the fulfillment of such a purpose.

From his patriotic and people-oriented point of view Jeong Yak-yong said that true Confucian scholars' Silhak should aim at "defeating foreign invaders, maintaining ample national wealth and resources, and educating the people to be equipped with both literary and military accomplishments."[13] Choi Han-gi's Silhak in the 19th century added the methods of strengthening the army to those of promoting the wealth of the nation through the study of the four classes (士農工商) of society.[14] In this way Late De-Neo-Confucian Silhak came to have a viewpoint quite alien to that of Neo-Confucian Silhak.

(3) Various Proposals or the Reform of Systems for the Improvement of People's Lives

In the 18th century Yi Ik, who had said, "The value of the study of the classics lies in whether it is useful or not in the future," expressed his view on politics, "The cardinal point of politics is the governance of the people and this governance involves being thoroughly acquainted with the actual conditions of the people." In this context,

---

11 Bak Ji-won, "Gwanongsocho·Jegachongronhubuseol", *Yeonamjip*, Vol. 4.
12 Ibid.
13 Jeong Yak-yong, "Sokyuron", *Dasanjeonjip*, Book 1, Vol. 12.
14 Choi Han-gi, "Samujinhakmun", *Injeong*, Vol. 11.

The Book of Odes (詩經) reads, "Only after taking care of the people's hidden and intimate sufferings can one enable the people to live in comfort."[15] Yi Ik's view was that the central point of politics was to provide the necessities of life such as food, clothing, and shelter, and to enable the people live in comfort. In fact, his primary achievement as a scholar was his *Seonghosaseol* (星湖僿說) in which he proposed the reform of various systems. The reason why his conception of Silhak was understood in terms of 'governance conducted to the advantage of the people (經世致用)' in academic circles was that he discussed the reform of various systems to enable the comfortable lives of the people.

The views, achievements, and reforming spirit of most late Silhak scholars were similar to those of Yi Ik. In the 17th century, earlier than Yi Ik, Yu Hyeong-won insisted on the comprehensive reform of various governmental systems in order to advance the welfare of the people who had been suffering from pain and constrains caused by inconsistent and unjust enforcement of laws and unfair burdens imposed by various systems. His *Bangyesurok* (磻溪隧錄) was famous for its most radical reform plans. It may not be an exaggeration to say that this book represented the views of the Late De-Neo-Confucian Silhak scholars who tried to promote the welfare of the people through the reform of various systems. So it may be said that Yu Hyeong-won was a precursor who led the Late Silhak scholars to focus on governance to the advantage of the people.

The main objects of reform that Yu Hyeong-won mentioned in his *Bangyesurok* were the five systems governing the land, taxation, education, the employment of officials, and slaves. Among them, in view of the contemporary situations, the systems governing the land, education and slaves were more important than the other two systems. I will investigate these three systems and the proposals for their reform.

---

15 Yi Ik, "Poems", *Seonghosaseol*, Book 1, Vol. 6, 'Gyeongsapyeon', 'Gyeongsamun'.

The Reality of the Land System and Proposals of Its Reform

In the Joseon Dynasty '*gongjeonbeop* (公田法, land taxation imposed by the State)' was originally enforced in accordance with the State ownership of land. In the 16th century, in accordance with 'the increase in private ownership of land', *gongjeonbeop* persisted only as a nominal system, which was the first factor behind the miserable lives of farmers. The unjust land taxation imposed on farmers also caused a problem. That is, the land taxation system in which the land tax was levied not relative to the area of land in question but to its yield instigated tax collectors into committing injustices and engaging in fraud, which was the greatest cause of the immiseration of farmers. Moreover, as the royal family and the aristocrats who were exempted from tax increased in number, tenant farmers' tax burden grew heavier. In addition, owing to the hereditary land system, the gap between rich land owners and poor tenant farmers seemed to grow ever wider.

Yu Hyeong-won was keenly aware of the aforementioned abuses and proposed a reform plan of the land system. In the plan he proposed the restoration of '*gyunjeonje* (均田制, the equal field system)', regarding '*jeongjeonbeop* (井田法, the system in which the private ownership and the State ownership of land were assigned in the ratio of nine to one)' as an ideal model. According to his plan, one *gyeong* (頃) of land would be distributed to each person regardless of his social status, whether he be a farmer, merchant, artisan, or even a slave. Land would also be distributed to incumbent officials, unpaid petit bourgeois town officials,[16] students of local and capital areas, the staff of offices, and the employees of educational institutes. But the area of land distributed to various parties would differ in accordance with their social status, with six gyeongs assigned to junior officials, 12 *gyeong*s to the most senior officials, and a half gyeong to petit bourgeois town officials. These

16 These officials refer to low officials of Yiseo (吏胥), Seori (書吏), and servant (僕隷).

were the specifics of his 'gyunjeonron (均田論, the view of the equal field system)'.

Yi Ik's '*gyunjeonje* (均田制)' and Bak Ji-won's '*hanjeonje* (限田制)', which stipulated the minimum area of land necessary for a family subsistence, were extended systems of Yu Hyeong-won's '*gyunjeonje*'. Jeong Yak-yong proposed a unique sort of revised *jeongjeonje* called '*yeojeonje* (閭田制, the system of joint farming per unit village comprising 30 households)'. Such a concerned approach to the problems inherent in the contemporary land system on the part of Silhak scholars reminds us of the fact that the just and competent operation of the land system was essential to the lives of the people. However, none of their proposals was put into practice.

Proposals for Educational Reform and the Abolition of the State Examination

The representative educational institutions of the Joseon Dynasty were the elementary school called Sahak (四學), the highest institution called Taehak or Seonggyungwan (太學 or 成均館) in the capital city, and elementary schools called *hyanggyo* (鄕校) in the regions. In addition, private schools called *seodang* (書堂) and *seowon* (書院) gradually became prevalent between the 16th and the 19th centuries. Masters in seodang and seowon taught sillabi ranging from elementary to advanced learning.

Education at that time aimed at producing persons qualified for government positions. In order to be a public official one had to pass the preliminary examinations called Saenwonsi (生員試) and Jinsasi (進士試), held at local schools, and the final civil service examination called Gwageo (科擧). Furthermore, one could be recommended to be an official on condition that one was acknowledged as a man of outstanding learning and moral behavior. One could also be made an official by Eumseoje (蔭敍制), which referred to the system of appointing individuals as officials on the basis of the merits of their ancestors. The subjects of the preliminary and final examinations were mostly concerned with the literature and fields of knowledge of the Confucian classics, which were irrelevant to administrative works, and contemporary education was focused on the subjects of the examinations. Corrupt officials were produced through the abuses of Eumseoje, which was from the start an unreasonable system, and 'Gwageoje (the format of the final civil service examination)' in the late period of Joseon. Gwageoje designed for the selection of high officials, was itself a misguided enterprise, for the subjects of the examination had little relevance to administrative work.

Yu Hyeong-won did not regard education merely as a means of developing public officials. Therefore he judged that the contemporary educational system was going radically astray, and thought that Gwageoje and Eumseoje should ultimately be abolished. He believed that a completely new educational system should be established and that officials should be selected on its basis. His plan was to establish separate educational institutions for liberal arts and for the cultivation of officials. 'Hyangsang (鄕庠)', to be established in each *myeon* (sub-county) of the provinces, and 'Bangsang (坊庠)', to be established in each *bang* (village) of the capital city, corresponded with the former while schools to be established in local districts such as the primary school called 'Euphak (邑學)', the secondary school called 'Yeonghak (營學)', and schools to be established in the capital city such as the primary school called 'Sahak (四學)', the secondary school called 'Junghak (中學)' and the most advanced school called 'Taehak (太學)' corresponded with the latter.

He laid special emphasis on education for the cultivation of public officials. First of all, he considered the treatment of students. In his plan the students of Euphak and Sahak were associate officials, so he believed they should be given special attention. All the educational expenses students owed were to be paid at national expense: they were to be provided with two to four gyeongs (1 gyeong=9917m) of land corresponding to two to four times the land distributed to farmers, and they were exempt from mandatory military service. All the schools' expenses were also paid at national expense. The number of students of each school was fixed in accordance with the population of the region each school was located.[17]

What was notable in Yu Hyeong-won's proposals was that students had to pass through a strict educational process. After entering the primary schools of Euphak and Sahak, only the students who passed the qualifying examination could enter the secondary schools of Yeonghak and Junghak. After completing the courses offered by the secondary schools, only the students who passed qualifying examination could enter Taehak. Only after finishing their studies at Taehak and the course of specialized practical training at Jinsawon (進士院), could students become officials. Instead of taking the civil service examination of Gwageo, students had to complete this strict process. Yu Hyeong-won's educational plan was designed to enable the appointment of new public officials in accordance with a student's ability or school record. What was also notable in Yu Hyeong-won's proposals was the qualification for entry to Euphak and Sahak. Almost all people regardless of their status (in Yu Hyeong-won's expression, 'all the talented citizens') were qualified to enter the schools. A youth more than 15 years old, even if he was a commoner or an illegitimate child, was permitted entry. However, the sons of tradesmen, artisans, shamans, and public and private slaves were excluded. (Slave here seems to indicate the slave who is engaged in a specialized job')

The sons of tradesmen and artisans were excluded apparently in consideration of the necessity of retaining diverse types of manpowers in Joseon, or because it was believed that they could do their work efficiently with only a basic humanities education. In any case, their proposed exclusion from entry to the reformed school system seems to have been a defect of Yu Hyeongl-won's educational reforms. However, in a period when education typically meant taking the next

17 Refer to Jeong Gu-bok, "Bangye Yu Hyeong-won's thought of social reform", *The Bulletin of History*, 1970, Vol. 45.

step to the status of public officials, his plan of providing education of the humanities in schools called Hyangsang and Bangsang should be evaluated highly in that the plan may have helped to reduce the illiteracy rate. And it would certainly have been a much needed reform to abolish Gwageoje, which was a locus of unjust practices, and Eumseoje, which was a means of strengthening the vested interests of powerful political parties. In addition, his plan of granting admission to schools to the sons of ordinary people and to illegitimate sons that had not been qualified to apply to Gwageo was a progressive one, for it implied the modern concept of equality of opportunity to education and employment. His plan, based on the abolition of class distinctions, was a radical break with tradition, which Neo-Confucian scholars could never have imagined. So it may be concluded that his proposal for educational reform reflected an important characteristic of De-Neo-Confucian Silhak.

Proposals for the Reform of the Slave System

The slave system, originating from ancient times, continued to exist in the Joseon Dynasty. A *nobi* (奴, male slave 婢, female slave), who used to be called a *jong* (從, attendant), was ineligible for citizenship, even though he or she was a citizen and a member of the nation, in this respect on an equal footing with other people. Slaves were classified into '*gongnobi* (公奴婢, public slave)' and '*sanobi* (私奴婢, private slave)'. In either case their names were recorded in a list, and they eked out an existence working like animals by order of their lords. Moreover, private slaves were traded for money and their descendants could not escape their status, which was hereditary. They had no rights whatsoever and suffered the hardship of all kinds of labor. In a word, they had the lowest status of all people.

Yu Hyeong-won realized the injustice of the slave system more keenly than anyone else, and passionately argued for its complete abolition. According to him, everyone is the same in that all were created by Heaven,[18] or in his words, "Everyone belongs to the same class."[19] Such a view of the human being was based on both biology and personality. It was also based on 'the theory of human rights endowed by Heaven (人權天賦說)', or on the equality of each human's rights. Holding such a view, he emphasized the dignity of the slave as a human being.

He vehemently argued that aristocrats' selling and buying a slave like property was an irrational activity. In view of his statement that in previous eras one's fortune had been estimated not by the number of slaves but of horses one owned, slaves seemed to have been usually regarded as properties in his own era. Yu Hyeong-won asserted that even emperors and feudal princes had not regarded a human being as property.[20] And he maintained, "Now, the treatment of slaves is contrary to the way of the human being."[21] Yu Hyeong-won criticized the injustice of the slave system not only on the basis of the equal dignity of human beings but also in terms of national defense. That is, as slaves were exempt from military service, he maintained, in order to prevent the weakening of national defense, the abolition of the slave system was a necessity.[22]

He also pointed out the injustice of the hereditary slave system. According to him, if a man committed a crime and was degraded in rank into being a slave, to regard even his sons and daughters as slaves was very unjust, for punishment of a crime was valid only for a certain period.[23] If the slave system could not be abolished immediately, he argued, at a minimum the system of hereditary slavery should be eliminated. In addition, he proposed the enforcement of '*Jongmobeop* (從母法)', by which the sons and daughters of a mother from a good family should not be made slaves even if their father had become a

18 Yu Hyeong-won, "Byeongje", *Bangyesurok*, Vol. 21, p. 409.
19 Ibid., "Noye", Book 2, Vol. 26, p. 509.
20 Ibid.
21 Ibid., p. 508.
22 Ibid. p. 509.
23 Ibid., "Nobi", Book 2, Vol. 26, p. 507.

slave.[24]

The proposals to partially abolish both the hereditary slave system on a preferential basis and *Jongmobeop* were temporary alternative plans to the complete abolition of slavery. As another alternative, he proposed the treatment of public slaves, who engaged in compulsory labor, as government workers and the payment of a salary to them which would be enough to engage in farming by employing workers.[25] In addition, he also proposed that the soldiers of Dongogun (東伍軍) who were private and public slaves should be qualified to take an examination and in the event that they passed it, that they could be raised in status to the rank of commoners.[26] This proposal was significant for it suggested a method of elevating the status of slaves.

It is very much worth noting that he insisted on the abolition of slavery on the basis of his 'view of the human being as a creation of Heaven (天民說)' and his proposition, "Every human being belongs to the same class (人間同類說)," because his insistence represented the equality of human beings based on the dignity of the human being. It may safely be said that this view of equality not only persuasively supported his proposal for the reform and eventual abolition of slavery but also enhanced the intellectual level of Korean Confucianism. His view of the equality of human beings, which already been suggested in his proposals for the reform of the land and educational system, became more philosophically concrete with his proposal for the reform of the slave system. Certainly, his firm belief in the equality of human beings was a hint of opening the modern age of Korea.

It was transparently obvious that his reform proposals could not be realized. If they had been, a society and nation centered on the aristocracy might have been dismantled and collapsed. Once, Yi Ik pointed out that Yi I's Neo-Confucian ideas for reform might have been realized but that Yu Hyeong-won's proposals were unrealizable.

---

24 Ibid., p. 506.
25 Ibid., "Gwanjigjije", Book 1, Vol. 15, p. 312.
26 Ibid., "Sokpyeon", Book 2, Vol. 26, p. 506.

It was a remark that really hit the mark. Although Yu Hyeong-won's proposals directed toward the modernization of Korea were radical in view of the norms of contemporary feudal society, their revolutionary characteristics were themselves the barrier to their realization.

(4) **Bukhakpa's Reform Proposals for the Betterment of People's Lives**

(A) The Emphasis on Iyonghusaeng and the Preference for Technological Civilization

The Late Silhak Scholars' reform proposals that called for the cessation or revision of the evil practices of Joseon society were inherited, for the most part, by several 'scholars of Bukhak (北學, Northern Learning)'. The most significant scholars of Bukhak were Hong Dae-yong (洪大容, 1731-1783), Bak Ji-won (朴趾源, 1737-1805), Bak Je-ga (朴齊家, 1750-1805) and Jeong Yak-yong (丁若鏞, 1762-1836), who were mentioned in the preceding section. In particular, Jeong was known as the scholar who compiled the views of the Bukhak scholars. Choi Han-gi (崔漢綺, 1803-1879), the last scholar of the Late Silhak school, also belonged to 'Bukhakpa (北學派, the school of Northern Learning)'.

The word 'Bukhak' which had been first used by Ch'en Liang (陳良), who was a contemporary of Mencius, was introduced to Korea by Bak Je-ga in the Preface to his work, *Bukhaui* (北學議). Bak borrowed the term 'Bukhak' because he thought that, for the sake of reform, Korean scholars should learn even from the northern country, Chinese Qing, what was practical and substantive. Conservative Neo-Confucian scholars could not permit the study of Qing learning for they despised it as the country of barbarians and displayed hostility toward Qing after its invasion upon Joseon in 1636. So Bak Je-ga who belonged to the Late Silhak school borrowed the term 'Bukhak' instead of 'the learning of Qing' to preempt criticism. De-Neo-Confucian Silhak scholars' determination to promote reform may be ascertained in light of Bak Je-ga's attitude of regarding Qing not as an entity to be conquered but as an entity to be learned from.

Bak Je-ga's core concept for the betterment of people's lives was '*iyonghusaeng* (利用厚生, promotion of the public welfare)'. He inherited this principle from his predecessor Bak Ji-won.

> "Even a slight defect of *iyonghusaeng* (利用厚生) may incur an effect detrimental to righteous virtue (正德)... Now, people's lives become poorer day by day and useful possessions become scarcer and scarcer. How can the gentry stand idly by with their arms folded without relieving the suffering of poor people? How can the gentry conveniently cling to unjust practices and be indifferent to people's poverty and distress?"[27]

> "Therefore, King Wŭ (禹) wisely ruled people always on the basis of *iyonghusaeng*, which should be founded on righteous virtue."[28]

> "Ah, only such an endeavor could safely be called '*iyong* (利用, promotion of people's lives)'. '*Husaeng* (厚生, public welfare)' comes only after *iyong,* and righteous virtue comes only after *husaeng*. Seldom is *husaeng* achieved without *iyong*. And if people do not live in plenty, how can they retain righteous virtue?"[29]

It becomes evident that Bak Ji-won and Bak Je-ga emphasized '*iyonghusaeng*' for the betterment of people's lives. The cultivation of 'righteous virtue (正德)' was also discussed in this context. However, unlike Neo-Confucian scholars who attributed more importance to the cultivation of righteous virtue than to *iyonghusaeng*, they placed more emphasis on *iyonghusaeng*. The subtex of Bak Ji-won's passage quoted above is that few people will devote themselves to the cultivation of self or moral behavior when they are hungry. His

---

27 Bak Je-ga, *Bukhakui*, 'Seo'.
28 Bak Ji-won, "Gwanongsocho" (Bangokhomajo), *Yeonamjip*, Vol. 17.
29 Ibid., "Yeolhailgi, Dogangrok", Vol. 11.

thought was very different from Neo-Confucian scholars' view that the best governance is moral governance or governance on the basis of propriety or of virtue. This was an aspect of the views of the Late De-Neo-Confucian Silhak scholars who laid emphasis on practical substance and advantage.

The emphasis 'Bukhakpa (北學派, the school of Northern learning)' scholars placed on practical substance and advantage was concretized by their advocacy of technological progress. Bukhakpa scholars came to recognize the practical usefulness or practical utility of technological civilization. They were interested in 'advanced tools and materials' and modern facilities, which they had seen during their stay in Qing, and proposed to produce similar tools and materials and to provide such facilities. Bak Ji-won included in such tools, materials and facilities, the cart, brick, and roof-tile and Bak Je-ga spoke of the cart, ship, castle wall, road, bridge, coin, medicine, paper, bow, rule (尺), irrigation facilities, and so on. His two volumes of *Bukhakui* (北學議) were replete with explanations of the usefulness of farming tools and other implements. Bak Je-ga explained that the improvement of irrigation facilities could help overcome drought and produce increased grain yields, and eventually result in the betterment of farmers' lives. And the improvement of carts and ships would facilitate the nation-wide distribution of local goods, which in turn would result in the accumulation of wealth and the development of commerce. As for castle walls, Korean walls were built with stones that were capital- and labor-intensive but which did not guarantee durability. On the other hand, brick walls were built with mud that required less money and labor but were more solid than stone walls. So he recommended the building of brick walls in order to decrease people's back-breaking labor and strengthen national defense.

In short, Buhakpa's *iyonghusaeng* aimed at the betterment of people's lives through the improvement of technology in every field. In addition, Silhak scholars belonging to Bukhakpa opened the door to the introduction of the modern technology of the West by emphasizing the scientific improvement of tools and the utility of improved tools. And this was also a characteristic of the Late Silhak school.

(B) The Advent of Modern Astronomy and the Consequent Philosophical Evolution

Among the theories Bukhakpa scholars newly learned from Qing, the most pivotal ones were those of 'modern Western science and Catholicism,' which were usually called 'Western Learning'. While Neo-Confucian scholars guarded against Western Learning, Bukhakpa scholars regarded it as a field of legitimate learning and attempted to acquire new knowledge of Western astronomy, geography and the contents of Western almanacs.

'The astronomical knowledge' transmitted by Catholic priests belonging to the Society of Jesus who came to China in the 17th century overthrew the traditional theories of East-Asian astronomy. In particular, Copernican theories of the earth and heliocentrism played an enormous role in this intellectual revolution. Until then, Neo-Confucian scholars had held 'the theories of *gaecheonseol* (蓋天說) and *honcheonseol* (渾天說)', according to which "Heaven is round and the earth is rectangular," or "Heaven moves from the west to the east and the earth stands still." In the past Chinese Zhuang Zhou (莊子) had not clung to *gaecheonseol* and *honcheonseol* and a Korean scholar named Kim Seok-mun (金錫文) who studied 'the changes of all things in the universe (易學)', held theories similar to Copernicus. However, their theories were not supported by scientific evidences while the theories of astronomy transmitted by Catholic priests could not be rejected for they had logical grounds.

The first Bukhak scholars who accepted the theories of Western astronomy was Hong Dae-yong. In 1765 (the 41st year of King Yeongjo's reign) he, as a military officer, had accompanied his uncle to Beijing and became familiar with Western astronomy while he was visiting a meteorological station there.[30] Soon after, Bak Ji-won was informed

30 Hong Dae-yong met in a Catholic church two Germans named Augustinus

of the theories of Western astronomy, which was sbusequently introduced in great detail in his work, *Yeolhailgi* (熱河日記). Hong Dae-yong also shared his knowledge of Western astronomy in his essay "Uisanmundap (醫山問答)":

> "Heaven is full of *gi*. The sun, the moon and stars are in heaven. The earth, the sun, the moon, and stars cannot be said to be above and below each other in the same way that we cannot determine the positions of east, west, south, and north for the parts of our body. Judging from solar and lunar eclipses, the earth is round. The earth circumnavigate the sun once a day. The circumference of the earth is about 90,000 *ri* (one *ri* = 0.4km) and there are 12 double hours in a day."[31]

Certainly, Hong Dae-yong's new astronomical knowledge was very different from the traditional astronomical theories (*gaecheonseol* and *honcheonseol*). And the difference inevitably brought about changes in Silhak-Bukhak scholars' views on the world, the human being and sinocentrism. I will now give a fuller explanation of these changes.

In the past Neo-Confucian scholars had understood the human being and the world on the basis of the theories of heavenly bodies called *honcheonseol* and *gaecheonseol*. Simply put, they established their view of the human being as the lord of all creation by comparing the circular heaven and the rectangular earth respectively to the head and the foot of a human being, and by regarding the human being as the product of heaven and earth. Moreover, they thought that the center of the flat earth was China, and that the nations around China were all 'barbarian'. Such a sinocentric view of the world was fundamentally based on Gaecheongseol and Honcheonseol.

---

von Hallerstein (Chinese name: 劉松齡) and Anton Gogeisl (Chinese name: 鮑友管) who were respectively director and vice-director of the meteorological observatory in Beijing. Hong Dae-yong learned from them up-to-date Western Astronomy.

31 Hong Dae-yong, "Uisanmundap",*Damheonseo* (Gyeonginmunhwasa), Vol.4, 'Naejip'.

However, the fact that the earth is neither flat or rectangular nor static but round and movable led to the supersession of the past world view. Actually, in the case of Korea, this intellectual revolution facilitated the recovery of the identity of Korean people. Hong Dae-yong was the first scholar who elucidated the change of consciousness of Koreans. He rejected the view of the human being as the lord of all creation together with sinocentrism as follows:

> "From the viewpoint of the human being, human beings are noble and things are base. On the other hand, from the viewpoint of things, things are noble and human beings are base. However, from the viewpoint of heaven human beings and things are equal."[32]

"The difference of longitude between China and the West is 180°. Chinese people think that China is located in the center while the other countries are located on the margins... However, every nation can insist that it is located in the center."[33]

> "Viewed from heaven, there is no distinction between inside and outside. Regardless of the location of a nation, its people are familiar with one another, serve their king, and are at one with their customs."[34]

Though he was a Confucian scholar, he asserted, like Zhuang Zhou, "From the viewpoint of heaven human beings and things are equal." In addition, abandoning the sinocentric world view, he established a Korea-centric world view on the grounds that there is no distinction between inside and outside, or center and margin on the spherical earth. In this context, he even said that Confucius would have written 'Korean History' instead of 'The History of the State of Lu' if he had

32 Ibid.
33 Ibid.
34 Ibid.

been born in Korea.[35] As he grasped the Copernican theory of the celestial bodies, he resolutely abandoned the old sinocentric view and took the lead in the recovery of the identity of the Korean people.

Bukhak-Silhak scholars including Hong Dae-yong, who were despised by Neo-Confucian scholars, investigated Bukhak with great daring and overcame the lack of autonomous Korean identity implied in Neo-Confucianism. This represented another paradigm shift achieved by Silhak scholars.

(C) The Novelistic Criticism of the *Yangban* Class

Silhak scholars belonging to the Bukhak School devoted themselves not only to the improvement of implements by relying on technological civilization, but also to the criticism of the perverted consciousness of the *yangban* (aristocratic) ruling class. Bak Ji-won was a case in point. Unlike Yi I, a Neo-Confucian scholar in the 16th century who suggested reform plans through his Memorials to the Throne, and unlike De-Neo-Confucian Silhak scholars such as Yu Hyeong-won and Yi Ik, who proposed reform measures in the form of 'records' and 'comments' respectively, Bak Ji-won, a Silhak scholar in the 18th century, severely criticized the perverted consciousness of the *yangban* ruling class and attempted the reform of the *yangban*'s consciousness through his short stories. His criticism was a kind of self-reflection in that, while himself belonging to the *yangban* class, he criticized *yangban* society.

From the late 16th century to the early 17th century Heo Gyun (許筠, 1569-1618) denounced through his novels the abuses of the social system that were already prevalent in the 16th century. In his novel, *Honggildongjeon* (洪吉童傳), he cast a critical eye on discriminations against illegitimate sons who were prohibited, according to the law, from being employed as senior officials. Since Heo Gyun had been put to death for high treason in 1618, the corruption of Joseon society

---

35 Ibid.

grew more widespread in the absence of specific reform measures over the course more than 100 years. The falsity and hypocrisy, the moral laxity and the privileged plundering of the *yangban* class were ultimately the main causes of the fall of the Joseon Dynasty. Bak Ji-won criticized contemporary destructive practices through novels such as *Yangbanjeon* (兩班傳, *The Story of a Yangban*), *Hojil* (虎叱, *A Tiger's Scolding*), *Heosaengjeon* (許生傳, *The Story of Heosaeng*) and *Yedeokseon-saengjeon* (穢德先生傳, *The Story of Master Yedeok*).

I will firstly give a summary of *Yangbanjeon*:

A poor *yangban* in Jeongseon County was in dire straits for he could not repay the grain he borrowed from the local government office. At that time a rich commoner wanted to purchase the status of *yangban* and the local magistrate permitted him to do so. So the commoner paid money to the poor *yangban* and acquired the status of *yangban*. After a while, however, the commoner wanted to abandon the status of *yangban* for he had become subject to too many restraints in the form of empty formalities. Moreover, he was compelled, in accordance with contemporary destructive practices, to exploit farmers through his privileged position of *yangban*. As his conscience would not allow him to do so, he abandoned the status of *yangban* and absconded from his responsibilities.[36]

From the above story I derived four concerns: ① the injustice of the *yangban*-oriented social system, ② the overabundance of empty formalities required of the *yangban* class, ③ the unjust tyranny of the *yangban* class, and ④ the *yangban*'s unproductive mental attitude of despising and avoiding labor.

Secondly, I will summarise the story of *Hojil*.

36 Bak Ji-won, "Yangbanjeon", *Yeonamjip*, Vol. 8, 'Byeoljip'.

A great hulking tiger comes down a mountain to a village with his followers seeking something to eat. In the village Master Bukgwak (北郭), famous for his moral virtue, is enjoying a secret meeting with a young local widow. The tiger, on the basis of the master's reputation, thinks that the man cannot be he but is instead a fox in the shape of the master, and he runs into the room with a heavy stick. Master Bukgwak, being driven out like a fox, suffers a bitter insult and falls into a dung-heap. As he manages to climb out, the tiger is waiting for the master with his mouth wide open in a snarl. The master becomes hysterical while begging for his life, and the tiger loudly scolds him and leaves. When morning breaks, some farmers catch sight of the unkempt figure and he is put to shame once more."[37]

Here the writer, with his dexterous writing, strips off the false mask of a *yangban* scholar. Regardless of whether they were male or female, the moral hypocrisy of members of the *yangban*-class was thoroughgoing in the 19th century. By denouncing their hypocritical attitudes, between the lines of the novel Bak Ji-won suggested his resistance to the Neo-Confucian valorization of the primacy of morality, which was the cause of the hypocrisy. The *yangban* in this novel was a hypocritical figure, or an actor wearing the mask of a virtuous man, who was even scolded by a beast.

Thirdly, I will summarize *Heosaengjeon*.

A budding Confucian named Heo Saeng was studying diligently, following his ten-year plan of study. However, he could not continue to study for he was poverty-stricken. So he started a business with an immense sum of money he had borrowed from a millionaire. As his business prospered, he was able to pay the principal and interest, the sum of which was twice as much as the money he had borrowed from the millionaire. Living in a shabby hut, he continued performing good

37 Ibid., "Hojil", Yeolhailgi.

deeds. The millionaire became familiar with Heo Saeng and introduced Heo to a minister named Yi Wan (李浣). The minister discussed current topics with Heo, but the latter only laughed upon hearing the minister's views. The minister became aware of something extraordinary in Heo. And when the minister desired to appoint him to a high government post, he could not, for nobody knew his whereabouts."[38]

In this story the writer not only pointed out the mistaken views of bureaucrats on current issues but also revealed his intention of abolishing 'the practice of putting government above people (官尊民卑)' together with the distinction between the four-class-segmented occupations of 'officials, farmers, artisans and tradesmen (士農工商)'. Contrary to the *yangban*'s established view of commerce as the meanest occupation, Bak Ji-won emphasized that the development of commerce was the optimal route to ensuing the wealth of a nation and tried to facilitate the improvement of people's lives. His emphasis on abolishing the distinction between occupations represented the Late Silhak's insistence on the equality of stations in life.

Finally, let's examine the characteristic views implied in *Yedeokseonsaengjeon*.

Master Yedeok is one of Master Seongyulja (蟬橘子)'s friends. Yedeok makes his living by removing dung from farm compounds. So the villagers call him Eom Haeng-su (Eom is his family name and haeng-su means an old man engaging in lowly work). A disciple of Seongyulja named Jamok (子牧) complains that his master does not keep company with noble men but with a lowly man like Eom Haneng-su. Seongyulja gives advice to his disciple on making friends with people. He says, "There are two bad ways of making friends with people: one is to form a friendship by taking advantage of an occasion, which means to make friends through calculating profit or loss; the other is to form

38 Ibid., "Okgapyahwa", *Yeolhailgi*.

a friendship by putting on a face, which means to make friends with flattery. Friendship formed in such ways cannot last long. Real friendship is moral friendship formed by mental communion and mutual veneration. My friendship with Eom Haeng-su is moral friendship." Eom Haeng-su seems to be foolish and lowly. However, he lives within his means without seeking fame, without disgracing himself, without reading a well-known book, without caring for domestic harmony... Though he engages in filthy work, his attitude is full of fragrance. Though he lives in squalid conditions, he firmly maintains his righteous attitude. Therefore, I cannot call him by name but by Yedeokseonsaeng (an unkempt but virtuous master).[39]

The core of this story is condensed in the sentences, "Though he engages in filthy work, his attitude is full of fragrance," and "Though he lives in squalid conditions, he firmly maintains his righteous attitude." Now I will not discuss the equality of occupations for I have already dealt with this subject. In this story Bak Ji-won shows that not only yangbans' ways of making friends but also their attitude to life are quite contradictory to those of Master Yedeok. The emphasis on innocent virtue was originally exclusive to Neo-Confucian scholars, but in this story they are shamed for the lack of virtue. Here Bak Ji-won discloses the *yangban*'s attitude of respecting only theoretical learning while neglecting the practical virtue of righteousness or the *yangban*'s devotion to vacuous learning that is symbolized as dung. Seen in this light, it may be wrong to insist that De-Neo-Confucian Silhak pursued only practical fact, practical substance and practical advantage, while neglecting the moral perspective represented by human nature or virtuous nature.

39 Ibid., "Yedeokseonsaengjeon", Vol. 8, 'Byeoljip'.

3. The Establishment of De-Neo-Confucian Silhak Thought

(1) The Rise of De-Neo-Confucian Classical Learning

The Late De-Neo-Confucian Silhak scholars who were critical of the governance promoted by Neo-Confucian scholars not only proposed reform measures to counter corrupt social practices but also criticized the impractical Neo-Confucian ways of study. As time went by, they were 'skeptical of and dissatisfied with Neo-Confucian thought' itself. With the critical frame of mind that proposed reform measures they sought the transformation of the trend of contemporary thought on the basis of classical learning. In other words, as the fundamental philosophical thought of Confucianism was essentiallly suggested in classical texts, the Late Silhak scholars attempted to critically reexamine Neo-Confucian understanding of the classical texts of Confucianism in order to initiate their own strand of philosophical thought.

Fundamentally, Silhak scholars' examination of classical learning was carried out in order to return to or begin from 'the Original Confucianism(本源儒學)'. Just as Neo-Confucian scholars had established their theories on the basis of 'the Original Confucianism', Silhak scholars' attempt to overcome Neo-Confucianism had to also start from their study of the Original Confucianism.

Their predecessors who had studied the classics in this context were Yun Hyu(尹鑴, 1617-1680) and Bak Se-dang(朴世堂, 1629-1703). The former had a profound knowledge of the Confucian proprieties[40]

40 Yun Hyu, belonging to 'the Southerners' together with Heo Mok, insisted conservatively that it only conforms to old rituals to wear funeral robe for three years in 'the first dispute on the propriety(禮訟)' and for one year in 'the second debate on the propriety'. Though he advocated De-Neo-Confucian classical studies and was killed as a rebel speaking and acting against Neo-Confucianism, he cannot be said to be a scholar of Late Silhak for his conservatism concerning the dispute on the propriety. However, he is considered to be a scholar who laid the foundation for 'the formation of Late Silhak' by his study of De-Neo-Confucian classics.

while the latter was not interested in them.[41] Both of them learned fundamental theories of Neo-Confucianism when they were young. It is not certain that their indifference to Neo-Confucianism can be ascribed to the fact that their teachers were not famous Neo-Confucian scholars. In any case, neither of them confined their interests to Neo-Confucian learning but instead both had a liberal attitude of learning, and came to have an interest in various fields. Consequently they did not cling to Cheng-Zhu's Neo-Confucianism, but attempted to surpass it.

Their De-Neo-Confucian study of the classics ranged over a variety of books including The Four Books (四書, *The Great Learning*, *The Analects of Confucius*, *The Doctrine of the Mean*, *The Book of Mencius*) and The Six Classics (六經, *The Book of Odes*, *The Book of History*, *The Book of Rites*, *The Book of Changes*, *The Spring and Autumn Annals*, and *The Book of Music*). Some of Yun Hyu's achievements were lost but his *Dokseogi* (讀書記) comprising 11 volumes alone represents the scale and depth of his classical study and focus. His classical study was mainly focused on *The Commentaries* on *The Doctrine of the Mean* and *The Great Learning* while Bak Se-dang's classical study was collated in his *Sabyeonrok* (四辨錄) comprising 14 volumes, in which his commentaries on *The Book of History* and *The Book of Odes* are compiled. He also published *The Commentaries* on the works of Laozi and Zhuang Zhou, who were regarded as heretics by Neo-Confucian scholars. Though they regarded Cheng-Zhu's achievements highly in their commentaries on classical books, they were not satisfied with Cheng-Zhu's Neo-Confucian view on classical study. Yun Hyu said that he once realized that the old sages' views in classical texts had not been adequately interpreted and insisted, "The truth of the universe cannot be fully comprehended by one man's intelligence."[42] And he tried to justify

41 Bak Se-dang was a retainer belonging to 'the Westerners' or 'the Faction of the Young Doctrine' and had some interest in the propriety but did not participate in the disputes on the propriety. Rather, he was critical toward the disputes that were nonproductive. He thought that the dispute on the propriety is only a vacant and nominal dispute without substance.

42 Yun Hyu, "Dogseogiseo", *Baekhojeonseo*, Book 2, Vol. 24, 'Seo'.

his break with Neo-Confucianism with the rationale that truth could not be the monopoly of a certain individual or school.

Bak Se-dang said, "Though a classical work may imply one meaning, there are many clues to the meaning," and he justified his own methodology of classical study, which was different from Cheng-Zhu's. Furthermore, (as mentioned above) he criticized Neo-Confucian scholars' impractical attitude of neglecting what is easy and familiar and researching what is vacuous and abstract. Such a criticism was also the justification for his attempt to formulate his own De-Neo-Confucian thought on classical learning.

In succession to Yun Hyu and Bak Se-dang, Hong Dae-yong and Jeong Yak-yong openly attacked Cheng-Zhu's classical learning and wrote their own commentaries on the classics. Though Hong Dae-yong read many classical texts, he was not deeply versed in classical learning. Jeong Yak-yong's *Jungyonggangui* (中庸講義) and *Noneojipju* (論語集注) marked the climax of De-Neo-Confucian classical learning not only in terms of quantity but also in quality. Choi Han-gi (1803-1879) devoted himself to the formulation and promulgation of his De-Neo-Confucian thought rather than to elaborating on its methodology.

Before these scholars, Yi Ik (1681-1763) expressed skepticism and disbelief about Cheng-Zhu's classical learning, not openly but in a circumlocuitous way. In effect, he adopted the prudent attitude of partially revising Cheng-Zhu's theories. Though he inherited Cheng-Zhu's viewpoint and suggested his own Neo-Confucian view, he presented theories corresponding to De-Neo-Confucianism, especially in the interpretation of classical history books. As he put forth revised theories of classical learning based on his own reinterpretation, without blindly accepting Cheng-Zhu's views, a considerable number of his theories corresponded to the ideas contained in De-Neo-Confucian Silhak thought. Therefore, considering his view of Silhak, which emphasized the importance of practical implements, it was highly probable that his reinterpretation of classical learning would also be seen as falling under the rubric of De-Neo-Confucianism (together with the views of Bak Se-dang and other Silhak scholars).

(2) The Philosophical Thought of Silhak with Respect to Classical Learning

The distinction between Cheng-Zhu school's classical learning and that of Lu-Wang school was based on the theory of '*gyeokmul* (格物, investigation of things)'. The tenets of De-Neo-Confucian Silhak or its fundamental character may also be elucidated through the theory of *gyeokmul*. In this context I will examine Silhak scholars' theories on *gyeokmul*. In order to avoid a lengthy explanation, my discussion will be limited to the theories of *gyeokmul* of the scholars in the early period of the Late Silhak.

The point of Zhu Xi's theories of gyeokmul was 'the ultimate pursuit of the principle of worldly affairs and arrival at the logical outcome of the principle (窮至事物之理, 欲其極處無不到也)' by interpreting '*gyeok* (格)' as '*ji* (至arrival) or *do* (到, arrival)' and '*mul* (物, thing)' as '*sa* (事, affair)'. On the other hand, the core of Wang's theories of *gyeokmul* was 'the correction of the biased source of intention (正意之不正)' by interpreting *gyeok* as '*jeong* (正, correction)' and *mul* as the source of intention.

Yun Hyu, who initiated the formation of the Late Silhak school through classical learning, objected to the interpretations of Cheng-Zhu's gyeok as 'ji (至)' and Lu-Wang's *gyeok* as '*jeong* (正)'. He also took issue with their interpretations of 'mul (物)' as '*sa* (事)' or as 'the source of intention'. According to Yun Hyu, *gyeok* means to feel something (物) with extremely sincere intention. And something here means 'illustrious virtue (明德)' and 'to renew people (新民之事)'.[43] 'To renew people' means 'to allow people to realize their virtue (盡人之性)'.[44] Therefore, he meant by *gyeokmul* to illuminate virtuous original nature and to allow people to realize their virtue. Such a

---

43 Yun Hyu, "Gobondaehakbyeolrok", *Baekhojeonseo* Book 2, Vol. 37.
44 He interpreted '*myeongmyeongdeok* (明明德)' of *The Great Learning* (大學) as 'fulfilling my own virtue' and '*shinmin* (親民)' as 'fulfilling other's virtue'.

new interpretation stood in almost complete opposition to Zhu Xi's interpretation of gyeokmul as the pursuit of objective knowledge, while being somewhat reconciled to Wang Shou-ren's tendency of emphasizing the subjective cultivation of virtue for the achievement of righteous morals.

Now let's examine Bak Se-dang's case. He explained the reason why he rejected Zhu Xi's interpretation of *gyeokmul,* as follows: "To interpret *gyeok* (格) as *ji* (至, arrival)" and to say "Gyeokmul means to arrive at *mul* (things) is invalid." He also said, "Zhu Xi added '*gung* (窮)' to '*ji*' (gungji窮至, to arrive at the ultimate destination), in spite of the fact that *gyeok* does not have the implication of *gungji*."[45] Bak Se-dang suggested his own interpretation: "Arrival (致) means to seek and to arrive (至). *Gyeok* means being principled and upright."[46] In addition, he said, "Mul (物) necessarily accompanies a principle (格). This is because we anticipate reaching a righteous principle."[47]

Bak Se-dang rejected Zhu Xi's theory of *gyeokmul* by interpreting, like Wang Shou-ren, *gyeok* as '*jeong* (正, uprightness)'. So one may presume that his theory is similar to Wang's. However, his meaning and usage of *jeong* are different from those of Wang. While Wang used *jeong* in the sense of correcting the bias of one's intention, Bak used it in the sense of the correct understanding of the principles of things and state of affairs. And while Wang used *jeong* to designate a focus on subjective cultivation, Bak used it in its objective aspects. In this respect Bak's theory seemed to be close to Zhu Xi's. We may conclusively say that Bak devised his new theory by synthesizing and sublating Chu's and Wang's theories. Now, let's examine the case of Yi Ik who opened the first chapter of the Late Silhak by pursuing the reform of the legal system and practical Confucianism while continuing to study Neo-Confucianism. Yi Ik variously interpreted '*gyeok*' as '*ji*(至, arrival)' or '*do* (到, arrival)', '*jeong* (正, uprightness)', and

45 Bak Se-dang, *Sabyeonrok*, "Gyeongiljangju", *Daehaksabyeonrok*.
46 Ibid.
47 Ibid.

‘*gak* (各, separateness)’.[48] He seemed to be influenced by Zhu Xi’s theory because he interpreted *gyeok* as *ji* or *do* like Zhu Xi.[49] However, while Zhu Xi was biased toward objective knowledge only with respect to *ji* and *do*, Yi Ik interpreted *gyeok* also as ‘*jeong* (正)’ like Wang Shou-ren. He said, “Mencius also advised people ‘to make a biased mind upright (格其非心)’.” Essentially, the ‘biased mind (非心)’ is opposed to rational principle. So according to Yi Ik *gyeok* means to elevate something to ‘the righteous standard (極)’ by making it upright in accordance with rules.[50]

Therefore Yi Ik seems to have borrowed the interpretation of *gyeok* from both Zhu Xi’s and Wang Shou-ren’s theories, but in fact he was not inclined toward either of them. He established his theory by meticulously synthesizing their theories according to his own view. His conclusion was that the proper meaning of *gyeokmul* is to acquire knowledge by making the mind of an individual upright. Furthermore, he interpreted *gyeok* (格) also as ‘*gak* (各, separateness)’, because *gak* implies discrimination.[51] He emphasized that the human being is not thrown into confusion because he has the capacity to discriminate. His emphasis on discrimination is evidence that he was not inclined toward either Zhu Xi’s or Wang’s theory. His position as such reminds us of his Silhak preoccupations, represented by his focus on the development of practical implements. Judging from the Late De-Neo-Confucian Silhak interpretations of *gyeokmul*, the classical learning of the period was certainly the duplication of neither Zhu Xi’s nor Wang Shou-ren’s learning but learning of their own devising.

---

48 Yi Ik, “Gyeokchiseongjeong”, ‘Gyeongsamun’, *Seonghosaseol*.

49 At this time Yi Ik explained that ‘ji (至)’ is the final arrival’ at the principle of things and that ‘do (到)’ is gyeokmul (格物) or the attainment of knowledge by ‘the final arrival’. He supplementarily explained that ‘do’ is the same as ‘ye (詣, arrival)’.

50 Yi Ik, “Gyeong”, “Daehakjilui”, *Seonghojeonseo*, Vol. 4,

51 Yi Ik, “Gyeokjiseongjeong”, *Seonghosaseol*,〈Gyeongsamun〉.

(3) The Conceptual Characteristics of De-Neo-Confucian Silhak

(A) The Nominalist View on Name and Substance

In the 17th century the conventional view on the supremacy of propriety facilitated the spread of 'nominalism under the guise of rationity' and 'the formalistic propensity' in contemporary society. The vehement disputes, called 'Yesong (禮訟)', around the choice of a one-year or three-year period of mourning for the deceased King Hyojong were fundamentally confrontations between the party who insisted on treating King Hyojong in accordance with the fact that he was the second son, and the other party who insisted on treating him as the first son, considering his special status of kingship. In this respect, they mirrored the nominalist debates among scholar.

As dissatisfaction with these disputes gave impetus to the rise of the Late Silhak, contemporary Silhak scholars rejected such nominalism as mere formalism. Bak Se-dang regarded 'Yesong' as futile because it had nothing to do with King Hyojong's virtue. With respect to the Confucian 'theory of name and substance (名實論)', Bak, as a Silhak scholar, attached more importance to substance than nomenclature. Another Silhak scholar, Choi Han-gi, expressed his view on nominalism: "A certain name is necessarily preceded by a thing. There is no name without a thing."[52] Choi's view represented Silhak scholars' general sense that the necessities of life such as grain and tools were more important than the formalities of rites. The philosophical tenet of Silhak scholars, 'seeking truth grounded on concrete evidences (實事求是),' also corresponded to the general trend of Silhak thought.

(B) *Gi*-principal Thought Based on Physical Quality or Technology

The Late De-Neo-Confucian Silhak scholars gravitated toward

52 Choi Han-gi maintained that a name comes after a real thing in his *Chucheukrok*.

‘*gi*-principal (主氣)’, which may have been related to their emphasis on experience based on sense or perception. According to them, *gi* unlike *ri* was akin to ‘the physical quality (氣質)’ or the original substance of the things perceived.

Among the Late Silhak scholars, Yu Hyeong-won and Yi Ik, who were in the vanguard of the promotion of reform, were not conspicuously biased toward either *gi* or *ri*. However, later scholars such as Bak Se-dang, Hong Dae-yong, Bak Ji-won, Bak Je-ga, Jeong Yak-yong and Choi Han-gi displayed growing concern about the theory of *ri-gi,* and were clearly biased toward the ‘*gi*-principal (主氣)’. So they rejected the theory of the real existence of *ri*, the description of *ri* as ‘the ultimate cause (所以然者)’, the view of *ri* as superintendent, and the idea that “Taegeuk (太極, the Great Ultimate) is *ri.*” According to them, *ri* is no other than ‘the order and coherency’ accompanying the functioning of *gi*. In this sense Jeong Yak-yong once compared *ri* to the texture of jade. Here, some may wonder whether there is any difference between the *gi*-principal of the Neo-Confucian scholars and that of the Late Silhak scholars, for Neo-Confucianism in its broad sense embraced not only the *ri*-principal of Zhu Xi and Yi Hwang but also the *gi*-principal of Zhang Zai (張載) and Seo Gyeong-deok (徐敬德). I will now focus on the issue.

There were some *gi*-oriented Neo-Confucian scholars who, like Seo Gyeong-deok, regarded *ri* as order and coherence accompanying the functioning of *gi*. But the Late Silhak scholars gradually came to have views on *gi* distinct from those of Neo-Confucian scholars. In Neo-Confucianism ‘*yin-yang* (陰陽, the cosmic dual forces)’ and ‘*ohaeng* (五行, the five elements forming the universe: water, fire, wood, metal, earth)’ were regarded as concrete *gi*, and *ohaeng* as comprising the fundamental elements forming the universe. However, Hong Dae-yong as a Silhak scholar said, “*yin* and *yang* originated from earth and fire respectively... Fundamentally, *yin* and *yang* refer to the shallowness and depth of the sunlight respectively.”[53] In other words, according

53 Hong Dae-yong, “Uisanmundap”, *Damheonjip*, Vol. 4, ‘Naejip’.

to Hong, *yin* and *yang* are merely the 'darkness and light' caused by sunlight. Jeong Yak-yong also understood *yin-yang* simply as the phenomena of light and shade, not as the elements or substance forming the universe. Bak Ji-won and Bak je-ga thought of *ohaeng* not as the fundamental elements of the universe but merely as the five substances existing in the phenomenal world.[54] With these views as a turning pont, the '*gi*-principal thought (主氣論)' based on 'physical quality (氣質)' transformed into *gi*-principal thought based on technology. As a result, the view of *yin-yang* and *ohaeng* as the fundamental elements or substance from which the universe is formed was rejected almost completely by Silhak scholars.

(C) The Principal De-Neo-Confucian Philosophy of the Late *Silhak*

Some Neo-confucian scholars in a broad sense advocated *gi*-principal, and not only regarded *ri* as the order and coherency accompanying *gi*'s functioning but also rejected Cheng-Zhu's principal propositions. Ihm Seong-ju, for one, substituted '*cheonjeukgi* (天卽氣, Heaven is *gi*)', '*seongjeukgi* (性卽氣, human nature is *gi*)', '*giilbunsu* (氣一分殊, one *gi* and its many variations)' and '*ohaeng* (五行, five elements)' for Cheng-Zhu's theories of '*cheonjeukri* (天卽理, Heaven is *ri*)', '*seongjeukri* (性卽理, human nature is *ri*)', '*riilbunsu* (理一分殊, one principle and its instantiation in many manifestations)', and '*osang* (五常, five constants)' respectively. Ihm was a great philosopher of *gi* and his theory of *ri-gi* was close to 'the monistic theory of *gi* (唯氣論)'. But he merely substituted *gi* for *ri*, and still adhered to Neo-Confucian ways of thinking. So his theory of the *gi*-principal, however close it might have been to the monistic theory of *gi*, cannot be said to have deviated from the fundamental tenets of Neo-Confucianism.

On the other hand, Silhak scholars such as Bak Se-dang, Hong Dae-yong and Jeong Yakl-yong rejected all the fundamental propositions

54 Bak Ji-won, "Hongbeomwuikseo", *Yeonamjip*, Vol 1, and Bak Je-ga, "Oepyeon", "OhaengYuljinjiui", *Bukhakui*.

of Neo-Confucianism such as '*cheonjeukri* (天卽理)', '*seongjeukri* (性卽理)', and '*riilbunsu* (理一分殊)'. Unlike Ihm Seong-ju, they did not try to substitute *gi* for *ri* in their theories, for the Late De-Neo-Confucian Silhak scholars rejected the Neo-confucian way of thinking itself. Jeong Yak-yong even rejected the Neo-Confucian propositions, "Mind is the sum of '*ri* and *gi* (心理氣之合)', " and "Mind is the combination (rule) of nature and feeling (心統性情)."[55]

Having rejected the principal propositions of Neo-Confucianism, Bak Se-dang, Hong Dae-yong and Jeong Yak-yong resuscitated the Original Confucian term '*Sangje* (上帝, Heavenly God)', which refers to '*Cheon* (天, Heaven)'. Accordingly, they substituted '*cheonjeuksangje* (天卽上帝, Heaven is God)' for the Neo-Confucian '*cheonjeukri* (天卽理, Heaven is ri)'. Originally, Neo-Confucianism had come to be distinguished from the preceding Confucianism on the basis of Cheng Yi (程頤), substituting *ri* for 'Sangje' and adopting '*cheonjeukri* (天卽理, Heaven is *ri*)' and '*seongjeukri* (性卽理, Nature is *ri*)' as the fundamental propositions of Neo-Confucianism. Thus I believe that the most conspicuous characteristic of De-Neo-Confucian Late Silhak, which distinguishes it from Neo-Confucianism, is its view of *Cheon* as *Sangje*.

(D) The Evolution of the View on Nature and its Influence

Neo-Confucian scholars generally upheld the view of 'the stimulus-response relationship between Heaven and human beings (天人感應說)' suggested by Dong Zhong-shu in the Chinese Han Dynasty. Cheng-Zhu also held this view and refined it philosophically. The seminal theory of this understanding was '*riilbunsu* (理一分手, one principle and its instantiation in many manifestations)'. On the basis of the one *ri* , which was believed to exist in actuality, scholars explained the homogeneity of man and nature. Zhang Zai (張載), who belonged to the Neo-Confucian school though he was deeply interested in the

55 Jeong Yak-yong, "Dapyiyeohong", *Dasanjeonseo*, Book 1, Vol. 19.

philosophy of *gi*, advocated 'the identity of self and object (物我一體論)' and thought that nature and the human being are essentially the same. 'The unity of Heaven and human beings (天人合一)' through the extremely sincere cultivation proposed in *The Doctrine of the Mean* succeeded the view of nature of the Neo-Confucian scholars. They thought that nature and human beings are homogeneous but different in that the former is 'the absolute ego (大我)' while the latter is 'the ego (小我)'. As shown in 'Cheonmyeongdo (天命道, The Diagram of The Mandate of Heaven)', they even thought that the figure of the human being is analogous to the shape of heaven and earth. Therefore they insisted that the human being is 'the progeny of heaven and earth'.[56] This is the basis of the view of the human being as the lord of all creations.

However, Late Silhak scholars like Bak Se-dang rejected the view of the reciprocal relationship between Heaven and human beings, for they thought that the relation between them is influenced only by *gi,* not by mind.[57] Bak instead attempted to demonstrate the distinction between nature and the human being. The Late Silhak scholars held the belief in common that all things are identical in that they are formed by *gi*. It is true that Neo-Confucian scholars held that nature and the human being are distinct from each other according to the purity or impurity of *gi*, and to the level of presence of original nature.[58] Silhak scholars went further in asserting the heterogeneity of nature and the human being. For instance, the Neo-Confucian scholar Han Won-jin 'classified human nature into three grades (性三品說)' and Hong Dae-yong and Jeong Yak-yong suggested a similar classification. But Hong's and Jeong's classificatory criteria were more complicated than Han's. His criteria were the 'existence or non-existence of life' and 'high or low perception', while Hong and Jeong added to Han's criteria 'high and low intelligence' and 'moral capacity', according to which they discriminated among plants,

56 Jeong Ji-un, *Cheonmyeongdo*. Refer to my own work, Book 1, *The History of Korean Confucianism*, p. 274.
57 Bak Se-dang, "Jungyongsabyeonrok", *Sabyeonrok*, Chap. 1.
58 The representative example is Han Won-jin's 'The Three Grades of Nature'.

animals and human beings.

As I have mentioned above, Hong Dae-yong, a Silhak scholar, visited a Catholic church in Beijing, and was informed of 'the spherical shape of the earth (地球說)', 'the rotation of the earth (自轉)', and the revolution of the earth (空轉)'. And Silhak scholars in general, having experienced the Copernican revolution, changed their views of the heavenly bodies. This radically new view of the heavens propagated among Silhak scholars through Hong Dae-yong's *Uisanmundap* (毉山問答) and his junior, Bak Ji-won's *Yeolhailgi* (熱河日記). This epoch-making discovery brought about a transformation of the past view of nature based on '*gaecheonseol* (蓋天說, the view that Heaven is shaped like a shell and earth like the yolk of an egg)' and '*honcheonseol* (渾天說, the view that Heaven is shaped like an umbrella and the earth is flat)', which regarded Heaven as the root and the earth as the branch and supported the idea that Heaven moves while the earth stands still. Furthermore, views on sino-centricism, human beings, and morality changed in succession. As a result, a 'Korea-centered world view' began to be suggested and helped to enhance the sense of sovereignty of Koreans, as was discussed above.

(E) The Change in the View on the Human Being and Morality

Neo-Confucian scholars regarded the human being as the lord of all creation for they believed that only the human being is endowed with the righteous morals of 'he five constants (五常, benevolence, righteousness, propriety, wisdom and fidelity)' and can practically live by them. So Neo-Confucianism was a philosophy which regarded the human being as the lord of all creation on the basis of his moral value. And this view was demonstrated by 'Cheonmyeongdo (天命圖, The Diagram of The Mandate of Heaven)' drawn by representative Neo-Confucian scholars in the 16th century such as Jeong Ji-un, Kim In-hu and Yi Hwang.[59] The intense disputes among Neo-Confucian scholars on 'the four

59 Refer to footnote 102).

beginnings and the seven feelings (四端七情論)' were in fact centered around the practice of ethics based on the theory of mind and nature. The 'Yesong', which was a dispute about the proper mourning robes of the royal family in the 17th century, was further evidence of the Neo-Confucian view of the supremacy of moral values. In the Late Silhak the human being was also regarded as the lord of all creation but on grounds different from those of Neo-Confucianism. The Late Silhak scholars' view on the human being was grounded on the moral capacities and 'numinous and luminous (靈明)' characteristic, and so they also attached importance to morals. However, unlike Neo-Confucian scholars, who vehemently rejected the significance of physical nature (氣質之性), they did not regard morality as an absolute value but as a relative value, for they saw sensual experiences as significant, and accepted human feeling and lust as intrinsic aspects of human nature. In a word they came to have a view of the human being as a desiring being'. In this context Heo Gyun said, "Man and woman are endowed with lust by Heaven, and prudent moral discipline was taught by the sages. As Heaven is higher than the sages, we may ignore the sages' virtuous teaching but we cannot ignore the original nature bestowed by Heaven."[60]

Jeong Yak-yong as a Silhak scholar rejected the endowment of original nature (or the five constants) emphasized by Neo-Confucian scholars, and said, "Original nature is only 'a matter of taste (嗜好)'." And citing the virtues of benevolence and righteousness, he asserted, "The virtues never exist like 'a seed in the mind' but are fulfilled by performing the deeds corresponding to them."[61] Morality, according to Silhak scholars, is put into practice not by the spontaneous generation of the original nature but by the autonomous effort of those who have unusual sagacity and will. In addition, Jeong Yak-yong's view of the human being performing good deeds driven by 'taste' derives from the view of 'the innate goodness of human nature (性善說)'.

60 Refer to Heo Gyun, *Seongsobokbugo* and Ahn Jeong-bok, *Sunamseonsaeng-munjip*, Vol. 17.
61-*Jeongdasanjeonseo*, Book 2, Vol. 6.

I mentioned above that the Late Silhak scholars accepted feeling as a physical attribute, and regarded the human being as a desiring entity. Such a view might have developed into utilitarianism. Actually, however, it evolved instead into Bak Ji-won's view of 'public utility (公利), not personal utility (功利)'.[62] While the dictates of personal utility encourage the pursueit of individual interests, public utility pursues the public interests as a matter of course. Therefore, Silhak scholars' striving for public utility was not very different from the tendency of Neo-Confucian scholars.

As Silhak scholars especially emphasized the goal of benefiting the people as a whole, as was discussed already, they proposed the people-oriented educational system, the reform of the slave system, and other reform based on the equality of human beings. I have already pointed out that the impulse for reform which opened the modern age began to merge from 'their view of the equality of human beings (The entire people including slaves are Heavenly People, 天民).' and from their dedication to the abolition of the slave system based on their view of inherent equality.

62 Bak Ji-won, "Gwanongsocho", *Yeonamjip*.

Chapter VIII.

Reflection on Korean Neo-Confucianism

1. Reflection on the Methodology of the Investigation

Now it's time to conclude this work. First, let's reflect on the methodology of my investigation. I grasped the characteristics of Korean Confucianism on the basis of 'the fundamental concepts of Confucianism' namely benevolence (仁), righteousness (義), propriety (禮), wisdom (智) and practicality (實)'. I adopted this methodology for I anticipated that it would be adequate to the task of highlighting the idiosyncrasy of Korean Confucianism. Perhaps for the first time this methodology has been adopted in the entire Confucian region of East Asia. So I took up the challenge posed by this methodology at the risk of possible error. I sincerely hope my work fulfills my intention.

Confucian scholars thought of themselves as follows: "Scholars are the primary force upholding the nation." With 'the spirit of devotion to people (愛民精神)' they sacrificed their lives in the purges of Confucian scholars in order to achieve rule 'by the people (民本)' and 'for the people (爲民)'. "Their sacrifice for the realization of the principle of benevolence is a characteristic of Korean Confucianism. When the Japanese invaded Korea, Confucian scholars roused themselves to action and volunteered for the righteous army at the risk of their lives. They fought against the Japanese invaders for the realization of the principle of righteousness. This was a distinctive phenomenon that could not be found in other Confucian countries of East Asia. In addition, Korea, befitting to its reputation as 'the country of courteous people in the East', embraced the age of the proprieties, even enduring a partisan struggle called 'Yesong (禮訟)' over the methods of observing the royal period of mourning. After many complications Korea practised rule by decorum in a thoroughgoing way. So as a place that fulfilled the principle of propriety, Korea was unrivaled by any other Confucian country. This is one more characteristic of Korean Confucianism. These characteristics have been grasped by means of my methodology, carried out in light of the fundamental Confucian concepts. However, this methodology may hinder a grasp of the historical progress of Korean Confucianism that can be captured by a general survey, for mine is a divergent approach based on the fundamental Confucian concepts of benevolence, righteousness, propriety, wisdom and practicality. In anticipation of such a deficiency, and as an antidote, I began my work with a survey of the history of Korean Confucianism. In addition, the investigation of each fundamental concept and its application was carried out in the light of the contemporary historical situation in which they emerged. Therefore, those who read this book in a linear way from start to finish may not be confronted with this deficiency.

2. The Idea of Human Nobility as a Characteristic of Korean Confucianism

The distinctiveness of Korean Confucianism that I have attempted to illuminate refers to its type of characteristic not its merits and weakness. In general, the investigation of a characteristic is related to a discussion of facts while the grasp of a phenomenon's merits and weakness is related to value judgment. Nevertheless, my discussion of facts also implies value judgment, for Confucian concepts themselves such as benevolence, righteousness, and propriety entail subjective value rather than denoting objective facts.

In retrospect, I think that the Confucian scholars of Korea appropriately applied the fundamental Confucian concepts to their historical situations. We can take as concrete examples the fulfillment of rule by the people and for the people on the basis of the spirit of devotion to the people, the display of patriotic zeal symbolized by the volunteers of the righteous army, the formation of culture based on the proprieties (禮文化), befitting Korea's reputation as 'the country of courteous people in the East', outstanding philosophical insights revealed in 'the disputes of the Neo-Confucian scholars', and the formation of Silhak on the basis of the spirit of 'practical endeavor (務實)'. These are the examples of universal concepts transformed into context-specific concepts'. In other words, these examples have shown that the concrete and unique characteristics of Korean Confucianism could be formed on the basis of the fundamental and universal concepts of Confucianism.

When we review the formative aspects of Korean Confucianism, we see a fundamental characteristic that cannot be found in China and other countries. It may simply be seen as the development of Neo-Confucianism and Silhak. It may not be implausible to state that these two philosophies are the axes representing Korean Confucianism. Therefore let's review the primary characteristics of these philosophies. The history of Korean Neo-Confucianism started with inquiries into The Mandate of Heaven or Cheonmyeongdo (天命圖) on the part of Jeong Ji-un, Yi Hwang and Kim In-hu, and continued with inquiries into 'Four Beginnings and Seven Feelings,' 'The Identity of or Difference between Human Nature and the Thing's Nature,' and ended with 'The Neo-Confucian View that *Sim* is *ri*'. We've already seen that the theories that emerged from these inquiries represented the unique characteristics of Korean Confucianism.

The study of The Mandate of Heaven (天命) was focused on the view of the human being as 'the lord of all creation (人間靈長觀)', and its conclusion was that 'the value of the human being as the lord' lies in exercising morality that other animals are incapable of. In addition, this strain of thought dealt with theories of the ethical grounds of human life that bolstered the logic of the conclusion of the study. In this context we found the notable idea of Korean Confucianism, 'Human Nobility'.

The most noteworthy characteristic of De-Neo-Confucian Silhak scholars in the late period of Joseon was their demand for reform that were more radical than those of Neo-Confucian Silhak scholars. They sought reform of various institutional and philosophical systems, all of which were appropriate to the contemporary circumstances. In the vanguard of De-Neo-Confucian Silhak scholars was Yu Hyeong-won in the 17th century, whose reform plans may safely be said to represent the entirety of the reform plans of Silhak scholars in the late period of Joseon. I think that his most significant proposal was the abolishment of slave system. He asserted, "All human beings are 'Heavenly People (天民)' who were created by Heaven." His assertion reminds us of the view of 'human right endowed by Heaven'. As the ideas of the liberty and equality of people were implied in his concept of 'Heavenly People', clearly the concept was directly connected with the idea of 'Human Nobility'.

Human Nobility', as we have seen, was a core idea suffusing both the Neo-Confucianism and De-Neo-Confucianism of Korea. So the conclusion of my investigation into Korean Confucian thought is that Koreans have thoroughly preserved the idea of Human Nobility since ancient times.

3. On the Alleged Defects of Korean Confucianism

The fact that Korean Confucianism has many unique characteristics is evidence that it is 'not an epigone' of Chinese Confucianism, that is, Korean Confucianism has maintained its own distinctive traits. Considering that originality is connected with the excellence of philosophical ideas and the quality of a culture, our task is to re-evaluate the status of Korean Confucianism.

However, before engaging in such a task, we must examine and reflect on the alleged defects of Korean Confucianism. The first thing that is usually suggested in this respect is that Korean Confucianism was the cause of 'flunkyism (事大性)' or puppetry which weakened the sovereignty of Korea. This critique, which disparaged Korean Confucianism, was made in the context of the common belief that Confucianism had taken the role of a bridge leading to a one-sided relationship between China as a major power and Korea as a minor power. In fact, however, showing politeness toward a major power was merely the diplomatic policy of a minor power, and Korea obviously maintained its sovereignty and independence in its diplomatic relationship with China. Of course, the relationship between the two countries might naturally have been accompanied by reciprocal Confucian etiquette but to some critics 'the accompanying etiquette' seemed to be one-sided and to have therefore constituted obeisance on the part of Koreans. Even today, however, isn't it essential in a diplomatic relationship to maintain etiquette between the countries concerned? Moreover, to Koreans the world before the modern age was made up of 'the East Asian countries surrounding China'. So at those times Korean scholars' study of Confucianism amounted to a kind of 'autonomous participation in the global order'. Thus, it may be said that the excellence of Korean Confucianism was the product of their positive participation in 'the globalization of Confucianism'.

Some people ascribe the fall of the Joseon Dynasty at the hands of the Japanese imperialists to Confucianism, for Neo-Confucianism was the governing ideology of Joseon at that time. They argue that the misrule based on Neo-Confucianism was the greatest defect of Korean Confucianism. I agree that Korean Confucianism was not free of blame for the fall of Joseon. Neither do I think that Confucianism did not play its moral and political part in the defeat, but I insisted that

Confucianism only bore 'partial' responsibility. Confucian scholars including myself have argued that the fall of Joseon could be ascribed to the king and governing bureaucrats rather than Confucianism itself. Such an ascription is based on the fact that Japan was also a Confucian country when it occupied Joseon by force.

There is another reason why I believe Confucianism bore only partial responsibility for the fall of Joseon. In the 16th century the king and the ruling class of Joseon did not put into practice the plans for strengthening national defense by building a strong military proposed by Yi I, a Neo-Confucian scholar, and in this defenseless state Joseon was invaded by Japanese soldiers in 1592, and was faced with a crisis. Learning the lesson of this shameful experience, Bak Ji-won, a De-Neo-Confucian scholar in the 18th century, tried to end political abuses more aggressively, and insisted on 'the extended scope of Silhak' or the reconfiguration of the concepts of Silhak. That is, he suggested that Silhak, the knowledge of which had usually been considered to be a necessity for securing government positions, should extend its scope and apply itself to knowledge of 'agriculture, manufacturing industry, and commerce'. Furthermore, on the basis of the pursuit of the 'public interest (公益)', he suggested proposals for making the people wealthier and the country affluent and powerful.

Jeong Yak-yong (1762-1836) who inherited his predecessors' views suggested that true Confucian scholars' conceptions of Silhak should aim at defeating foreign invaders, accumulating ample national wealth and resources, and educating people to be equipped with both literary and military skills. And in his Memorial to the Throne he advised on the need to build up national wealth and defenses through the cultivation of experts in both the literary and military fields. Choi Han-gi, a Silhak scholar, uniquely suggested the opening of trade with Western nations, and didn't hesitate to include military science in Silhak's pedagogical arsenal in order to strengthen national defense.

These Silhak scholars repeatedly stressed the necessity of reforms in order to build up national wealth and defenses. However, the king, ministers, and especially the king's maternal relatives and those in high government posts disguising themselves as Confucian scholars, far from putting Silhak scholars' reform plans into practice, would not even consider them. The king's maternal relatives, using the authority of the royal order, tyrannized the people and were bent on satisfying their self-interest and desires.[1] In view of such a situation it's legitimate to say that the incompetence and corruption of the king, the rapaciousness of his maternal relatives, and the intellectual vacuity of mediocre scholars were the cause of the fall of Joseon.

In the face of this, Neo-Confucian scholars who adhered to the philosophy of 'defending orthodoxy and rejecting heterodoxy (爲政斥邪)' also strove to maintain the sovereignty of Korea. Some of them (Ki Sam-yeon and so on) fought against the Japanese imperialists and were killed as soldiers of the righteous army, and some of them (Hwang Hyeon and so on), displaying the agony of the intellectual in the face of futility in times of crisis, killed themselves, thereby thoroughly revealing their sense of identity.

4. The Prospect of Korean Confucianism

I have reflected on Korean Confucianism starting from the question of whether Confucianism as a traditional system of thought retains its value in modern times. Its value, in view of circumstances in which modern science, technology, and economics dominate human lives, may be similar to that of the humanities *per se*.

Koreans are little concerned with both Korean Confucianism and the humanities. However, scholars of the humanities maintain that the value of their field should be emphasized all the more in the modern age. Likewise, scholars of Korean Confucianism believe that the value of Korean Confucianism lies in its role of finding an escape from

---

1 The representative ones were Pungyang Jo clan, Andong Kim clan, and Yeoheung Min clan.

the destructive practices Korea is now faced with, and furthermore in its possible contribution to solving the current stalemates humanity confronts.

'Benevolence (仁)', in view of its classical meaning of favorable consideration of others as if they were oneself, can ultimately be extended to the concepts of 'freedom and equality'. Therefore, the concept of benevolence can be productive in the future through its reinterpretations and through ideas that complement it. The concept of 'righteousness (義)', which originally meant duty and justice, may be extended and thereby can contribute to improving the lives of Koreans and humankind. 'Propriety (禮)', in its broad meaning, may take the role of a guide to moral deeds. The value of 'wisdom (智)', by dint of intellectual development and technological aids, may come to be highly regarded--all the more so in this unpredictable age. On the premise that the dignity of the human being should be maintained in accordance with the knowledge that wisdom imparts, its utility may be recognized. The fact that the prospects of Confucianism as a whole are not so gloomy also suggests the bright prospects of Korean Confucianism.

What is the most representative thought of Korean Confucianism? It's the thought of 'human nobility' consistently suffusing Korean Neo-Confucianism and De-Neo-Confucian Silhak. Neo-Confucian scholars promoted 'human nobility' in connection with the moral values entailed in the study of 'The Mandate of Heaven'. The proposition that, "Everyone is created by Heaven," was suggested by a De-neo- confucian scholar named Yu Hyeong-won, who proposed measures of reform so radical that the administrative and economic systems of the Joseon Dynasty could have been dismantled if his proposals had been acted upon. They supported the abolition of the slave system and also had something in common with the concept of human nobility.

In a word, human nobility was a core idea widespread throughout all the schools of Korean Confucianism. Moreover, it is related to the spirit of 'devotion to the welfare of mankind (弘益人間)' implied in 'Dangun Mythology (檀君神話)' which consists of the myths of the Korean people. The view that, "The human being is Heaven (人乃天)" advanced by Choi Hae-wol's (崔海月) Donghak (東學, Eastern Learning) was not an arbitrary one--it also had something in common with human nobility. Needless to say, human nobility is a concept that should be propagated in the future.

I've already mentioned that theories of 'Four-Seven', 'The Identity of or Difference between Human Nature and Thing's Nature', and 'Neo-Confucian *simjeukri*' are all concerned with morality. In view of the fact that morality itself is the product of human nobility these venerable theories cannot be said to be worthless in the context of today. It will be demonstrated that these theories are a legacy to be cherished in the effort to strengthen morality in this era and in the future. In particular, these theories will contribute 'considerably' to the elaboration of the realm of the philosophy of mind.

If we intend to take the characteristics of Korean Confucianism as a stepstone on the path to cultural development, our task is 'to closely reexamine and critically improve' the philosophical heritage handed down to us by Korean Neo-Confucianism. And we should not underestimate the views of De-Neo-Confucian Silhak scholars as a remnant of the past, given that they creatively and courageously proposed reform measures appropriate to their own eras. Their proposals should also be assimilated as assets guiding Korean Confucian scholars today and in the future.

In passing, I want to add some incidental words. When Korean Confucian scholars today submit the results of their philosophical works connected with given social problems, I hope that politicians and public officials will show interest in these works and respond reasonably to them. I have already emphasized the importance of politicians' sympathetic participation in overcoming national crises in the context of discussing the causes of the fall of the Joseon Dynasty. The promising prospects of Korean Confucianism are not irrelevant

 244

to reflection on the bitter lessons of history and the practical attempt to resolve critical problems.

Appendix I.

Moral Awakening in the Service of the Unification of Korea

(Modern Korean Society and the Obstacles to Living Moral Lives)

1. The Dual Task of Koreans

The tasks of establishing righteous morals and improving 'the quality of life' in a society have been the common themes of human kind in all ages and countries. Since the beginning of human history there have been many cases in which a certain standard of morality, however temporarily, was instrumental in the establishment of social order. For instance, East Asian countries, especially Korea under the Joseon Dynasty, developed stable politics, society, education and culture on the basis of *samgangoryun* (三綱五倫, the three fundamental principles and the five moral disciplines in human relations) and its resultant ethical systems.

However, today when the distinction between East Asia and Western Europe has become economically and culturally meaningless, Confucianism cannot take the role of a persuasive ideology. As the moral values of North, South, East and West have become intermingled these days, human beings have lost their ways. Owing to the absence of a strong moral code Koreans wander aimlessly through their lives, and the Western nations are in a similar position, unable to foster a social order in which people can lead orderly lives based on their own sense of morality.

Though the whole world suffers from the lack of a productive moral code and consequent social fragility, only Korea bears the additional burden of 'the partition of the nation'. Korea has the dual task of reestablishing desirable morals and achieving peaceful unification based on the reconciliation of South and North Korea.

Strong morality alone cannot accomplish the tasks of overcoming the ideological confrontation between South and North Korea and realizing the unification of Korea. But it should not be overlooked that it can have an influence on that issue to a significant degree. In this connection, the rehabilitation of a just morality of Koreans should be pursued so that it may helpful to the realization of the long-cherished wish for the unification of Korea. This is the reasonable way of responding to the situation of Korea that Koreans should bear in mind in the discussion of morality.

To relate the rehabilitation of morality to the unification of Korea may seem too tenuous a connection to mention in this kind of investigation. However, turning away from a burden as if it were not ours because it is too heavy cannot be the true method of philosophizing. The really desirable attitude may be to seriously approach a problem and endeavor to find its solution, however difficult the problems we are faced with in the course of our lives may be. In this context I'd like to focus on the rigorous role Korean philosophers should play.

2. The Present Situations of the Korean Confucian Circle

These days amorality or lack of moral sense is fundamentally ascribed to a 'poor sense of ethical value'. In addition, it is also attributed to the destructiveness of modern civilization. The tendency of taking the selfishness and avarice of the human being as a matter of course and the trend of vitiating altruism are not irrelevant to modern scientific and technological civilization. The view of the human being as an avaricious being originated from 'the modern view of attaching importance to nature(自然)', but, this view, in spite of critical reflection on it, hardly withers away owing to the influence of the superlative development of scientific and technological civilization.

Today science and technology have brought about 'the convenient lifestyle of mechanization and automation'. However, such a lifestyle is a primary factor behind the dilution of both human relationships permeated by affection and intimacy and the sense of moral value that was the nucleus of the humanities. Moreover, citizens can't afford to prioritize morality owing to the irresponsible behavior and speech of businessmen with political affiliations, the severity and mercilessness of the various strands of the law, and the ferocity of the economic system that makes subsistence itself impossible without limitless competition.

People of this era not only do not care about moral introspection but also about the laxity of moral fiber, and their resultant callousness is even regarded as generosity. The present situation is too coarse to allow people to pursue moral self-development which can be achieved only by diligence, sincerity, and self-improvement. As people cannot live meaningful lives, they lose their strength of personality and fall into the state of alienated solitude, helpless solipsism and further, the crisis of losing their humanity. These are the actual conditions modern people are generally faced with.

The situations of Korea is worse than this, for Neo-Confucianism, which almost arbitrarily has taken on the responsibility of establishing a Korean moral code since the middle ages, is now degraded into a hackneyed philosophy. The situation of Korea is often illustrated by saying, "Confucius must die for the revival of morals in Korea." However, this quasi-curse becomes a truth. Seonggyungwan, which once represented Korean Confucian circles and was the central locus of moral thought, has recently lost its *'raison d'être'* owing to its corrupt and illegal practices. As Seonggyungwan has lost its prestige, it is an undeniable fact that the moral function of the whole Korean Confucian circle is currently almost paralyzed.

'The three fundamental principles and the five moral disciplines in human relations (三綱五倫)' that represented Korean ethical codes have long been considered outmoded and useless. In addition, 'the ceremonies of coming-of-age, marriage, funeral, and ancestral rite (冠婚喪祭)' that represented Confucian manners and ceremonies have long gone unobserved. Since Western manners and ceremonies were introduced to Korea, Korean traditional rituals have rarely been performed in spite of their merits. Considering that manners are naturally formed in accordance with the customs of a certain period, it may be a natural consequence that they cannot be maintained as before. Manners and moral codes are subjected to change in accordance with a changing world. What matters here is that it is not a simple matter to develop an alternative ethical system that can replace the existing one.

Some Confucian scholars' endeavor to newly illuminate the established moral principles of Confucianism and investigate proposals to apply them in the present age. However, for decades, Confucian academic circles have not been able to go further than pretending to examine, with respect to self-cultivation, aspects of the Neo-Confucian theory of *simseong* (心性, mind and nature) such as 'the view on four-seven (四端七情, the four beginnings and the seven feelings)'. I said 'pretending' because they do not meet the urgent demands of times for the development of human nature, though there is a clear onus on them to do. There has been little, if any, research starting anew from the ethics of the Original Confucianism, which comprises fundamental concepts such as benevolence (仁) and righteousness (義), and the other virtues of sincerity (誠實), fidelity (信義), reverence (恭敬), and friendship (友愛). There has been such little research that the studies that do exist are regarded as superficial. After all, the completion of worthwhile research might take more time and effort.

3. The Moral Consciousness Found in the Populace

Although newly elaborated ethical theories have not yet been presented, we should not be disappointed or abandon our attempt to establish a desirable moral system. Hasty withdrawal is like the abandonment of a task after 'seeking wool on an ass', for we have not yet investigated the primordial concepts of morality itself and their formation.

Moral character, formed by autonomous will, is different from the forced norm called law. But Koreans seem to habitually neglect the practice of autonomous will. It is arguable whether such neglect originated from the patriotic rejection of the illegitimate legalism forced upon Korea during the period of Japanese occupation. In any case, it should be pointed out that these days the law-abiding spirit of Korean law-makers and the autonomous will of ordinary Koreans to observe moral code have been much attenuated, and steps should be taken to correct this.

Self-cultivation like that of a monk is necessary for the formation of moral codes because of their characteristic of autonomy. In other words, the autonomous mental attitude and control of a monk aimed at the attainment of a so-called 'pure heart' correspond to the preparatory stage of the formation of moral codes. So self-cultivation is a necessary, but not sufficient condition of morality because morality is not achieved through self-cultivation or self-ordained training alone but ultimately through the relation to others.

Moral consciousness can be recovered when we don't do harm to others and show consideration for them. Moral consciousness means the will to harmonize my way of living with another person's, based on 'the common denominator called living'. Therefore, it is essential to have a practical reason for the control of one's own feelings. This is the reason why Kant said that we should regard others not as a means but as end in themselves.

Moral consciousness is evidently formed not only through self-awakening but also through our relations with others, judging from the fact that the proprieties originated from 'secular custom'. So, first of all, let's have a look at the moral aspects of ordinary people, not of scholars of ethics and morals, for their moral consciousness formed through their variegated and vivid lives may surely be helpful to our investigation.

In the course of our lives immoral and good deeds coexist like 'shade and light (陰陽)'. Not a few good deeds shine like luminous constellations in the pitch-black night sky. I will introduce some examples I am familiar with. Nowadays, we deplore the fact that fellow-feeling between even brothers and sisters has disappeared. However, there are not a few people who do not hesitate to donate their internal organs to those who are seriously ill, and improve their conditions without any reward. Some doctors, though they are not a Schweitzer in Africa, devote their whole lives to curing the diseases of the poor. There are teachers who also devote themselves to the education of children in remote corners of the planet and on isolated islands. Many people unsparingly spend time and money to alleviate the hunger of the homeless. Those who adopt babies, especially handicapped babies, though they may not be well-off, are also the people who practise love of neighbor or love of human beings. A passer-by who risked his life, by dangling in the air by attaching himself with a rope used for cleaning windows in order, to save people in a burning skyscraper, and a diver who plunged into the water to save people in a submerged vessel, these are our brethren. Those who presented themselves as 'the patriotic keeper of Dokdo Island' are today's soldiers or generals of the righteous army. These memorable good deeds were performed not by scholars but by ordinary people.

I, as a Confucian scholar, think that these people are 'supporters of noble causes (志士)', models of 'self-sacrifice to preserve integrity (殺身成仁)', and the vanguard of ethics and morals. As we can see in these examples, the warmth and the seeds of moral consciousness are still alive in our society. These real and vivid examples are both reprovals of and lessons to Confucian scholars and constitute 'the lamplight of the future'.

4. The Universality and Sociality Inherent in Moral Principles

With respect to the Confucian moral view, the above examples seen in actual life may be said to be the expression of the 'benevolence (仁)' and 'righteousness (義)' latent in us. And the examples show that the seeds of benevolence and righteousness have naturally sprouted into the virtues of filial piety (孝), friendship (友愛), loyalty (忠), fidelity (信) and brevity (勇).

These examples also evidence the unchanging universality inherent in moral principles or virtues, and allow us to realize that the indispensable virtues of 'benevolence, righteousness, propriety, wisdom, and fidelity' that were called 'the five constants' in the past should not be forgotten and thoughtlessly abandoned. Our task is to discover the means of applying universal normative principles to the present situations and to clarify the characteristics inherent in these principles. The manner of relationship, to which the three fundamental principles (三綱) and the five moral disciplines (五倫) are applied, may differ in accordance with places and times but the relationship between human beings itself", corresponding to 'sociality', cannot be denied and can hardly disappear. So in practising the three principles and the five disciplines, only the elements that are not appropriate to the present situation should be rejected and the sociality of a relationship should be flexibly put into practice regardless of the three principles or the five disciplines. In fact, the three fundamental principles and the five moral disciplines were consolidated not synchronically but gradually with the addition of moral codes in relation to the political and social systems of the past such as monarchy and patriarchy. So it may be said that the revision or reinterpretation of the appropriate methods of practising moral principles is perennially required. And the revision or reinterpretation process should be accompanied by a new doctrinal effort in which new understanding and new meaning are incorporated into moral principles and virtues.

Some Neo-Confucian scholars, bearing in mind today's circumstances and the predictable future, have attempted to reinterpret moral principles and virtues as well as the applicable Confucian moral codes of the past. In particular, it's a long time since the investigation of the core principles of Confucianism such as 'benevolence' and 'righteousness' with respect to their 'ethical virtue (德性倫理)' commenced. Once I also suggested, bearing in mind 'social development', a definition of benevolence as 'the nature of creating things (産物之性)' based on the human being's fecund creativity in addition to the existing definitions of 'love of the human being (愛人)', 'the nature of loving things (愛物之性)', and 'the nature of creating things (生物之性)'. I also suggested a definition of righteousness (義) as a complex concept implying both the characteristics of ethical virtue and ethical obligation. Owing to these characteristics, the Confucian concept of righteousness is at once the same as and different from the Western concept of justice.

5. The Reinterpretation of Fundamental Moral Principles

Now it's time to discuss the necessity of the reinterpretation of moral principles and the issue of establishing a new doctrinal code by developing new theories. Recently, I critically investigated the concept of benevolence (仁) that is the core principle of Confucianism. Needless to say, the most outstanding and originary interpretation of benevolence is Confucius' 'loving people (愛人)' which is actualized as 'consideration of others'. However, I don't believe that loving people is the first prerequisite for the formation of morality because the existence of the human being precedes the function of loving people. As *The Book of Mencius* and *The Doctrine of the Mean* say, "Benevolence is the human being."

As Confucius also said, "Benevolence is love toward people," the act of loving is meaningless if the human being, the subject and object of the act, does not exist. And if a human being does not lead a life worthy of a human being, the inevitable norms of morality become vacuous and meaningless to the human being. In this context, the interpretation of 'benevolence as the human being' in *The Book of Mencius* and *The Doctrine of the Mean* logically precedes Confucius' view of benevolence as 'loving people'.

The interpretation of benevolence (仁) as the human being (人) also implies the problem of confusing the human being with benevolence

— all the more so because benevolence and the human being have the same pronunciation of [in] in Korean. What matters here is why benevolence is interpreted as the human being. As we cannot discover any explanation, we have to assess it for ourselves. Confucius once said, "To be benevolent is to be wise and brave." and in this context Zhu Xi said, "Benevolence is the whole of virtue and the other virtues are all partial." In this way sages in the past judged that benevolence is the highest principle or virtue of original nature'. Mencius once said that the four virtues of benevolence, righteousness, propriety and wisdom belong to original nature that differentiates the human being from animals, and scholars following Mencius assimilated his thought. From Mencius' thought we may believe that benevolence as the whole of virtue is the essence of making a human being a moral human being. It may be in this context that classical texts regard benevolence as human being. In the early period of Joseon Gwon Geun's proposition that "The human being is benevolence" in his *Iphakdoseol* (入學圖說) also meant that, "The human being is the embodiment or the energeia (actuality) of benevolence."

From this we may derive a proposition, "Benevolence is the fundamental virtue or principle that makes a biological human being a moral human being." This proposition corresponds to a reinterpretation of human nature or the establishment of a kind of new doctrinal code based on *The Book of Mencius* and *The Doctrine of the Mean*. With this proposition we come to secure a fundamental base on which we can make ourselves moral human beings. And this proposition, locating the essence of the human being at the starting point of moral pursuit, agrees with the original humanistic characteristics of Confucianism. On this fundamental base we should pursue and practise concrete morality.

6. Moral Awakening in the Service of the Unification of Korea

Looking at the contemporary Korean situations, we discover

another task we have to take on. This is the resolution of moral problems entailed by the reunification of Korea which has been the long-cherished wish of the Korean people. Of course, the task of national reunification cannot be approached in its moral aspects alone for it is a matter of overcoming the political confrontation of modern ideologies. However, it cannot be said that reunification is completely disconnected from morality, for moral ideology is itself a guide to the proper ways of living, and politics is closely connected to morality. Moreover, as the reunification of Korea is a matter of using all of our capacities, it is desirable for us to consider some aspects of moral awakening necessary for the reunification of Korea.

The most urgent condition that must be met for the reunification of Korea is the maintenance of the attitude of co-existence aimed at the mutual prosperity of North and South. The freedom and equality that support the political systems of North and South are not incompatible ideologies in social life, but essential ones for guaranteeing human and civil rights. Just as we believe that the best policy for the pursuit of reunification is 'the peaceful harmonization of North and South', 'co-existence for mutual prosperity' should also be pursued even from the viewpoint of morality.

Confucianism teaches us the lesson of 'mutual col-existence'. The seminal example is 'the theory of sincerity (誠論)' or 'the theory of the completion of self and others (成己成物論)' mentioned in *The Doctrine of the Mean*. The following statements about sincerity are introduced in Chapter 25 of *A Commentary on the Doctrine of the Mean*: "Sincerity itself is the Way of Heaven and to become sincere is the way of the human being," "Sincerity is the beginning and end of things. Without sincerity things cannot exist. Therefore, a true gentleman evaluates highly the attempt to be sincere." Then the statement below follows:

> "Sincerity not only means the completion of self but also of others. The completion of self is benevolence and the completion of others is perception (知). The characteristic virtue of nature (性) embraces

> both self and others. (Chap. 25,《中庸章句》, *A Commentary on the Doctrine of the Mean*)

According to the above statement, the existence of others is completed by perception while the existence of self is completed by the characteristic of benevolence. Considering the aforementioned proposition that "Benevolence is the human being," benevolence here means a kind of 'personification', that is, the resolution to live like a human being with firm belief in self-consciousness. Benevolence and perception help to complete the self and others, and sincerity, especially profound sincerity, helps to achieve benevolence and perception to the full, as discussed in Chapter 22 of *The Doctrine of the Mean*. Therefore, we may conclude that sincerity helps to complete both self and others. That is, 'the co-existence' of self and others can be achieved through sincerity.

Originally *seong* (誠, sincerity) had diverse meanings such as 'flawless truth', 'consistent purity', and 'sincere devotion'. The view of sincerity itself as 'the Way of Heaven' can be ascribed to the universality of its unchanging faithfulness and purity. On the other hand, the sincere attempt at the embodiment of faithfulness and purity should become 'the way of the human being'. When a host regards his guest with a faithful, pure and sincere mind, he will be viewed by his guest as a man of noble personality, and his guest in turn, susceptible to the host's influence, might also try to become a mature person. Then, it can be said that the two have formed 'a co-existent and symbiotic relationship', and that sincerity has become the moral principle or virtue that achieves co-existence.

It is clear in our present situation that a sincere attitude toward co-existence is a moral virtue required for the reunification of Korea. Today the authorities of the North and South mutually request the other party to show good faith. Considering that good faith means nothing other than sincerity, the value of a sincere attitude in the talks between North and South becomes self-evident.

In addition to sincerity, there is another concept whose moral aspects should be illuminated for the reunification of Korea. That is the concept of the symbiotic relationship that emerges from the concept of coexistence. As I believe that 'a symbiotic relationship' is essential to forming the foundations of reunification, I have previously examined it together with the potential method of coexistence of North and South. (Refer to Volume 30 of *A Study of Yulgok's Learning*). It is summarized as follows.

The Confucian view of 'the symbiotic relationship' was proposed in the context of profound speculation on 'the formation of nature'. This is frequently discussed when the mutual relationship of *yin* and *yang* (陰陽) is grasped as 'complementary cooperation'. When two contrasting entities like *yin* and *yang* harmoniously co-exist through 'mutual accompaniment (待對, 相須)' and complementary cooperation, such a form of co-existence develops into 'a symbiotic relationship'.

The mobility and tranquility of *yin·yang* detailed in 'the theory of the formation of the universe' in Zhou Dunyi (周敦頤)'s *Taegeukdoseol* (太極圖說) represent the quintessential 'symbiotic relationship'.

> "It's at once 'Endlessness and the Great Ultimate (無極而太極)'. Taegeuk moved and produced *yang* (陽). Mobility in its extremity changed into tranquility. *Yin* (陰) was produced by tranquility. Tranquility in its extremity changed into mobility again. Mobility at one time and tranquility at another time alternately took the role of root... *Yang* changed and combined with *yin* to produce *ohaeng* (五行, the five elements: water, fire, wood, metal, and earth)... All things were created by the mysterious combination and condensation of the essences of *yin·yang* and *ohaeng*... by the association of the two kinds of *gi* called *yin·yang*."

In particular, the remark, "Mobility at one time and tranquility at another time alternately took the role of root," refers to 'a symbiotic relationship' based on mutual accompaniment because the remark implies that mobility can arise owing to tranquility and *vice versa*.

To regard the relation of two contrasting objects not as that of mutual opposition or struggle but as a symbiotic relationship is a meritorious characteristic of Confucianism. The symbiotic relationship is connected with Zhu Xi (朱熹)'s definition of benevolence as 'the mode of enabling things to maintain their lives' based on the view of the universe as a life-form mentioned in *The Book of Changes* and Cheng Hao (程顥)'s view on the life-generating function of benevolence. So 'the symbiotic relationship' that guarantees 'mutual prosperity' is an indispensable moral principle for the reunification of Korea and for the survival of mankind.

We know from our experience that the virtue of the symbiotic relationship is embodied as 'the spirit of mutual help'. Moreover, considering the geographical environment of Korea, surrounded as it is by powerful states, the spirit of mutual help cannot be over-emphasized, not only for the reunification of Korea but also for the achievement of national prosperity after reunification. I believe that 'the moral reawakening' of Koreans should aim at the fulfillment of such goals.

7. Concluding Remarks

My investigations are classified into three areas. The first is that the seeds of morality are produced by the nameless multitude. This phenomenon has been ascribed to the disposition of love or benevolence toward others and to the disposition of righteousness or the chivalrous spirit. I'd like to regard this phenomenon as offering the possibility of the revival of the fundamental moral principles of Confucianism in these desolate modern times. Our fundamentally noble-hearted populace clearly display the will 'to revive Confucian morality'.

The second area is my 'reinterpretation of benevolence (仁),' which is one of the fundamental moral concepts of Confucianism. The point of my reinterpretation was that the meaning of benevolence is not only loving others and consideration of others but also the human being. The basis of my reinterpretation was that moral norms are hard to establish without our acknowledgement that we are human beings. Only when we recognize ourselves as such and are seen as such by others can indispensable concrete moral norms be effective. So it may not be implausible to say that the self-recognition of "We are human beings" or "We will live like human beings" is the prerequisite to human beings becoming the agents of morality. We should not forget that Confucianism is based on the humanitarian thought implied in Confucius statement that he is a being that can live only with human beings but not with animals.

The third issue is my suggestion that Korean scholars today who assume the task of moral revival should morally awaken themselves in order to play a part in national reunification, not to speak of the comprehensive re-examination of morality. This suggestion is based on humanitarian thought. The misfortune caused by national division is not only a matter of the families separated during the Korean War. The manacles of ideological confrontation between North and South block the path to the greater affluence and happiness of the Korean people, which is the reason why reunification is the long-standing task of Koreans that must be fulfilled. So it is only natural that Confucian scholars today should also participate in the challenge.

I have not been able to provide even an inkling to the method of fulfilling the above-mentioned tasks. Even in the fields of ethics and philosophy my performance of these tasks has not been sufficient. I have merely displayed my commitment to facing up to those challenges. I will feel satisfied if the interest I've shown draws a little attention to the tasks at hand from passionate young scholars.

(This article was presented as the keynote speech at <The International Academic Conference> sponsored by the Korean Academic Society of Confucianism. The Conference was held on November 11th in 2015 in the auditorium of Jungang University.)

Appendix II.

A Study on Mencius' Virtue Ethics[*][1]

1. Introduction

This work starts from the question of how ethical theories, which facilitate amicable communication between persons and the establishment of social ethics and social order, can be formulated. I will discuss this question by focusing on the thought of Confucius, and of Mencius in particular, who laid the foundation of Confucianism. Therefore this paper will mainly deal with Mencius' theories of ethics and its characteristics.

Some may ask why I attempt to grasp contemporary issues by relying on an age-old, traditional system of thought. The reason is that as these are universal questions that can be raised in any time and place, Confucius and Mencius, who represented Confucian thought, might well have pondered over similar issues. In other words, my methodology is to reexamine the wisdom of the classics by "reviewing the old and learning the new" (溫故而知新).[2]

Let's take as an example "the five cardinal human relations" (*wulun* 五倫). Though the past modes of practice of the five moral formulas pertaining to father and son, king and vassal, husband and wife, the elderly and the young, and among friends have become

---

* Youn Sa-Soon, professor emeritus at Korea University.

1 The English translation of the texts of *Lunyu* 論語 (*The Analects of Confucius*), *Mengzi* 孟子 (*Mencius*) and *Zhongyong* 中庸 (*Doctrine of the Mean*) cited in this article is my own.

2 *Analects* 2.11.

very outmoded, the moral formulas *per se* have been and will be maintained as in the past. Moreover, some formulas constituting the relations between people have retained a universality that makes them vital in the present and future. The reason why we recall Confucius' and Mencius' thought is that though the modes of human relations may change with the passage of time, human relations *per se* have retained essentially unchanging features and the modes or principles underlying them in the past are still valid.

Here I will not discuss in detail the five moral disciplines (principles or virtues) underlying human relations, namely affection, loyalty, distinction, orderliness, and faithfulness. However, the fundamental principles underlying human relations must not be neglected and ignored, for they have a universality transcending the passage of time. The fundamental principles Confucius and Mencius especially observed were *ren* 仁 (benevolence) and *yi* 義 (righteousness). So I cannot but pay attention to the theories of *ren* and *yi* in my investigation of Mencius' theories. As he inherited and philosophically developed Confucius' theories, I will focus my attention on Mencius' thought.

2. Confucius' and Mencius' Definitions of *Ren* and *Yi*

Before the eras of Confucius and Mencius the literal meanings of *ren* 仁 (benevolence) included "wisdom", "wise person", "thou", and "person" and those of *yi* 義 (righteousness) included "uprightness", "truthfulness", "matter-of-course", "significance", "criterion", "duty", and "reasonableness".

Confucius accepted, on the whole, the literal meanings of *yi*. However, he personally defined *ren* as "loving others" (愛人)[3], and thought that the method of practicing *ren* is *shu* 恕[4], that is,

3 *Analects* 12.22.

4 *Analects* 15.24.

to treat others as if they were yourself, "not to impose on others what you yourself would not desire" and let others do something insofar as you yourself wish to do the same.[5] To sum up, displaying consideration for others is Confucius' method of practising *ren*.

Mencius also explained *yi* on the basis of its literal meanings, and defined *ren* by adding his own gloss to its literal meanings. According to him, *ren* is "the path of the human being" (人路)[6], in particular, "the righteous path of the human being" (人之正路)[7]. In addition, he described *ren* as "the mind of the human being" (人心)[8], "the peaceful abode of the human being"[9], and "the human being *per se*."[10]

Mencius suggested as manifestations of *ren* and *yi* not only concrete instances but also states of mind or 'the beginning' (端緒) of original nature. He thought that the representative instances of *yi* are "showing respect for or being obedient to one's elder brother(s)"[11] and serving the King with loyalty[12], and that 'the beginning' of the fulfillment of obedience and loyalty is "the mind of shame and hatred" (羞惡之心).[13]

The concrete practical instance or the starting point of *ren*, according to Mencius, is the display of filial piety or the rendering of service to parents. In this respect he said that "filial piety is the kernel of *ren*" (仁之實).[14] He thought that 'the beginning' of *ren* is "the mind that cannot be aloof from others' sufferings" (不忍人之心)

5 *Analects* 15.24; 6.30.
6 *Mengzi* 6A11.
7 *Mengzi* 4A10.
8 *Mengzi* 6A11.
9 *Mengzi* 4A10.
10 *Mengzi* 7B16.
11 *Mengzi* 4A27.
12 *Mengzi* 1A1.
13 *Mengzi* 2A6.
14 *Mengzi* 4A27.

or "compassion" (惻隱之心).[15]

In the practice of *ren* one should firstly devote oneself to one's parents, and secondly love elders, children and the people. Mencius proposed "governance by *ren*" (仁政) as a form of extended practice of this principle. In this context he said, "Those who govern with the mind not being aloof from others' sufferings can rule over the whole country as if it were in their own hands."[16]

3. *Ren* and *Yi* Theorized on the Basis of the View of Human Nature as Fundamentally Good

(1) Confucius' Original Conception of Ren *and* Yi

Confucius related *ren* to the desirable characteristic of a man. In this context he said, "A sycophant's false expression and words are remote from *ren*"[17] and "Being steadfast, dignified, simple and slow in speech are akin to the attributes of *ren*."[18] Judging from his dicta, he seems to have meant by *ren* the characteristics of innocence and honesty above all else.

He also related *ren* to virtues such as politeness, generosity, fidelity and propriety. As befits his former occupation of 'propriety master' (儒者), he particularly related propriety to *ren*, and said, "to subdue one's self and return to propriety constitutes *ren*" (克己復禮爲仁).[19] He always emphasized to his disciples the filial piety toward their parents, love between brothers and intimate friendship with benevolent persons.[20] One of his disciples named Youzi (有子) stated that filial piety and brotherly love are the means

15 *Mengzi* 2A6.

16 Loc. cit.

17 *Analects* 1.3; 17.17.

18 *Analects* 13.27.

19 *Analects* 12.1.

20 *Analects* 1.6.

of achieving *ren*.[21] His words were an echo of Confucius' view.

Since The Age of the Warring States, *ren*, due to Confucius' influence, had become the fundamental principle informing the formation of the system of family ethics based on filial piety. In East Asia filial piety evolved into the virtue of practicing *ren* and came to be understood as the fundamental principle underlying the maintenance of ethical order. The practice of *ren* through filial piety was compatible with the characteristics of premodern East Asian societies composed of large families that lived mainly by means of agriculture.

The Chinese letter '仁' (*ren*) symbolizes 'two persons' (二人). Confucius noticed the symbolic meaning of '仁' and interpreted it as love and scrupulous care, which facilitate the unity and mutual understanding of people. Mencius' attempt at the political embodiment of *ren* also originated from Confucius' dictum, *Ren* and its application is far more vital to the lives of ordinary people than water and fire are.[22]

As for *yi* 義 (righteousness), Confucius seemed to rely mainly on its literal meanings and to not clearly formulate his own opinion. But this was not always the case. Confucius once mentioned *yi* as if it designated personal character. However, at another time he discussed it as a principle of ethical order, and alluded that concentrating on loyalty and fidelity (忠信) leads to righteousness (*yi*).[23] As 'loyalty and fidelity' means the reliability of the sincere mind, according to Confucius, it is similar to *yi*.

Once Confucius used *yi* as the antonym of *li* 利 (profits). In this context he said, "A virtuous person is well-versed in *yi* while a mean person is well-versed in *li*,"[24] and "one should seize on *yi* at the

21 *Analects* 1.2.

22 *Analects* 15.35.

23 *Analects* 12.10.

24 *Analects* 4.16.

sight of *li*."[25] Moreover, he used *yi* as the norm of conduct and the principle of ethical order. As a result he states that a virtuous man "enters government service in the event that the country pursues *yi*,"[26] and "nurtures people with generosity and then employs their services on the basis of *yi*."[27]

(2) Mencius' Comprehensive Conception of Ren *and* Yi

Mencius acknowledged Confucius' definition of *ren* as 'love toward others', and reinforced his concept of filial piety by emphasizing that *ren* is achieved through it. He argued, "If one has affection toward others, but is not devoted to one's parents, one is acting against *ren*."[28]

This belief was related to the circumstances of The Age of the Warring States, and was formulated in reaction to Mozi (墨子, 470? BC - 391? BC) who advocated 'the equality of affection' (兼愛). Mencius, in order to refute Mozi's doctrine, asserted that *ren* starts from filial piety and is gradually disseminated to other people.

Mencius' definition of *ren* as 'the mind of the human being' was based on the premise that it is representative of original nature. And his other definition of *ren* as 'the comforting home of the human being' was based on the premise that it is the 'good' original nature. Still another definition of *ren* that he advanced, that it is 'the human being *per se*', was based on his judgment that the good original nature of the human being makes man behave like a human being. This definition was supported by his assertions that *ren* starts from 'the compassionate mind' and 'the mind that cannot be aloof from others' suffering', and those "bereft of such minds cannot be said to be human beings."[29] What is at issue here is whether he could

25 *Analects* 14.12; 19.1.
26 *Analects* 4.10.
27 *Analects* 5.16.
28 *Mengzi* 4A4.
29 *Mengzi* 2A6.

suggest a reason why the original nature of the human being is good. Mencius emphasized that a younger brother should revere and obey an elder brother. This emphasis illustrates the uniqueness of Mencius' concept of *yi*, for originally reverence and obedience had been regarded as principles to be observed in the relationship between vassals and the king, as is evidenced by 'vassals' loyalty to the king' (君臣有義), which is an element of 'the five moral hierarchies in human relations' (五倫). As aforementioned, Mencius emphasized not only filial piety as the embodiment of *ren* but also reverence for elder brothers. Consequently, the view that elder brothers have authority second only to parents in the familial hierarchy came to be settled in Confucianism.

The principle of *yi*, according to Mencius, is no other than original nature revealed by an individual's mental state or attitude. He thought that *ren* springs from compassion and *yi* from 'the sense of shame or hatred'--that is, those senses are 'the beginning (端緖) of *yi*'. Needless to say, Mencius regarded *yi* as the good original nature of the human being, so it is necessary to investigate his 'view of human nature as fundamentally good' (性善說).

(3) Outline of Mencius View of Human Nature as Fundamentally Good

Mencius' alluded to 'the view of human nature as fundamentally good' (性善說) when he talked about *liang-zhi* 良知 (innate wisdom) and *liang-neng* 良能 (intuitive ability).[30] At that time, however, he did not emphasize his view of human nature, perhaps because he was satisfied with peoples' observance of conventional etiquette, even without their obtaining the benefit of education on the proprieties.

Mencius has dual theories of human nature as fundamentally good. One theory rests on the proposition that all human beings

[30] *Mengzi* 7A15.

have something in common.[31] According to him, the human mind is commonly endowed with *liyi* (理義, truth and justice).[32] He thought that just as broiled beef satisfies the tastes of people, so too *liyi* pleases people.[33] However, this remains merely a relative theory, not a universal one, and his other theory was more practical and concrete. He classified aspects of human nature into instinctive desires such as appetite and sexual desire, and the fundamental virtues of *ren*, *yi*, *li* 禮 (propriety), and *zhi* 智 (wisdom) rooted in one's heart, and only acknowledged the latter as part of human nature because the former is something that the animals also follow.[34] He argued that only the fundamental virtues comprise the original nature and the attributes unique to the human being,[35] and that the fundamentally good nature is the natural manifestation of *ren*.

Mencius thought that *ren* is actually manifested by compassion, *yi* by the sense of shame or hatred, propriety by modesty or reverence and wisdom by discrimination between right and wrong, and called these four virtues collectively 'the mind of the four beginnings' (四端之心). Among these, he gave a concrete example of compassion and through it tried to promote his theory.

Mencius said, "If a baby crawls to a well, anyone who sees the baby will attempt to hold it from falling in."[36] According to him, this is evidence of compassion or the mind that cannot be aloof from or indifferent to others' sufferings, real or potential.[37] He believed that acting out of compassion is not artificial but the natural manifestation of the original nature of *ren*, and argued that the issuance of compassion is proof of the essential goodness of

31 *Mengzi* 6A7.

32 Loc. cit.

33 Loc. cit.

34 *Mengzi* 7A21.

35 *Mengzi* 6A6.

36 *Mengzi* 2A6.

37 Loc. cit.

human nature.

Though he did not provide concrete examples of *yi*, *li* (propriety) and *zhi* (wisdom), he argued that the four beginnings are the natural manifestations of these concepts, as well as of *ren*. He asserted that if there are those who do not feel compassion, shame and hatred depending on circumstances, they cannot be said to be human beings.[38] This is the summary of Mencius' view of human nature as fundamentally good.

4. A Reinterpretation of the Compassionate Mind and the Mind of Shame and Hatred

(1) Reflection on Mencius' Theories of Xin, Xing *and* Qing

Mencius regarded only the 'four beginnings' (四端), namely *ren, yi, li* and *zhi*, as *xing* 性 ([human] nature). He did not regard instinctive desires such as appetite and carnal desire as *xing*. Though the fact that the four beginnings constitute good nature does not require verification, it is necessary to consider the relation of *ren* to compassion in that the former corresponds to *dynamis* (可能態) and the latter to *energeia* (現實態).

Neo-Confucian scholars since Zhu Xi (朱熹, 1130-1200) thought that the relation of *in* to compassion is analogous to that of *ti* 體 (substance or principle) to *yong* 用 (function or realization). In *The Doctrine of the Mean* (中庸) the relation of *ti* and *yong* is regarded as analogous to that of 'before issuance' (未發) and 'after issuance' (已發), which represent the activity and inactivity of *xin* 心 (mind) respectively. In this context the text maintains that, "*Xing* (human nature) issues in order to become *qing* 情 (feeling)" and "*Qing* is the issuance of *xing*."[39] Though Mencius discriminated *xing* from *qing*,

38 Loc. cit.

39 As the theory of *li-qi* (principle-life energy) developed in Neo-Confucianism,

he does not seem to have comprehensively studied their relation.

Mencius sometimes called the four beginnings *qing*, but not always. In fact, he called them *xin* (mind) more frequently, as in the case when he discussed *ren* and said that it is 'the compassionate mind'. Originally, his usage of *xin* subsumed both *xing* and *qing* but he often used *xin* instead of *qing*. In particular, the *xin* mentioned in his discussion of the four beginnings actually meant *qing* or 'emotion' (情感).

This confusion in the usage of words may be ascribed to the fact that the cerebral functions that have been disclosed by the science of anatomy were totally unknown to people in Mencius' times. So it is necessary to understand Mencius' theories in light of the contemporary situation before hastily criticizing them.

(2) A Reinterpretation of the Compassionate Mind

Mencius, while illustrating the innate goodness of human nature through the instance of a baby crawling toward a well, maintains that the manifestation of the compassionate mind is proof that one's mind enables one to avoid being aloof from others' sufferings.[40] He also formulated his thinking contrariwise, saying that owing to the mind that cannot bear to watch others' sufferings, man comes to have a compassionate mind.[41] This means that Mencius regarded the compassionate mind as a synonym of 'the mind that cannot be aloof from others' sufferings'.

Though they are synonymous, Mencius regarded only 'the compassionate mind', and not 'the mind that cannot be aloof from others' sufferings,' as 'the beginning of *ren*'. This is because he

---

Yi Hwang's (李滉, 1501-1507) theory of the four beginnings as the issuance of *li*, and of the seven feelings as the issuance of *qi*, was the extension of this thinking. Refer to Yi Hwang, "Tap Ki Myŏng-ŏn" (In reply to Ki Myŏng-ŏn), *T'oegye chŏnsŏ* 1958, vol. 16, p. 405.

40 *Mengzi* 2A6.

41 Loc. cit.

used the latter in a broader sense than he did the former. In other words, he seems to have applied the latter to the discussion of shame in the context of *yi*, and that of modesty and reverence in terms of propriety, as well as that of the concepts related to *ren*.

What does it mean not to be aloof from others' sufferings? It may refer to the empathetic attitude displayed toward a person who is faced with a perilous situation. So avoiding aloofness from others' sufferings may refer to the case when we feel compassion for a person in hardship and actively attempt to help the person overcome it.

This view of Mencius' seems to support Confucius' definition of *ren* as 'love of others' (愛人) and 'consideration for others' (恕). As the compassionate mind displays naturally overflowing emotion, so do love of and consideration for others. I think that Mencius' intention of interpreting *ren* as the compassionate mind was to show that love of others and consideration for them are also spontaneously arising emotions.

To show *ceyin* (惻隱, compassion) is to be sorrow-stricken at or to sympathize with someone's suffering. Originally, Mencius used the term *chuti-ceyin* (怵惕惻隱).[42] The word *chuti* essentially means 'fear' with the connotations of 'sympathy' and 'concern.' So, why did Mencius add 'fear' and 'sorrow' as well as 'the mind that cannot be aloof from others' sufferings' to Confucius' definitions of *ren*?

Here 'fear' may be interpreted as 'restraint' or 'caution'. However, as *ceyin* accompanies sorrow, 'fear' may not simply imply 'restraint' or 'caution'. Just as sorrow arises when fear is intensified, fear is the emotion arising before sorrow. What is necessary in this context is to elucidate the reason why sorrow is preceded by fear.

It can be argued that this is so because fear refers to the psychological tension brought about by the anticipation of hearing about the unforeseen danger, hardship and misfortune of the

42 Loc. cit.

person concerned. In other words, as the person toward whom we show compassion might have suffered from adversity or danger, we cannot but be anxious and worry about our own possible shortcomings before talking with him.

Another reason why fear precedes sorrow derives from the need to take precautions against succumbing to egoism. Seen from an ethical perspective, avoiding the display of egoism may be more important than worrying about our possible shortcomings. As sympathy toward others is characterized by altruism, Mencius mentioned fear in the sense that we should guard against egoism, so that we can demonstrate altruism.

Another issue is why sorrow accompanies our love of others. Mencius' example of 'a baby crawling toward a well' may help us to arrive at an answer to this question. Those who witness the sight of the baby may be surprised, embarrassed, frightened and sorrowful, but never happy. In particular, the feeling of sorrow arises from thinking of the approaching crisis as our own, which results from compassion based on altruistic love.

My interpretation of *ren* on the basis of compassion has some relevance to *maitri-karuna* (慈悲, true friendship and compassion or sympathy), which is mentioned in the Buddhist canon. In Buddhism 'carnal desire' (渴愛) is prohibited for it is the cause of 'suffering' (苦) and 'karmic rebirth' (輪回). On the other hand, Buddhism encourages the practice of *maitri-karuna* for it is a kind of altruistic love. Considering the era in which Mencius lived and in light of the interpretation of this issue in the Korean translations of the Buddhist canon, I feel that the Buddhist emphasis on *maitri-karuna* might have been influenced by Mencius' thinking on compassion.[43]

43 Originally, *cibei* 慈悲 was a compound word composed of two Sanskrit words, *maitri* (true friendship) and *karuna* (compassion or sympathy). The concepts of *ci* and *bei* first appeared as two of the four immeasurable minds, that is, *ci* 慈 (true friendship), *bei* 悲 (compassion), *xi* 喜 (joy), and *she* 捨 (equability), which were the virtues to be cultivated in early Buddhism. The compound word *cibei* first appeared as a translation of its original Sanskrit word in the Mahayana Buddhist canons of East Asia such as *Niepan jing* 涅槃經 (Nirvana sutra) and

When compassion, which is 'the beginning of *ren*', is understood as Buddhist *jabi,* the aspect of mercifulness implied in Mencius' *ren* comes to the fore. Sorrow-stricken compassion provides the impetus to offer support to a person in adversity. To have a compassionate mind is to sympathize with the suffering of a person, and so it is usually identified with sympathy. So it may be concluded that Confucius' practice of *ren* through consideration was inherited and sustained to a greater degree by Mencius' 'compassionate mind'.

(3) A Reinterpretation of the Mind of Shame and Hatred

At this juncture, I will discuss 'the beginning of *yi*', that is, 'the mind of shame and hatred' (羞惡之心). The cause of shame may be one's own mistakes or unwarranted actions, or the comparison of one's own acts with others'. In addition, my discussion will also be focused on one's hatred of others caused by their acts.

When does one feel ashamed and hateful in one's association with others? It may be when others do not show consideration. Mencius did not explain why the mind of shame and hatred is 'the beginning of *yi*'. He only gave an example that demonstrates how such a mind is formed, as follows:

> Here is a basketful of rice and a bowlful of soup. Getting them will mean life; not getting them will mean death. When these are given to a wayfarer in an impolite manner, he won't accept them. Even a beggar won't take a bowl of food that has been tossed at him by a host.[44]

Bore jing 般若經 (Perfection of wisdom sutra). In particular, in a commentary of the latter entitled *Mahāprajñāpāramitāśāstra* (Great Treatise on the Perfection of Wisdom 大智度論), the term frequently appeared, even in the compound words such as *wuai daci dabei* 無碍大慈大悲 and *tonti dabei* 同體大悲. I believe this is not a fortuitous phenomenon, but a consequence influenced Mencius' idea of compassion.

44 *Mengzi* 6A10.

If others insult one with ill-treatment, shame and hatred are the natural responses to the insult. But why are these emotions 'the beginning of *yi*'? It is possible that Mencius would answer that such an insult conflicts with one's attitude of not being aloof from others' sufferings, adding that the insult is an act that is contrary to the tenets of the original mind or *yi* of the human being. But such an answer is difficult to accept as a satisfactory explanation of 'the beginning of *yi*', and a more plausible explanation is required.

As Mencius offers no further elaboration, I will provide my own interpretation here. To issue an insult that arouses the sense of shame and hatred is to ignore the person concerned and further, to deny the equality of human beings. Therefore, the hatred anticipated in the above parable awakes both the wayfarer and the beggar to the humane conception that all human beings are equal. Such a rational thought is the norm of conduct that is conducive to the concept of *yi* (righteousness or uprightness). Therefore, in the above quotation Mencius seems to have conceived of *yi* as rooted in the feelings of shame and hatred, which are motivated by situations in which contempt is present.

To ill-treat or insult others is in Mencius' terms 'to remain indifferent to others' sufferings' or to do what one should not do. It is an unrighteous and ill-disposed attitude. Conversely, to refrain from insulting others and to avoid arousing the hatred of others are the constituent elements of *yi*. In other words, these are the impetus for realizing the concept of *yi*.

Even when I engage in wrongdoing or make a mistake, *yi* is involved, or it informs me that I should not engage in misconduct that will lead to shame and hatred. For instance, in the relationship between parents and child the *yi* of the child consists of not being ungrateful to the parents. Mencius in fact educated his followers in the elements of filial piety as a form of concrete practice of *ren,* and he furthermore emphasized 'governance by *ren* or the compassionate mind' (仁政).

While discussing the four beginnings, Mencius insisted that the realization of 'governance by *ren*' is very important. Governance by *ren* is the *yi* that a ruler should realize. If a ruler does not govern people in a way that is thoroughly informed by *yi*, Mencius asserted that the people will hate him and be angry with him, and eventually dismiss him.[45] This view of 'governance by *ren*' ultimately aimed at governance by the people and for the people.

We have seen that the feelings of shame and hatred arise from our self-reflection that we are at fault in our relation with others as well as from others' insulting attitude toward us. In the light of the notions of filial piety and governance through *ren*, it may be said that self-reflection functions as the beginning of *yi* to a greater extent than does our response to others' insulting attitude.

5. The Characteristics of Virtue Ethics Implied in the Theory of *Ren* and *Yi*

Insulting ill-treatment arouses acute shame and hatred on the part of the insulted person. The person's feelings of shame and hatred may eventually lead to the conclusion that such ill-treatment is a form of misconduct that should not be engaged in and that it is contrary to the concept of *yi* 義. However, ill-treatment also implies the concept of *ren* 仁 in that it reminds us of the compassionate mind or the mind that cannot be aloof from others' sufferings. In other words, it may be said that *yi,* originating from the feelings of shame and hatred, is a concept subordinated to *ren* in that shame and hatred evoke compassion which is 'the beginning' of *ren*. At a minimum, they are concepts that should be considered in the same context.

According to Mencius, *yi* refers to righteousness and justice

45 This is the view of Mencius' "Revolutionary Change of Dynasty" (易姓革命) in the name of "the expulsion of a tyrant" (放伐論).

based on 'virtuousness' (德性), like *ren*. Mencius rejected Gaozi (告者)'s theory of 'internal *ren* and external *yi*' (仁內義外)[46] and argued that both *ren* and *yi* issue from the inner mind or virtuousness, which shows that his theories of *ren* and *yi* belong to virtue ethics.

Yi, originating from the feelings of shame and hatred, is a normative principle facilitating the manifestation of the compassionate mind. *Ren*, owing to the beginnings of *yi*, that is, shame and hatred, becomes a more unswerving virtue while *yi*, owing to the beginning of *ren*, that is, compassion, adds warmth to its attributes. Compassion, shame, and hatred are related to one another like two sides of the same coin owing to the presence of consideration toward others and reciprocal respect between persons. This is the central feature of Mencius' virtue ethics.

Mencius' system of ethics, which is an objective norm formulated on the basis of the human ideal and wisdom, also entails objective norms such as *yi* and *yili* 義理 (sense of duty). A system of ethics than encompasses objective norms is generally called 'duty ethics'. In this context *The Doctrine of the Mean* stipulates that "Only when my feelings of joy, anger, sorrow and pleasure accommodate themselves to norms, can I attain the state of harmony and equilibrium, the penetration of Way through all-under-heaven."[47]

It should also be remembered that the beginnings of *ren* and *yi* such as compassion, shame and hatred, are relative. Though Mencius argued that human nature is fundamentally good, he argued in his discussion of 'the four beginnings' (四端), that "feelings have the possibility of becoming good."[48] However, this does not mean that they are good *per se*. So Mencius asserted that it is necessary to extend the implications of 'the four beginnings' by uncovering the

46 *Mengzi* 6A4.

47 *Doctrine of the Mean*, chapter 1.

48 *Mengzi* 6A6.

possibility of goodness and demonstrating 'good will' (善意志).

It is a historical fact that there were not a few mistaken practices in the Confucian circles of East Asia resulting from the indiscriminate applications of *ren* and *yi* based on compassion, shame and hatred. The unjust and unethical applications of *ren* and *yi* based on the feeling of compassion, and the extending of generosity even to ill-disposed persons, were mainly ascribed to the view of *ren* and *yi* as absolute values or the view that *ren* and *yi* have priority over everything else in any time and place. In order not to repeat such a misguided practice we have to selectively apply the concepts of *ren* and *yi* to the appropriate person in the apposite place.[49]

6. Conclusion: The Significance of Mencius Virtue Ethics

Critically speaking, the practice of *ren* as love based on pity or the compassionate mind may remain a passive attitude, for pity and compassion are relative feelings that are dominated by personal mood and circumstance. Though they may be evaluated as the manifestation of altruistic good intention, they lack consistency and intensity. So it is necessary for the compassionate mind to be channeled into institutional arrangements for the relief of suffering people. Then we may preserve the implications of love and empathy that are subsumed in the concept of *ren*.

However, a focus on such complementary arrangements should not be permitted to devalue Mencius' age-old theories. Rather, we should now evaluate whether Mencius' theories of *ren* and *yi* have relevance to the aims of this study.

This study aimed 1) to unearth a basis for the relations or mutual understanding between persons, 2) to locate archetypal normative

49 In Chapters 4 and 5 I was compelled to repeat some of the discussions that I mentioned in my paper "Yuhak ŭi haeksim wŏlli in in kwa ŭi e taehan yŏn'gu" (A study on '*ren*' (benevolence) and '*yi*' (righteousness) as the core principles of Confucianism) (2016).

principles for the establishment of an ethical social order, and 3) to examine the general characteristics of ethical theories that help maintain social order. As these aims have been philosophical tasks throughout the ages, and have relevance to the concepts of *ren* and *yi*, which are the fundamental principles of Confucianism, I have examined Confucius' and especially Mencius' theories to further them.

The results of my study are summarized as follows:

1) Mencius interpreted Confucius' definition of *ren*, that is, 'love toward others' (愛人) as 'not being aloof from others' sufferings' or 'the compassionate mind'. In other words, according to him, love based on pity or the compassionate mind and sympathy toward suffering persons has the role of linking person to person.

2) Like Confucius, Mencius' normative principle was *yi*. And he believed that the feelings of shame and hatred are the beginnings of *yi*. We have seen that these feelings motivate our attitude of refraining from insulting others. In addition, this study has concluded that reciprocal reverence, which is based on not being aloof from others' sufferings or on the compassionate mind, is required for the maintenance of ethical social order.

3) I have argued that Mencius' ethics based on *ren* and *yi* was a form of virtue ethics. As for virtue ethics, no further explanation is necessary here as the subject was treated extensively in Chapter 5.

The compassionate mind arouses sympathy and consideration for others, which is the basis of reciprocal reverence between persons. Conversely, enmity toward others causes discord, conflict, hostility and confusion, and heaping insults upon others on the basis of enmity is evil. In a word, it is the seed of injustice. Therefore we should cherish the display of consideration and sympathy toward others and reciprocal reverence based on the compassionate mind.

We have seen that the fundamental characteristic of *yi* based on shame and hatred lies in the imperative to 'treat a person like a human being', and that such a characteristic is related to human rights or the equality of human beings. I believe that it is one of my noteworthy arguments that the consciousness of human rights or equality is facilitated by the feeling of hatred. Moreover, my argument does not rely on Hsun-tzu's 'view of human nature as fundamentally depraved' (性惡說), but instead rests on Mencius' 'view of human nature as fundamentally good' (性善說).

Though Mencius' virtue ethics has some limits and inconsistencies, it also has its merits, one of which can be viewed in the relation of his ethics to duty ethics. The practice of the latter, which is contrasted with virtue ethics, has the fundamental requirement of being preceded by 'autonomous intention'. As obligation is motivated by autonomous intention, virtue ethics precedes duty ethics, and in this respect the importance of the former should not be neglected.

In the past virtue ethics was neglected because it was considered to be mainly based on subjective emotion, not on objective value judgment. However, I disagree with this assessment for the following reasons: First, a person of high intelligence, as Mencius pointed out, "gains pleasure from attaining truth and righteousness."[50] This remark suggests that virtue ethics implies objectivity. Second, as almost all ordinary persons are endowed with a compassionate mind, they are willing to save a person in a perilous situation, like the baby crawling toward the well. Such a universal disposition is proof of at least 'the relative objectivity' of the human mind. Lastly, the historical fact that numerous benevolent and righteous Confucian scholars engaged in virtuous deeds is also proof that virtue ethics imply objectivity.

50 I have mentioned this in section 3 of chapter 3, entitled "Outline of Mencius' View of Human Nature as Fundamentally Good."

References

Yi Hwang. 1958. "Tap Ki Myŏng-ŏn" 答奇明彦 (In reply to Ki Myŏng-ŏn), In *T'oegye chŏnsŏ* 退溪全書 (*The complete works of T'oegye [Yi Hwang]*). Vol. 16, Seoul: Daedong Institute for Korean Studies at Sungkyunkwan University.

Youn Sa-Soon. 2016. "Yuhak ŭi haeksim wŏlli in in kwa ŭi e taehan yŏn'gu" (A study on 'ren' (benevolence) and 'yi' (righteousness) as the core principles of Confucianism). *Taehan minguk Haksurwŏn nonmunjip: inmun sahoe kwahak p'yŏn (Research Collections of The National Academy of Sciences, Republic of Korea: Humanities and Social Sciences*), vol. 55 (1).

INDEX

E

F

O

P

Q

R

S